Researching Women's Lives from a Feminist Perspective

Edited by

Mary Maynard and June Purvis

Taylor & Francis
Publishers since 1798

UK   Taylor & Francis Ltd, 4 John St., London WC1N 2ET
USA   Taylor & Francis Inc., 1900 Frost Road, Suite 101, Bristol, PA 19007

First published 1994

A Catalogue Record for this book is available from the British Library

ISBN 0 7484 0152 0
ISBN 0 7484 0153 9 (pbk)

Library of Congress Cataloging-in-Publication Data are available on request

Typeset in 10/12pt Times
by Graphicraft Typesetters Ltd., Hong Kong

Printed in Great Britain by Burgess Science Press, Basingstoke on paper which has a specified pH value on final paper manufacture of not less than 7.5 and is therefore 'acid free'.

Contents

Introduction

Doing Feminist Research

Mary Maynard and June Purvis

Why this Book?

In 1981, Helen Roberts published her influential text *Doing Feminist Research* (reprinted in 1988). The appearance of this book was significant for a number of reasons. At a time when feminism was still treated with open hostility and ridicule in the academy, it indicated that feminist work comprised a serious intellectual pursuit, with important insights to contribute to our understanding of the social world. It helped to open up debate as to how taking account of women and adopting a feminist perspective affects the research process. Further, the book, which was based on the personal accounts of a number of people involved in research, argued that the problems which emerged from these accounts were themselves methodologically important. The various authors demonstrated that research is not a linear process, as is often implied in the polished descriptions published from completed studies. Instead, a focus on autobiographical analyses of what it is actually like to do research can provide a useful insight into issues often hidden in conventional methodology textbooks.

In the intervening period, discussions about the nature of feminist methodology and feminist research have become both more acceptable and more complex. As Maynard describes in the first chapter of this volume, debate no longer concentrates solely on the question as to which research techniques should be employed and how they should be implemented, although these are still important concerns. Feminists are now involved in exploring a whole range of wider issues concerned with practical, political and ethical matters in undertaking research. There is also a burgeoning literature on epistemology, which is concerned with the nature and status of feminist knowledge.

Despite the high profile now given to discussing feminist research, however, much of the material published, with a few notable exceptions, tends to focus on the principles involved in a rather abstract way.[1] This can sometimes be at the expense of exploring the dynamics of actually *doing* research in the field. Although individual researchers are increasingly drawing attention to the difficulties and contradictions arising in their own specific work, there is little material which addresses these in a readily accessible and comprehensive way. As Kelly, Burton and Regan point out in chapter 2 of this book,

> Feminists have been stern critics of 'hygienic research'; the censoring out of the mess, confusion and complexity of doing research, so that the accounts bear little or no relation to the real events. But many of our accounts are full of silences too. (p. 46)

It is the intention of this book explicitly to address the 'silences' referred to, which is why we have invited a number of well-known feminist researchers to write about the process of conducting their research, warts and all. Substantive areas of focus have been chosen for their significance in feminist thinking during the last decade, although, of course, it is impossible to be exhaustive about this. In addition to a concern with issues such as sexual violence, femininity, employment, sexuality and political activity in the past, contributors also pay attention to the impact of 'race', class, lesbianism and disability. Each chapter provides a reflexive account of the research process, offering the insights of the insider as to how it proceeds, its difficulties and compensations. In doing so, it becomes apparent that the debates and arguments are far more complicated than they were fifteen or so years ago. No longer can it be argued that there is a 'right' way of doing things and there is no clear consensus as to what feminist research definitionally might comprise. Rather, what does emerge from the pages of this volume is a sense of the parameters within which feminists feel they, minimally, must operate, in order to be rigorous about, and maintain integrity towards, their work. This, together with continual reflection on the research process itself, contributes to the rich and dynamic discussions which emerge when we consider what is meant by 'doing feminist research'.

Themes and Controversies

Although the various contributors to this volume have focused their chapters in differing ways, there are important emphases which unite them. The chapter by Kelly, Burton and Regan, for example, which draws on their work on domestic violence and child sexual abuse, raises a series of general questions about feminist methods, methodology and epistemology which are also the concern of Maynard. Skeggs' account of conducting an ethnographic study with working-class young women, over an extensive period of time, focuses more specifically on the practicalities of day-to-day research, thus complementing similar discussions by Glucksmann, by Holland and Ramazanoglu and by Phoenix. Marshall's angry critique of the racism of academic life, and discussion of her strategies for fighting and coping with this, parallel Stanko's analysis of how she is continually 'dancing with denial' in the face of criminology's failure to take feminist work on male violence seriously. Marshall, together with Holland and Ramazanoglu, ground their accounts of doing research in work which has focused on the meanings of sexuality. Similarly, both Glucksmann and Purvis adopt historical approaches, reflecting respectively on the merits of oral history in understanding women's experiences of employment and of using diaries and letters as personal texts when studying the political activity of the suffragettes.

In addition to such common ground, however, a number of other themes also emerge from the pages of this book. These foreground issues to do with power, politics and responsibility in the research process. Four of these themes, identified as being crucial to understanding the concerns of feminists currently engaged in research, are discussed below under the headings: mixing methods; the impact of involvement in research; validity in feminist knowledge; and politics and academe.

Mixing Methods

In chapter 1, Maynard draws attention to the orthodoxy which seems to have become something of a feature of discussions on feminist research methods. A gulf has been drawn between quantitative and qualitative approaches, with the implication that it is qualitative work, particularly the semi-structured or unstructured interview, which is quintessentially feminist. Maynard takes issue with such a stance, as do Kelly, Burton and Regan. In chapter 2, the latter authors question the assumptions that implicitly underpin such a position and discuss how they have used the survey method and self-report questionnaires in their work on child sexual abuse.

This dissatisfaction with the idea that feminist research must involve interviews appears in a number of other chapters in this book. Instead, the view is put forward, on a number of occasions, that not only should the method adopted be that most appropriate to a specific set of research questions and the overall research context, but it is frequently useful to select a range of methods, with a view to maximizing input to the research. Glucksmann, for instance, refers to her approach as being 'multi-sourced' (p. 158). For one project, in addition to working with women on an assembly line, she also interviewed supervisors and managers, examined company archives and trades union journals, as well as consulting census data and other official statistics. Marshall's analysis of the social construction of Black female sexuality has involved combining an anonymous questionnaire with semi-structured and unstructured interviews. Skeggs, who argues that ethnography is not a method but a theory of the research process, used interviews, questionnaires, participant observation, statistical analysis, historical documentation etc. in ways which were all part of a more general framework relating research practice to the theories that underpinned her research.

In putting forward an argument for multiple methods, feminists are not suggesting, in some naive fashion, that combining approaches will ensure the increased validity of their data. Nor do they argue that the information constructed through different methods can simply be aggregated to produce a single unitary picture of the 'truth'. Rather, along with other researchers, they acknowledge that the differences generated from different research techniques are likely to be as illuminating as the similarities.[2] The challenge to feminists now lies less in the critique of a simplistic qualitative/quantitative polarization and more in how it might be possible to make all methods 'feminist user-friendly'. As Kelly, Burton and Regan point out, much effort has been expended by feminists in adapting the traditional interview format to comply with feminist research practice. Perhaps it is now time to consider transforming questionnaire and survey methods, making them sensitive to feminist principles concerning how to treat participants and how to use the information to which their testimonies give rise.

The Impact of Involvement in Research

As the discussion immediately above indicates, a major concern for feminists has always been with the process of conducting research. Questions about the inevitability of a power dimension to the relationship between the researcher and the researched, about the ethics of research practices, and matters of exploitation and control have featured prominently in the debate. This is still the case. Yet, less attention has been paid to the direct impact and meaning that participation in a research project can have on both the person undertaking the work and those being studied. This, then, is a second significant theme which our contributors address.

Perhaps the most striking example of the effect that research can have on the researcher is Marshall's account of studying Black women's sexuality. Marshall analyzes the tremendous effort involved in opposing the trend to pathologize and dehumanize Black womanhood within the racist context of academia. As a Black researcher, she describes the sense of isolation felt as an insider/outsider and the pressure of being treated as a Black superwoman. Although arguing that Black feminist research can be an empowering process in many ways, Marshall notes the lack of attention paid in the literature to stress as part of the research experience, arguing that 'doing research can seriously damage your health' (p. 121).

Other contributors explore the impression, often given, that feminist research is a rather comfortable and cosy activity. Purvis, for instance, describes her personal feelings on reading the autobiographical accounts of forcible feeding written by the suffragettes, some of which referred to acts of gross humiliation and torture. Holland and Ramazanoglu discuss the difficulties involved when researching a sensitive subject such as sexuality, particularly when respondents reveal, possibly for the first time, serious violence and abuse which has been committed against them. In her chapter, which focuses on the experience of being a Black researcher, Phoenix outlines a number of areas in which the practice of research can have a deleterious effect, especially where racism is involved. Skeggs admits that the longer she spent with the young women in her study, the more confused she became. This confusion, to do with how to write about the young women's lives in a way that would properly reflect their experiences and understandings, only really finally resolved itself when she began to write her chapter for this book.

Another dimension to the way in which research participation can have an impact on the researcher is in terms of being a member of a research team. This is another under-considered area of research practice. Phoenix, for example, points out that the very notion of conducting feminist research presupposes that those doing it have some power in and, hence, control over the research hierarchy. Yet, as both she and Holland and Ramazanoglu indicate, the majority of women working within research are at the bottom of research hierarchies, where they have only limited control over the research process. They may not, in fact, have as much influence on activities, such as the analysis and interpretation of data, as might appear to the research respondents. Kelly, Burton and Regan also address such issues. They include in their chapter an edited version of a taped discussion amongst themselves, which, in drawing on their experiences as a research team, considers whether it is possible to break down power and hierarchical relationships in order to work collectively.

Of course, it is not only the researcher who may have to face the consequences, positive or negative, of involvement in a research project. In this context, part of Phoenix's chapter reports on work which asked for respondents' views of and responses to research, as well as monitoring the nature of the questions asked of interviewers by interviewees. She reports that although many women say that they enjoyed being interviewed, some found being a research participant intrusive and might feel vulnerable later, fearing that they might be compromised if information they conveyed fell into the 'wrong' hands. Phoenix's chapter, along with several others in the book (for example, those by Holland and Ramazanoglu; Kelly, Burton and Regan; Maynard; and Skeggs), signals the necessity for feminists to consider further the likely impact on the researched of participation in a research project.

Validity in Feminist Knowledge

The question as to what constitutes valid and reliable feminist knowledge is of increasing concern to feminists. Much of the debate so far, however, has been carried out at an abstract epistemological level, as Maynard's discussion of the area in chapter 1 indicates. The major focus has been to critique masculinist notions of science and/or proffer postmodern criticisms of Enlightenment forms of knowledge.[3] But there are difficulties in adapting the validity arguments advanced in such discussions to the day-to-day practicalities of conducting empirical research. This is a theme taken up in several of the chapters in the book. The arguments, broadly speaking, are of two kinds. The first is concerned with the role of experience in feminist research. The second focuses on the process of interpretation.

It has generally been regarded as an axiomatic feature of feminist social research that it is grounded in women's experiences. The contributors to this book would not demur from this point of view. As Purvis indicates, for example, it is only by considering the suffragettes' own testimonies about their imprisonment that we can challenge the distorted and mistaken views about them offered by many histories of the period. What is at issue, however, is whether focusing on experience alone is sufficient for the conduct of feminist research. Kelly, Burton and Regan acknowledge disquiet over such a position when they argue that whereas, initially, experience was viewed as a starting point for feminist analysis, it has now become an end in itself. They write:

> Whilst personal experience undoubtedly influences one's perspective and understanding, many current references to it are determinist and essentialist. Experience/identity is substituted for, or deemed to be equivalent to, politics, as if critical awareness and understanding are inscribed on a person through forms of oppression, with an implicit or explicit presumption that such awareness is inaccessible to those who have not 'lived' such experiences. (pp. 29–30)

A similar concern about the use of experience in feminist research is expressed by Glucksmann. She argues that the researcher and the researched are positioned differently in relation to both the production of knowledge and the kinds and range of knowledge they possess. In her research on women assemblers, Glucksmann could not rely entirely on the women's own accounts of their situation, precisely because a central aspect of their subordination was that they acquired only a fragmented and partial knowledge of the assembly line. She, therefore, had to complement her analysis with material from other sources.

It is clear, then, that the notion of experience needs to be problematized, since individuals do not necessarily possess sufficient knowledge to explain everything about their lives. Accounts will vary depending on such factors as where respondents are socially positioned, memory etc. There is no such thing as 'raw' or authentic experience which is unmediated by interpretation.

Another issue here is that a focus on *women's* experiences and lives alone detracts attention from the fact that a lot of feminist research has been on men and masculinity. Stanko, along with Kelly, Burton and Regan, makes the point most forcefully that a lot of the research on violence towards women focuses on men and challenges masculinity. She explains how her own experiences as a feminist criminologist have led her to focus on how men view violence in their own lives, as a way of trying to understand how they characterize this in the lives of women. Despite reluctance to stop researching women's personal safety, Stanko argues that understanding how men manage male hierarchies can contribute to knowledge about violence towards women, which is itself rooted in such hierarchies.

The second issue which arises in the context of establishing validity in feminist research is that of how we carry out the process of interpretation. This is addressed in a number of the chapters and is echoed in Purvis' concern about the imprisoned suffragettes, and whether she is interpreting these women as they would want. In her chapter, for instance, Skeggs indicates how the repeated listening to tapes of interviews and other forms of conversations with respondents is an essential, yet often neglected, area of analysis. She describes how letting the young women in her research re-listen to and respond to their tapes provided a useful way of monitoring the legitimacy of the interpretations she had made of their initial responses. Glucksmann usefully outlines and discusses a continuum of interpretative approaches as used in oral history, considering the arguments about establishing the validity of interpretations proposed for each. Like Holland and Ramazanoglu, she unpacks the research process to show those factors which contribute to various strategies of constructing interpretations.

Those writers in this book who address the question of validity in feminist research seem to agree that reaching conclusions is a social process and that interpretation is a political, contested and unstable activity. Feminists have to accept that there is no technique of analysis or methodological logic that can neutralize the social nature of interpretation. Rather, as Holland and Ramazanoglu suggest, feminist researchers can only try to explain the grounds on which selective interpretations have been made by making explicit the process of decision-making which produces the interpretation, and the logic of the method on which these decisions are based. This entails acknowledging complexity and contradiction which may be beyond the interpreter's experience, and recognizing the possibility of silences and absences in their data.

Politics and Academe

The fourth, and final, of the major themes identified as emerging from the chapters of this book involves a consideration of the relationship between politics and the academy. The contributors address this issue in differing ways, but with two significant and related aspects.

The first is a concern to re-examine the possible transformatory aspects of feminist research, particularly in terms of facilitating social change and empowering the participants. As Maynard points out, bringing about social change for a group and individual empowerment are clearly very different activities. Along with Kelly, Burton and Regan, she warns against overly simplistic and glib notions of what the two might mean and how they might be brought about. In a similar vein, Glucksmann considers some of the dangers, which she identifies in the arguments of some feminists, of conflating politics and research. Writing of a tendency to imply that feminist research *is* feminist politics, she counsels against a slippage which substitutes establishing egalitarianism in the research situation for egalitarianism in the real world. In developing her arguments, Glucksmann problematizes, as do other contributors to the volume, earlier, simplistic, notions that research is identifiably feminist when it is 'by', 'for' and 'about' women.

The second aspect to this debate involves confronting the relationship between academic research and writing and politics, head-on. Kelly, Burton and Regan, for example, like Glucksmann, decry the increasing lack of a relationship between feminist research, much of which is conducted by academics in academic institutions, and the struggle for women's liberation. They argue that the point of doing research is to create useful knowledge which can be used to 'make a difference' (p. 28) and voice the concern that a masculinist hierarchy between theory and practice is being reproduced in academic feminism.

It is in this context that a number of contributors express their anxieties about the current influence of some forms of postmodernism which are so far removed from practical concerns that they imply that social research is pointless. Glucksmann, for instance, suggests that 'for many of us there is an ongoing struggle to avoid being submerged either by political defeatism or by postmodern paralysis' (p. 150). Kelly, Burton and Regan write about the 'current "romance with epistemology"' which

> seems more concerned with attempting to convince the predominantly male academy that a privileged status should be accorded to 'women's ways of knowing' than with enabling us to better discover and understand what is happening in women's lives, and how we might change it. (p. 32)

Purvis also reflects on these issues. She notes how the 'turn to culture', to post-structuralism and to postmodernism, particularly in the USA, threatens to transform feminist women's history by focusing on gender rather than women. She argues that women must be brought 'back' into historical studies. Purvis also stresses that we need to focus on the material forces that have shaped women's lives and experiences, even though these may be mediated through the discourses of the day. Such a view finds resonance with others expressed throughout this book.

In discussing four themes which link the concerns of our contributors, we have, of course, been able to highlight only some of the ways in which their approaches overlap. The remaining chapters in this volume develop further our initial analysis and demonstrate, in detail, the range of experiences involved when undertaking feminist research.

Notes

1 See, for example, Stanley (1990a).
2 Brannen (1992).
3 Harding (1986, 1991); Nicholson (1990); Smith (1988a).

Chapter 1

Methods, Practice and Epistemology: The Debate about Feminism and Research

Mary Maynard

The question as to what constitutes feminist social research has been an issue for feminists for over a decade and there is now a considerable literature addressing the topic. It seems to be widely accepted by feminists themselves that there is a distinctively feminist mode of enquiry, although there is by no means agreement on what this might mean or involve. In fact, as Sandra Harding has pointed out, scrutiny of the arguments reveals some confusion in the terms that are central to the debate.[1] Harding usefully makes a distinction between discussions of method, of methodology and of epistemology. Whereas method refers to techniques for gathering research material, methodology provides both theory and analysis of the research process. Epistemology is concerned with providing a philosophical grounding for deciding what kinds of knowledge are possible and how we can ensure that they are both adequate and legitimate. Harding contends that the term 'method' is often used to refer to all three of these elements of research. This lack of clarity has impeded feminists in their quest convincingly to set out what is specifically 'feminist' about their work.

Despite the fact, however, that feminists have increasingly quoted and endorsed Harding's arguments, defining what feminism means in terms of doing research is still no easy matter. Different claims abound. Indeed, the task is made more difficult since there are disagreements both *within* each of the components which Harding has identified and *between* them. In this, of course, feminism is no different from the rest of the social sciences. One particular problem is reconciling the abstract analyses and recommendations made at the epistemological level, where there is burgeoning interest and writing, with the more concrete concerns of method and methodology faced by those carrying out empirical research. It is the concern of this chapter to disentangle and explore some of these issues. First, it will provide a critical overview of those arguments that have been central to feminist interest in method, research practice and epistemology. Secondly, it will consider some of the difficulties raised by this literature. Finally, the chapter will address selected key issues important to feminism if our work is to be taken seriously and be influential.

The Debate about Methods

The idea that feminism has a method of conducting social research which is specific to it has increasingly come under attack.[2] However, this was certainly a view put forward in the early stages of second wave feminist scholarship and it is one which continues to be espoused.[3] These arguments advocated and defended a qualitative approach to understanding women's lives as against quantitative methods of enquiry. The arguments were rooted in a critique of what were perceived to be the dominant modes of doing research which were regarded as inhibiting a sociological understanding of women's experiences. Quantitative research (particularly surveys and questionnaires) was seen to represent a 'masculinist' form of knowing, where the emphasis was on the detachment of the researcher and the collection and measurement of 'objective' social facts through a (supposedly) value-free form of data collection. By contrast, the use of qualitative methods, which focus more on the subjective experiences and meanings of those being researched, was regarded as more appropriate to the kinds of knowledge that feminists wished to make available, as well as being more in keeping with the politics of doing research as a feminist. Semi-structured or unstructured interviewing has been the research technique most often associated with this stance, although this can, of course, produce both quantitative and qualitative data.

Initially, the feminist critique of quantification drew from the arguments of phenomenological sociologists, which were particularly influential in the early 1970s.[4] These sociologists claimed that the assumptions as to how actors structure their everyday worlds to be found within most questionnaire or interview schedules produce a falsely concrete body of data, which distort rather than reflect actors' meanings. Similarly, feminists have argued that the production of atomistic 'facts' and figures fractures people's lives.[5] Only one tiny part of experience is abstracted as the focus for attention and this is done in both a static and an atemporal fashion. Often the result of such an approach is a simple matrix of standardized variables which is unable to convey an in-depth understanding of, or feeling for, the people under study. Further, research practices which utilize either pre-coded or pre-closed categories are often of limited use when trying to understand women's lives. This is because they are based on assumptions, often at an unrecognized and common-sense level, that the researcher is already sufficiently familiar with the phenomenon being investigated to be able to specify, in advance, the full range of experiences being studied and how these can be encapsulated, categorized and measured. Sociological research which is based upon such assumptions, it is argued, is neither exploratory nor investigatory. Rather, it assesses the extent, distribution or intensity of something which has been defined in advance of the research undertaken, by the researcher. Feminists have argued that there are aspects to women's lives which cannot be pre-known or pre-defined in such a way.

This position was particularly important at a time when feminist research was in its infancy and when women's lives and experiences were still largely invisible. What was most usefully required then was an approach to research which maximized the ability to explore experience, rather than impose externally defined structures on women's lives. Thus feminists emphasized the importance of listening to, recording and understanding women's own descriptions and accounts.[6] This strategy enabled researchers to extend knowledge of areas such as schooling and paid work, previously understood mainly from a male perspective. It also facilitated the development of new, woman-oriented fields of research, for example violence towards women, sexuality, childbirth and domesticity. At its heart was the tenet that feminist research must begin with an open-ended exploration of women's experiences, since only from that vantage point is it possible to see how their world is organized and the extent to which it differs from that of men.

With hindsight, however, it can be seen that this approach, which proved so beneficial to feminists in their early work, gradually developed into something of an unproblematized orthodoxy against which the political correctness, or otherwise, of *all* feminist research could be judged.[7] It began to be assumed that *only* qualitative methods, especially the in-depth face-to-face interview, could really count in feminist terms and generate useful knowledge. Despite the fact that a number of feminist commentators *did* advocate the use of a range of research techniques and several deployed survey material and the statistical analysis of data to very effective critical ends,[8] the tendency to equate feminist work with a qualitative approach has persisted. One reason for this is the way in which quantification has been identified with the position of positivism, and positivism has become something of a *bête noire* in the quantitative versus qualitative debate.

Historically, what counts as positivism and its defining characteristics have been contested and have also changed.[9] The stereotypical view, however, and the one to which many feminists tend to subscribe, has focused on what counts as science. The emphasis here has been on deductivism. This involves the formulation of hypotheses about the world and the development of statements from them which are then tested to assess their validity. The existence of an independent and objective test (as is supposed to occur in laboratory experiments, for example), is crucial. It is this which ensures the facticity and reliability of the knowledge produced because it is uncontaminated by the subjective bias of the researcher. Science is thus characterized in terms of the objectivity of its method and the value-neutrality of the scientist. In textbook notions of positivism the resulting findings are fed back into and absorbed by the initial theory. This linear model of how research supposedly proceeds in the natural sciences is one which, some have argued, the social sciences need to pursue if they are to match the achievements of the other sciences.

The first point to be raised about this picture of positivism is, does it correspond to how science actually works? Developments in the sociology of knowledge and in the philosophy and sociology of science suggest otherwise and, although there are differing positions in the ensuing debate, plausible claims for the socially constructed nature of and investigator involvement in *all* research have been made.[10]

A second issue is to do with the implied relationship between the philosophical doctrine of positivism and empirical methods of research which involve measurement to provide numerical or statistically manipulatable data. In his very clear exposition of the nature of quantitative research Alan Bryman, for example, suggests that positivism and the use of quantitative methods are not necessarily the same thing, as is often assumed, and that there are 'aspects of the general approach of quantitative researchers which are not directly attributable to either positivism or the practices of the natural sciences'.[11] Bryman also questions the extent to which the terms qualitative and quantitative actually denote divergent assumptions about the nature and purpose of social research. He concludes that this is little more than an academic convention which took root in the 1960s and which 'has little to recommend it, either as a description of the research process or as a prescriptive view of how research should be done'.[12]

We also need to ask how far those doing quantitative research agree with the practices and assumptions which are attributed to them and used to criticize their work. Whilst it is no doubt the case that some *do* regard themselves as neutral researchers producing objective and value-free 'facts', others are more circumspect, acknowledging that providing figures involves as much of an act of social construction as any other kind of research. What is at issue, then, is whether positivism is *intrinsic* to quantitative research, and the answer appears to be that it is not. Catherine Marsh, for instance, has defended survey research against the charge of positivism, although she concedes that most of the textbook discussions do not allow a distinction between the two. Marsh suggests that there have been two kinds of attacks on surveys. One focuses on crude data collection and analysis and involves criticisms of poor research which most would agree with but which are not synonymous with surveys *per se*. The other focuses on the fact that the subjects of social research are conscious, language-speaking and meaning-creating. But, she argues, 'this is a problem for any social scientist, from the experimenter to the ethnographer, and is not confined to surveys'.[13] It is likely, then, that it is not so much quantification *per se* as naive quantification which is the problem.

A final point to be made is that in rejecting quantification, feminists have overlooked the contribution that research involving enumeration has made to our knowledge and understanding of women's experiences. Further, the *political* potential of such work must not be underestimated. The significance of violence in women's lives, for example, is underlined by studies showing the extent and severity of its incidence. Issues such as the feminization of poverty and women's lack of progress in achieving equality, on a number of dimensions, with men in paid work also benefit from work which demonstrates the problem numerically. This is not to argue that only work of this kind is useful or of interest. Such a position would be absurd. It is, however, to suggest that the time has come for some rethinking in terms of what are regarded as acceptable methods for feminists engaged in empirical research. This seems to encompass a recognition of the need for breadth as well as depth, as I have discovered in my own collaborative work on the Careers Service and on women's employment in the tourist industry, both of which used surveys in addition to other research techniques.[14]

Three things, in particular, are leading feminists to reconsider their position on method. First there is the need to acknowledge that the qualitative techniques they have tended to favour are not in and of themselves specific to feminism. Indeed, they are all an integral part of social science research and have their own histories of development and change outside and independent of feminism. Feminists may have appropriated these techniques, but they did not create them. They have also modified them, although they are not alone in doing so. In addition, a number of researchers have recently drawn attention to the ways in which the polarization of quantitative versus qualitative impoverishes research, and there have been calls for the use of multiple methods to be used in a complementary rather than a competitive way.[15] In their chapter for this book, for instance, Liz Kelly, Sheila Burton and Linda Regan clearly illustrate how this can be done to advantage in their work on child sexual abuse.[16] They argue that using questionnaires produced more reliable information than interviewing, because it allowed respondents anonymity in revealing distressing and sensitive experiences. This indicates that it is no longer tenable for the old orthodoxy to remain.

Feminism and Research Practice

If the arguments for the existence of a distinctive feminist method can be dismissed, what other grounds might there be for defining research as feminist? Another way in which feminists have answered this question is to turn to issues of methodology, which involves the theory and analysis of how research should proceed, how research questions might best be addressed and the criteria against which research findings might be evaluated. In doing so, feminists have tended to concentrate attention on two main areas of concern, the position from which distinctively feminist research questions might be asked and the political and ethical issues involved in the research process. Kelly has suggested the term 'feminist research practice' as helpful in this context, since it signals more clearly the wide-ranging nature of the points which feminists customarily address. Kelly argues that what distinguishes feminist research from other forms of research is 'the questions _we have asked, the way we locate ourselves within our questions, and the purpose of our work'.[17] She thus draws attention to a range of issues which go beyond those relating specifically to method.

Many of those who have written about feminist research practice have indicated that a theoretical perspective, acknowledging the pervasive influence of gender divisions on social life, is one of its most important defining characteristics.[18] There are, however, differences over what this might mean. To begin with, there are different theoretical emphases. Perceiving the significance of gender in terms of division and inequality, for instance, implies a different theoretical perspective to that which emphasizes the importance of patriarchal power and control. Each approach is likely to lead to the posing of different sorts of questions and to the production of different kinds of knowledge and analysis. Further, it is not entirely clear what focusing on gender means in terms of the subjects of research. Some have argued that it entails a preeminent concern with women alone, and given their previous neglect this was especially important early on in feminist work.[19] Others have suggested that 'gender' implies women's relationship to men and that this also needs to be included, although examined from a woman's perspective, in any enquiry involved in understanding how women's experiences in a male world are structured.[20] Stanley and Wise have always maintained that a concern with gender necessarily means being prepared to focus on men and masculinity, with the intention of researching the powerful as well as the powerless.[21] Although this is still a relatively underdeveloped aspect of feminist research, it raises important questions about whether such work is solely about women's experiences, as has so often been claimed. A further issue here, and one which is currently a particularly important aspect of feminist debate, is the relationship of gender to other forms of oppression, for instance those of race, class and disability, and the need to include an awareness of this within the parameters of our research.

A second way in which an understanding of the feminist research process has developed, and a consequence of gender-conscious theory and politics, is in the modifications which have been made to existing techniques. It has already been pointed out that feminists have largely used interviewing in their work. But they have not, as is now well-known, adopted this strategy blindly. Feminists have been critical of the ways in which sociological research involves hierarchical power relationships.[22] Even non-scheduled interviewing and ethnographic methods can entail a deliberate separation of the researcher from the 'subject' of the researched. The researcher using qualitative methods may not be constrained by pre-coded questions, but is, nevertheless, exhorted by textbook guidelines to be emotionally detached, calculating and in control of the collection of data. Those researched are regarded, in this view of research, as the passive givers of information, with the researcher acting as a sponge soaking up the details provided. Feminists have rejected the inevitability of such a power hierarchy between researcher and researched. Instead, they have argued for the significance of a genuine, rather than an instrumental rapport between them. This, it has been claimed, encourages a non-exploitative relationship, where the person being studied is not treated simply as a source of data. Research becomes a means of sharing information and, rather than being seen as a source of bias, the personal involvement of the interviewer is an important element in establishing trust and thus obtaining good quality information.

The problem is that it is not entirely clear what the term 'good quality' might mean in this context. Does it refer to the authenticity of women's accounts, to reliable and valid information, or to material which has not been violated by researcher (re)interpretation? Who is to judge on these issues and using what kind of criteria? Further, it is not always so easy to reduce the power dynamics that are likely to be present in research and it is unlikely that they can ever be eradicated completely. As Janet Finch has indicated, if the researcher is educated and articulate it is very easy to encourage women to talk about aspects of their lives concerning which, on reflection, they might have preferred to remain silent.[23] It is easy too for feminists to deny that they have knowledge and skills in order to minimize differences between women, as Gelsthorpe has noted.[24] The problem of power dynamics may become particularly acute when men are the subjects of research. But here the difficulty is likely to be reversed, with the male respondent rather than the female researcher engaged in manipulation, as both Scott and Smart have described.[25]

A number of ways of dealing with these kinds of dilemma have been suggested. For example, feminist research is characterized by a concern to record the subjective experiences of doing research.[26] This concern with reflexivity, also to be found in some forms of ethnography, may be expressed in two rather differing ways. It can mean reflecting upon, critically examining and exploring analytically the nature of the research process in an attempt to demonstrate the assumptions about gender (and, increasingly, race, disability and other oppressive) relations which are built into a specific project.[27] It may also refer to understanding the 'intellectual autobiography' of researchers. This is important for Stanley and Wise who have been critical of the way in which social research dichotomizes objectivity versus subjectivity. They argue that the researcher is also a subject in her research and that her personal history is part of the process through which 'understanding' and 'conclusions' are reached.[28] In both cases gender is seen, not just as something to be studied, but as an integral dimension of the research process and therefore also to be examined. Such work on reflexivity means that feminists have been at the forefront of discussions about the need to be open and honest about the research process, although, clearly, there are no easy solutions to the issues which have been raised by them.

A final way in which feminist research practice might be said to be distinctive has been in its insistence on its political nature and potential to bring about change in women's lives. At one time this was summed up in the slogan that feminist research was 'on', 'by' and 'for' women and that it should be designed with the aim of producing knowledge which would transform patriarchy.[29] Such a claim is not, however, uncontentious, as Glucksmann's chapter in this volume indicates. It implies, for instance, that studies which cannot be directly linked to transformational politics are not feminist. It raises the question as to how far the researcher is in control of the extent and direction of any change which her research might bring about. In fact, different kinds of change are potentially involved. One is that associated with empowerment, literally helping to give people knowledge, energy and authority in order that they might act. Anne Opie has argued that there are at least three ways in which an individual may be personally empowered through participation in a research project.[30] These are through their contribution to making visible a social issue, the therapeutic effect of being able to reflect on and re-evaluate their experience as part of the process of being interviewed, and the generally subversive outcome that these first two consequences may generate. It is also possible, of course, that the researcher may be empowered in these ways as well.

Yet these are rather limited notions of the effects that research may have. To start with, it is by no means the case that all outcomes will be positive. It may be possible for participants in a study to have their consciousnesses raised without the corresponding channels for action being available. Feminists have raised questions about the ethics of research which, having generated all sorts of issues in respondents' minds, then abandons them to come to terms with these on their own. Kelly, for instance, has described the kind of support which she felt it necessary to provide for the women who talked to her about surviving sexual violence.[31] Writing about her research on women who have left violent partners, Kirkwood reveals that one of them declined to return for a second interview because she had found the first so traumatic.[32] Of course, it may be that a particular study has little or even no effect on participants. Still, it is important to be aware of the possible negative, as well as positive, outcomes that might arise.

Feminists have also written about the personal consequences on the researcher of undertaking particular kinds of research. Stanley and Wise, for example, argue that their consciousnesses as feminists were raised in such a profound way, as a result of their work on obscene telephone calls, that it affected their views of men, patriarchy and feminism.[33] Kirkwood found her research so emotionally stressful that she eventually sought counselling, although she argues that, retrospectively, she can see that these emotions played an important role in the quality of her analysis.[34]

Finally, it should be noted that even if research has little impact on the lives of those included in it, it may be important for the category of persons they are taken to represent. Thus, work on rape or women's housing problems may be too late to alleviate the suffering of those directly involved in it, but can contribute to legislation, policy or the behaviour of agencies in ways which later enhance the experiences of others.

This discussion of feminist research practice has drawn attention to a number of issues and debates in the field. Whilst it is clear that there is no one methodological approach or research practice specific to feminism, as some critics have erroneously claimed,[35] this should come as no surprise since feminism embraces a number of theoretical positions and perspectives. What *is* obvious, however, is the challenging and wide-ranging nature of the discussion which has developed; a discussion which has implications for the whole of social research and not just for the feminist variant of it. The next section addresses some of these implications further in an epistemological context.

Epistemology and the Nature of Feminist Knowledge

The feminist concern with epistemology has centred on the questions 'who knows what, about whom and how is this knowledge legitimized?'. An early feminist writer on this subject, Dorothy Smith, argued, for instance, that sociology was not just the study of men in society, it was also a 'male science of society' because its whole approach to the study of the social world was coloured by a masculinist bias.[36] Catharine MacKinnon has referred to this as the 'male epistemological stance' which she defines as men's power to create the world from their own point of view, which then becomes the truth to be described. For MacKinnon, although objectivity and science represent supposedly neutral positions, they are, in fact, gendered and partial.[37] Feminism not only challenges this partiality; it also critiques the purported generality, disinterestedness and universality of male accounts.

The main way in which this has been done is to confront the dichotomizing that is characteristic of Enlightenment thinking and the view of science which developed out of it. The Enlightenment pictured humanity as engaged in an effort to find universal moral and intellectual self-realization. Important here was the notion that reason, as employed philosophically and scientifically, could provide an objective, reliable and universal foundation for knowledge.[38] This, of course, is the origin of the pursuit of rationality and the positivistic position discussed previously. The knowledge generated would then be used to improve the quality of life and enable societies to develop and progress to higher forms of civilization. The legitimacy that such knowledge lay claim to was, however, rooted in a series of dualisms: reason and rationality versus emotion; mind versus body; subject versus object; objective truth versus ideology and the distortion of 'interests'. Feminists have pointed out not only that these polarizations mirror the dichotomy male/female, but that they are false in the way in which they imply opposite, unconnected extremes and consistently devalue the second component of these.[39]

One writer whose work in this area is well known is Sandra Harding. In Harding's view there are three stages in the development of feminist epistemology. The first of these, 'feminist empiricism', argues that it is possible to remove sexist and other biases from the processes of research, particularly when problems for study are initially being identified and defined, in the belief that, once these have been eliminated, value-neutral work will be produced.[40] Harding regards this as an attempt to reform 'bad' science, simply by 'adding' women into existing frameworks, rather than questioning the prejudiced assumptions that are constitutive of science *per se*. The second stage, and the one in which we are currently located, according to Harding, is that of the 'feminist standpoint'. Here the argument is that understanding women's lives from a committed feminist exploration of their experiences of oppression produces more complete and less distorted knowledge than that produced by men. Women lead lives that have significantly different contours and patterns to those of men, and their subjugated position provides the possibility of more complete and less perverse understandings. Thus, adopting a feminist standpoint can reveal the existence of forms of human relationships which may not be visible from the position of the 'ruling gender'.

In addition to 'feminist empiricism' and 'feminist standpoint' Harding suggests that there is a third epistemological position, that of feminist postmodernism. This, along with other variants of postmodernism, is critical of universalistic grand theories and rejects the existence of an authentic self. Its focus instead is on fragmentation, multiple subjectivities, pluralities and flux. Harding clearly does not regard these three stages of feminist epistemology as being absolutely distinct and she argues at one point, for instance, that the empiricism and standpoint positions are locked into dialogue with each other. Further, although she refers to the latter as 'transitional' she is also uneasy about any postmodern alternatives. While apparently agreeing with the postmodern critique of science as a doomed project, she also sees problems in adopting it wholeheartedly, because of the way in which it deconstructs and demeans gender as an issue. Thus, feminists cannot afford to give up the standpoint approach because it is 'central to transferring the power to change social relations from the "haves" to the "have-nots" '.[41] Postmodernism, in contrast, provides a vision of the future by deconstructing the possibilities as to what this might mean.

The idea of a 'feminist standpoint' has gained currency, although there are variations on precisely what this involves.[42] Harding herself identifies the standpoint position as a 'successor science'. She argues that objectivity should involve the critical scrutiny of *all* evidence marshalled as part of the research process. Conventional notions of objectivity are 'weak' because they include the researchers' hidden and unexplicated cultural agendas and assumptions.[43] 'Strong' objectivity, as represented by the feminist standpoint, includes the systematic examination of such background beliefs. It thus 'avoids damaging forms of relativism ... and transforms the reflexivity of research from a problem into a scientific resource'.[44]

This idea of a successor science has been challenged by Stanley and Wise. They draw attention to 'silences' in Harding's work, particularly the lack of any real consideration of Black feminist and lesbian feminist points of view and argue that, rather than there being one standpoint, there are a range of different but equally valid ones.[45] Harding has recently attempted to overcome this problem and, in *Whose Science? Whose Knowledge?*, has included a section on 'others' (rather an unfortunate term suggesting deviation from some 'proper' norm). However, she does not deal with Stanley and Wise's central point; once the existence of several feminist stand*points* is admitted, then it becomes impossible to talk about 'strong' objectivity as a means of establishing superior or 'better' knowledge because there will, necessarily, be contested truth claims arising from the contextually grounded knowledge of the different standpoints. Stanley and Wise reject the idea of a successor science which, they say, still retains the implication that there is a social reality 'out there' that research can discover. Such 'foundationalism' is based on an insistence that 'truth' exists independently of the knower. They argue instead for a 'feminist fractured foundationalist epistemology'.[46] Whilst not disputing the existence of 'truth' and a material reality, judgments about them are always relative to the context within which such knowledge is produced.[47]

Those who defend the 'standpoint position', or one of its variants, deny that it signifies a collapse into total relativism, arguing, albeit sometimes for different reasons, that it occupies middle ground[48] in what is, conventionally and mistakenly, perceived as a foundationalism versus relativism dichotomy. There is still, however, the problem of the differing accounts which may emerge from different standpoints. While Stanley and Wise do not seem to regard this as an issue and write positively about such pluralism, others see difficulties.[49] Although it may be tempting to regard each standpoint as equally valid, this may be difficult when the power relations between women themselves differ. Things become particularly problematic, for example, when one standpoint contains elements or assumptions which are racist or heterosexist in nature. Another issue relates to whether it is the standpoint of the individual or the group which is being referred to and what the relationship between them might be. Neither is it clear whether it is the standpoints of feminists or of women more generally which are to be the focus of attention. The terms 'feminist' and 'women's' are often used interchangeably in the literature and, although a feminist approach is almost definitionally one which starts out from women's experiences, most women are not feminists and would not necessarily agree with accounts of the social world generated from a feminist stance.[50]

The 'standpoint' debate is an important one for the ways in which it systematically sets out the specific characteristics of a feminist epistemology and shows how these have relevance for a number of issues (relativism and objectivity, for instance) which are continually debated within sociology more generally. As has been seen, however, there are still areas of contention so that the notion of standpoint is not as definitive as the term itself might imply. Other matters also pertinent to the debate will be addressed in the more general discussions which follow.

Methods, Research Practice and Epistemology: Linking the Terms of Debate

The above sections have considered some of the significant arguments and developments in the debate about the constitutive features of feminist research. The focus of this debate seems to have changed over the years. Initially concerned with the rather narrow issue of method, it then broadened out to include different aspects of research practice. Recently, interest has been more epistemological in nature. One reason for this has been feminists' involvement in discussions about postmodernism which involves questioning many conventional notions about the nature of science, the legitimacy of theory and the status of empirical research.[51]

Although there is no one particular model of what feminist research should be like, recurrent themes appear throughout the literature. There is the focus on women's experiences, for example, and the concern for ethical questions which guide research practices. Feminists are concerned with the role of the researcher in the research, and with countering the scientistic philosophy and practice which is often associated with it. Although these themes, along with others, may not be specific to feminist work, the ways that they are treated (informed as they are by feminist theorizing about gender and feminist politics more generally), together with the manner in which they are combined, mean that it is possible to identify specific feminist research practices and epistemological positions.

There is a problem, however, in linking some of the arguments made at an epistemological level with what happens, or should happen, in terms of research practice and the use of particular research techniques. The discussion about feminist methods, for instance, which tends to have polarized qualitative versus quantitative approaches, is clearly at odds with the critique of the inhibiting effect of dualistic categorization that has been mounted by some feminists in the debate on epistemology. The methods literature has, thus, tended to reproduce the binary oppositions that have been criticized elsewhere, although there is now a move to advocate the importance of quantitative work, as indicated previously. Yet it is difficult to see how some of the issues currently at the forefront of epistemological concerns could really be empirically explored in anything other than qualitative work. The concern with the body and emotions as legitimate sources of knowledge, for example, with reflexivity and the critique of subject/object polarizations seem more appropriate to, and have more affinity with, research which employs relatively open-ended strategies. In many ways this should not surprise us. After all, as we have already seen, it was largely because of philosophical critiques of science and positivism that feminists developed their antipathy to quantification. But this now poses something of a problem because, despite feminists' disclaimers, the epistemological discussions still point to the overall legitimacy of qualitative studies, while researchers themselves are attempting to rehabilitate approaches that involve measurement and counting. This seems to indicate that arguments about what constitutes knowledge and discussions about methods of doing research are moving in opposite directions.

There is also divergence between the abstract analytical philosophizing which characterizes the literature on epistemology, particularly in its post-modernist form, and the more concrete language of that on methods and methodology. Can the former be translated into the practicalities of the latter? Whilst feminist postmodernism usefully directs attention to the fractured nature of womanhood, the possibilities of multiple identities and the dangers of totalizing theory, taken to their logical conclusions many of its precepts are inimical to the principles, never mind the practice, of undertaking empirical research. There are two main reasons for this. The first is that the social world is pictured as so fragmented, so individualistic, so totally in a state of flux that any attempt to present a more structured alternative, which, by its very nature, much social research does, is regarded as, a priori, mistaken. Not only is the task impossible, it is also seen as ill-conceived. A second reason is that the kind of research currently identified with the social sciences (be it surveys, interviews etc) is associated with precisely that, previously described, modernist Enlightenment tradition which postmodernism is trying to transcend. Whilst analyses of discourse and text are possible from within a postmodern perspective, anything which focuses on the materiality of human existence is virtually impossible, unless analyzed in terms of discourse and text. This does not mean, of course, that a postmodern approach has nothing to offer feminists. What it does mean is that because it contains radically different assumptions from those of other epistemological positions it has, potentially, different things to offer. Addressing this issue, Smart has described for example, how, in explaining rape, it is necessary to explore 'how women's bodies have become saturated with (hetero)sex, how codes of sexualized meanings are reproduced and sustained and to begin (or continue) the deconstruction of these meanings'.[52]

While this kind of work clearly makes a contribution to understanding the relationship between sexuality and sexual violence, it cannot be, and should not be regarded as, a substitute for other kinds of research. Two things are at issue here. The first relates to the problem of political intervention. If one major goal of feminist research is to challenge patriarchal structures and bring about some kind of social change, however conceived, then the postmodern approach, which eshews generalizations and emphasizes deconstruction, can only have a limited role in that endeavour. The second is the development of another kind of orthodoxy among feminists which advocates the postmodern approach as *the* way forward and appears dismissive of other kinds of work.[53] Not only does such a stance attempt to undermine other feminist positions, it also refutes the pragmatism which has been argued for in feminist research.[54] One element which is missing in most discussions of such work is the nature of the *external* constraints which are frequently faced. Not least of these are lack of time, money and other resources, in addition to the requirements imposed by funding bodies. That such facts intrude into and colour the research undertaken needs to be acknowledged. To the hard pressed researcher, being asked to reflect on intractable epistemological concerns can sometimes appear to be something of a dispensable luxury.

Critical Issues for Feminist Research

Currently, behind all the issues so far discussed in this chapter, there would seem to be three major and related concerns confronting feminists engaged in empirical social research. These are to do with the role of experience, the importance of 'race' and other forms of diversity, and the question of objectivity. One of the early driving forces of feminism was to challenge the passivity, subordination and silencing of women, by encouraging them to speak about their own condition and in so doing to confront the experts and dominant males with the limitations of their own knowledge and comprehension. Thus, the legitimacy of women's own understanding of their experiences is one of the hallmarks of feminism. An emphasis on experience is not, however, unproblematic. To begin with there is no such thing as 'raw' experience. Post-structuralist thinking clearly demonstrates that the very act of speaking about experience is to culturally and discursively constitute it.[55] People's accounts of their lives are culturally embedded. Their descriptions are, at the same time, a construction of the events that occurred, together with an interpretation of them.

The researcher is also, of course, involved in interpretation. There has been some discussion about this amongst feminists, with the suggestion that to do anything other than simply let women 'speak for themselves' constitutes violation. The problem with this is that it overlooks the fact that *all* feminist work is theoretically grounded; whatever perspective is adopted, feminism provides a theoretical framework concerned with gender divisions, women's oppression or patriarchal control which informs our understanding of the social world. It is disingenuous to imply otherwise. No feminist study can be politically neutral, completely inductive or solely based in grounded theory. *what* This is a contradiction in terms.

Also at issue here is that, although women's experience may constitute a starting point for the production of feminist knowledge, it is not sufficient for understanding the processes and practices through which this is organized.[56] Dorothy Smith has written that

> A sociology for women must be able to disclose *for* women how their own social situation, their everyday world is organized and determined by social processes which are not knowable through the ordinary means through which we find our everyday world.[57]

To repeat and describe what women might have to say, while important, can lead to individuation and fragmentation, instead of analysis. Feminism has an obligation to go beyond citing experience in order to make connections which

may not be visible from the purely experiential level alone. When researching women's lives we need to take their experience seriously, but we also, as
Maureen Cain argues, need 'to take our own theory seriously' and 'use the
theory to make sense of . . . the experience'.[58] This is an interpretive and
synthesizing process which *connects* experience to understanding.

One example, which draws particular attention to this issue, is the question of difference (as opposed to *differance*) in feminist literature[59] and the
importance of diversity in women's experiences, based on social attributes
such as class, sexuality, race, ethnicity and disability. To focus on such differences in terms of experience alone has several consequences. First, it
encourages benign description which concentrates largely on distinctions in
lifestyle, cultural practices etc. Second, it can exclude practices which oppress
people with disabilities, an analysis of racism, classism, homophobia, heterosexism and detailed structural explorations of how specific forms of oppression
are legitimated and maintained. Third, to imply that matters of class are
significant to the experience of the working class alone, that 'race' is important
for only some ethnic groups (for to be 'white' is also to have ethnicity), or
that sexuality is relevant only to lesbians and gays is to miss the point. For
these things structure *all* our lives, no matter how invisible they might be in
experiential terms, and we are not excused from confronting them because
we are not members of a particular oppressed group. The points made here
are also relevant to the position of the standpoint epistemologies. It is not
enough for each of the issues, so conveniently lumped together in the category
'difference', to be located in the experience of oppression of particular groups.
If feminism is to fully confront racism and heterosexism, if it is to be able to
analyze the interrelationships between class, race, gender and other forms of
oppression, then it cannot let its focus of research remain with experience
alone. One way of going beyond this is to use our theoretical knowledge to
address some of the silences in our empirical work. It is not always necessary
to include women who are white, black, working-class, lesbian or disabled in
our research to be able to say something about racism, classism, heterosexism
and disableism.

A final matter here concerns objectivity. Ramazanoglu has explained this
in terms of how to produce scientific knowledge about meanings and social
relationships, when people understand and experience these differently.[60] This
is a problem that feminism shares with sociology more generally, although, as
already discussed, some have advocated a feminist notion of 'strong' objectivity, while others have dismissed it as a problem altogether. But perhaps the
issue is not so much about objectivity (with its positivistic connotations of
facticity), nor of value-neutrality (and the supposed null effect of the researcher
on her research), as about the soundness and reliability of feminist research.
Feminist work needs to be rigorous if it is to be regarded as intellectually
compelling, politically persuasive, policy-relevant and meaningful to anyone
other than feminists themselves. At the moment, it appears that this is
more easily dealt with on a practical level than on an epistemological one. At

the very least this call for rigour involves being clear about one's theoretical assumptions, the nature of the research process, the criteria against which 'good' knowledge can be judged and the strategies used for interpretation and analysis. In feminist work the suggestion is that all of these things are made available for scrutiny, comment and (re)negotiation, as part of the process through which standards are evaluated and judged.

This chapter indicates that there is no one answer to the question 'what is feminist research?' and many contested issues of method, methodology and epistemology remain. It is clear, however, that, in contrast to more conventional discussions of research, which have a tendency to be somewhat arid, the debate within feminism is vibrant and dynamic. The issues that have been discussed here are important for feminism in several ways. Not only do they inform the research process, they also influence the empirical knowledge to be produced and the theoretical knowledge which will be constructed. The outcomes are, therefore, crucial for feminism taken as a whole.

Notes

The author is grateful to Bob Coles and Rosemary Deem for comments on an initial draft of this chapter.

1 Harding (1987), p. 2.
2 See, for example, Kelly *et al.* (1992a); Reinharz (1992); Stanley and Wise (1990).
3 See, for example, Bowles and Duelli Klein (1983); Reinharz (1983); Graham (1983).
4 For example, Cicourel (1974); Filmer *et al.* (1972).
5 Graham (1983, 1984).
6 Bowles and Duelli Klein (1983); Graham (1983, 1984); Stanley and Wise (1983).
7 Kelly *et al.* (1992a).
8 For the former see, for example, Stanley and Wise (1983); for the latter see, for example, Martin and Roberts (1984).
9 Maynard (1989), ch. 2.
10 The various positions are discussed in Harding (1986).
11 Bryman (1988), p. 42.
12 *Ibid.*, p. 125.
13 Marsh (1979).
14 Research on equal opportunities policies in the Careers Service, conducted with Bob Coles and Jo Riding, involved sending a questionnaire to all Principal Careers Officers in Great Britain to find out what kind of policies, with regard to gender, were in place, and what sorts of administrative procedures were being followed to ensure such policies were being pursued successfully, and to construct a catalogue of innovatory or good practices. A content analysis of policies and all relevant literature received was also undertaken. See Coles *et al.* (1988) and Coles and Maynard (1990). The research on women employed in the tourist sector was directed by Roy Carr-Hill and myself. In this, questionnaires delivered to the place of work were supplemented by interviews. See Carr-Hill and Maynard (1989).

15   Brannen (1992); McLaughlin (1991).
16   See also Kelly *et al.* (1992a).
17   Kelly (1988), p. 6.
18   Cook and Fonow (1986); Bowles and Duelli Klein (1983).
19   Duelli Klein (1983).
20   Cook and Fonow (1986); Gelsthorpe (1990).
21   Stanley and Wise (1993).
22   Oakley (1981).
23   Finch (1984).
24   Gelsthorpe (1992), p. 216.
25   Scott, S. (1984); Smart (1984).
26   Gelsthorpe (1990), p. 93.
27   Fonow and Cook (1991a).
28   Stanley and Wise (1993).
29   Duelli Klein (1983).
30   Opie (1992), p. 64.
31   Kelly (1988).
32   Kirkwood (1993).
33   Stanley and Wise (1991).
34   Kirkwood (1993).
35   Hammersley, M. (1992).
36   Smith (1988b).
37   MacKinnon (1982), pp. 23–4.
38   Flax (1987).
39   Harding (1986).
40   *Ibid.* It should be noted that Harding's critique is of empiric*ism*, which fetishizes facts as the only valid objects of knowledge, and not of empirical work *per se*.
41   *Ibid.*, p. 195.
42   Haraway (1988); Rose (1983); Stanley (1990a).
43   Harding (1991), p. 149.
44   *Ibid.*, p. 164.
45   Stanley and Wise (1990), p. 28.
46   Stanley and Wise (1993).
47   Stanley and Wise (1990), p. 41.
48   *Ibid.*; Harding (1991), p. 138.
49   Ramazanoglu (1989b).
50   *Ibid.*
51   Flax (1987); Nicholson (1990).
52   Smart (1990), p. 83.
53   For example, Hekman (1990).
54   Kelly *et al.* (1992a); Stanley and Wise (1990).
55   Foucault (1981, 1986).
56   Ramazanoglu (1989b).
57   Smith (1986), p. 6.
58   Cain (1986), p. 265.
59   Whereas 'difference' relates to diversity conceived in experiential terms, '*differance*' refers to competing constructions of meaning in a post-structuralist or postmodernist sense.
60   Ramazanoglu (1989b), p. 437.

Chapter 2

Researching Women's Lives or Studying Women's Oppression? Reflections on What Constitutes Feminist Research

Liz Kelly, Sheila Burton and Linda Regan

The central question which this chapter explores is what counts as 'feminist research'. Our discomfort with some definitions is linked to our work to-gether in the Child Abuse Studies Unit (CASU), set up to develop feminist theory and practice, based in the Polytechnic (now University) of North London. CASU was established in 1987 by Esther Saraga and Mary MacLeod with an explicit intent: to link feminist concerns and initiatives in academia and the statutory and voluntary sectors, through a combination of research, networking, training, conference organizing and campaigning. In late 1992, we are the remaining staff of CASU, and whilst our job titles involve 're-search', we are committed to maintaining the original vision of CASU's role. Since 1988 all the full-time staff in CASU have had to 'income generate' – our own salaries and all the running costs of the Unit. The context we work in is, therefore, contradictory; whilst we have the safety of an explicit femin-ism both our personal job security and the long-term future of CASU are tenuous.

Our discussion is structured through three connected themes: the theo-retical grounding of feminist research, which has shifted from a link between the academy and activism to a concern to explicate a 'feminist epistemology'; questioning what we see as an orthodoxy in definitions of 'feminist research' reflected to some extent in the provisional title for this collection 'Studying Women's Lives'; and exploring the structural location of researchers in higher education and relationships within research teams. These themes move from the intellectual foundation within which we locate our work, to putting these ideas into practice (or not), to the social relationships between women who conduct research. Feminism ought to provide us with a coherent way of con-necting these aspects of 'doing research', our concerns are with the gaps and silences which we have had to 'fill in' for ourselves.

Liz Kelly, Sheila Burton and Linda Regan

Our Definition of 'Feminist Research'

Feminism for us is both a theory and practice, a framework which informs our lives. Its purpose is to understand women's oppression in order that we might end it.[1] Our position as feminist researchers, therefore, is one in which we are part of the process of discovery and understanding and also responsible for attempting to create change. This orientation draws on what we understand as the liberatory intention and method of consciousness-raising (CR) – to use our experiences of living as women as a starting point from which to build explanatory frameworks which would inform activism. Our hope is that the research we do reflects the dynamic and cumulative process of CR, combining personal and social change in a continuing and reflective process. Our strongest networks are with women (and a few men) outside the academy who want and need critical research to support/inform their work. As Liz Stanley has noted,

> feminism outside of the academic mode has insisted on the crucial need for useful knowledge, theory and research as practice, on committed understanding as a form of praxis ('understand the world and then change it'), and also on an unalienated knowledge.[2]

Our desire to do, and goal in doing, research is to create useful knowledge, knowledge which can be used by ourselves and others to 'make a difference'. Feminism as a praxis is not based on the simple fact of women sharing a gender in common, but on a common agenda – the liberation of women. Many of the commentaries published in the 1980s interpret the first decade of 'second wave' feminism as an idealistic universalizing of women's experiences. Whilst much of the more academic work published in the 1970s (and into the 1980s) can be read in this way, activist literature and history tells a somewhat different story; a story in which differences between women were sometimes recognized[3] and where conflicts and struggles about race, class and sexuality were commonplace within feminist groups, campaigns and organizations.[4] Our respective, and different, involvements in this 'inside' story inform our understanding of, and practice as, feminists.

That said, however, it is nonetheless the case that the 1980s placed differences between women on every feminist agenda, and demanded a reworking of what feminism means. Our goal now is to develop an anti-oppressive feminist praxis[5] which aims to both account for, and take account of, the complex interplay of multiple sources of oppression (and areas of privilege) in women's lives. We see this as a goal to be striven for, to be constructed in the individual and collective 'doing' of feminism in various locations. It is certainly not the preserve of academics; the most committed attempts to create it which we have either witnessed or been part of occurred outside the academy.

Shifting Connections between Theory and Practice

In the twelve years since *Doing Feminist Research*[6] was published, 'Women's Studies' has become a growth area in publishing. The extent and range of this growth is breathtaking – especially for those of us who remember scouring bookshops, library shelves and journal contents pages for anything that would help us ask, not to mention answer, our urgent questions.

The earliest definitions of feminist research centred on the creation of knowledge about women through research with women. The link between research and action/activism was tenuous, critical reflection on personal experience and awareness of differences between women muted. An orthodoxy developed in social science, but with wider ramifications, perhaps best summarized in the phrase 'research on, with and for women', and which asserted or implied that 'feminist method' involved face-to-face interviewing.[7] Whilst the differences between research 'on', 'with' and 'for' women were explored, it was not until the mid 1980s that this orthodoxy was questioned in any fundamental way. Two strands of criticism predominated: the failure to address the question 'which women', both in terms of who the researcher and participants were; and the implicit presumption that 'experience' was unproblematic. The relationship of feminist research to the struggle for women's liberation has regrettably ceased to be a central concern.

Both the initial conceptions of feminist research and recent rethinking have led many feminist theorists into the most complex and contested areas of philosophy, particularly the relationships between epistemology and method. Engagement with the fundamental question of the creation and validity of knowledge has produced a rich, but inaccessible, literature concerned with what a feminist epistemology and/or feminist methodology might consist of.[8] Whilst fascinating and challenging, these explorations take place at an abstract level, seldom connected to the practice of either research or activism – with a few notable exceptions[9] relatively few of the published reflections on feminist method are written by research practitioners. In our cynical moments we ponder whether the masculinist hierarchy between theory and practice is being reproduced within academic feminism – demonstrated by the fact that the 'new' books which excite and exercise feminists are no longer held in common, that a language/discourse has developed which increasingly separates women inside and outside the academy.

Two factors influencing this increasing disconnection in the 1980s, which have implications for how feminist research is understood and undertaken, are 'identity politics' and postmodernism. Whereas in the 1970s experience was viewed as a necessary starting point, in the 1980s it has become an end in itself. Whilst personal experience undoubtedly influences one's perspective and understanding, many current references to it are determinist and essentialist. Experience/identity is substituted for, or deemed to be equivalent to, politics, as if critical awareness and understanding are inscribed on a person through forms of oppression, with an implicit or explicit presumption that such awareness is inaccessible to those who have not 'lived' such experiences. Whilst not seeking to deny differences in experience, critical consciousness involves developing a perspective on, a politics of, experience. For domination to be challenged it has to be, in principle, possible to develop an inclusive, liberatory feminism which encompasses the range of differences between women, where what we share is a politics within which experiences can be located, explained and struggled with/against.

The social experience of, for example, living in the world as a lesbian is influenced by other aspects of women's identity and biography. Our class origins, race, nationality, physical abilities and religious upbringing will connect in complex ways with our sexual identity; as will our early (and subsequent) sexual experiences, which could be abusive or chosen, heterosexual or lesbian. Alongside these differences are a range of others which do not connect in any determined way with either identities or personal biography. They include, but are not limited to:

- accounting for sexuality in terms of biology or choice;
- whether individuals claim either lesbian or gay as a positive identity, or view either or both as negative, or eschew any form of 'labelling';
- the extent to which individuals are 'out' to kin, colleagues and friends and in public settings;
- the extent to which lesbian identities and relationships reflect or are constructed in opposition to conventional femininity and heterosexuality;
- the extent to which lesbianism is understood to connect with feminism.

How both sets of differences are understood, and acted in relation to, has more than a little to do with politics; and there is currently no unifying 'lesbian' or 'lesbian feminist' politics. Conservative, liberal and radical positions exist, as do complex configurations which draw on more than one tradition/source. Changes in political perspective/understanding result in experience being thought about, and accounted for 'differently'.

Changes in our political understandings and commitments influence what we notice, what we take account of, and what we see as needing to be accounted for – and change is not determined by identity. The passage from Liz Stanley quoted earlier refers to 'committed understanding'. One does not have to have experienced an event or a form of oppression in order to attempt to develop 'committed understanding'. One recent example from our work involves being commissioned to conduct a research review on the connections between disability and child abuse.[10] Looking in detail and critically at a literature, and working alongside disability activists, produced a shift in consciousness, with implications for both research methods and social theory, which we are now collectively committed to exploring. Most basic social research methods require forms of physical ability – especially speaking and writing. The exclusions that this creates are 'taken for granted' in methods texts, research training, and descriptions of how specific samples were created.

Most, if not all, high-profile, large-scale, well-funded surveys make no reference to either the inclusion or exclusion of people with disabilities. The consequences of this failure to develop 'inclusive methods' extend to studies of disability, where others – usually carers or clinicians – 'speak' for children and adults with disabilities. On a more philosophical level these same presumptions of ability thread through recent published work on what constitutes the self. On a practical level our discussions of these issues led to a realization that many of the powerful metaphors about women's resistance to oppression refer to these forms of physical ability – 'speaking out', 'having a voice', 'writing our lives'. The challenges to our praxis which including people with disabilities involve are extensive and profound, creating for us a series of new questions.

Whilst 'inclusion' is a central theme in recent feminist theory, it is through practice that we discover what the 'taken-for-granted' processes of exclusion consist of, and are confronted with the necessity of finding ways to overcome them. It was 'doing' a piece of work which challenged us in relation to disability. Similarly, it was not academic theory but rather the insistence by women who were not white, able-bodied, educated and/or heterosexual that they wanted access to, and influence in, women's organizations which created an impetus for change.

We use these examples to suggest that the specifics of our particular locations in systems of oppression need not be determining of either our understanding or our practice. Some of the issues which appear intractable in theory are being addressed by many (but by no means all) feminist services, campaigns, national and international coalitions. The 'pessimism of theory' which threads through much recent academic feminist writing needs to be tempered by an acknowledgment and recognition of change occurring in practice. Whilst this is uneven, and the struggles to achieve change painful, we do each other and the movement we are part of a disservice if feminism outside the academy is represented as something abstract, or historical, rather than a movement in process.

Postmodernism's claims to the moral high ground are frequently predicated on an insistence that it can rectify the failure of feminism to take account of 'difference'. These claims rest in part on a rewriting of the history of feminist activism we noted earlier. We question representations of 1970s feminism which assert that differences between women were persistently and deliberately ignored in order to create an illusion of solidarity and sisterhood, or that one can generalize from what was published (and even here selective sources are used) to what was happening everywhere in the Women's Liberation Movement.

Postmodernist concerns are discussed at a level rather far removed from the practical questions which preoccupy researchers: how to get access; how to build a sample; what methods to use; what questions to ask and how to word them; how to make sense of the information we have collected. If taken in its strong form postmodernism suggests that most recognized forms of social research are pointless exercises. Rather than feminist 'research' – the creation of new knowledge which addresses aspects of women's oppression and which is a resource in the creation of social change – the task now becomes to deconstruct already existent forms and examples of cultural production. (The ultimate goal of many who adopt this framework appears to be reconstruction through becoming cultural producers themselves – filmmakers, journalists, novel writers).

In this context, to admit to being a researcher, to maintain that there are things we do not know, and that there may be strategies which might enable us to find out, is to risk the charge of being deemed an 'essentialist' or an 'empiricist' or even a 'positivist'.[11] This relativism and loss of connection to the original concerns of women's liberation movements is disturbing. If we cannot speak of 'women' how can there be such a thing as 'women's oppression' or a political analysis of it? This is not answered by a sleight of hand – 'feminisms' – since multiples are logically dependent on there being a singular.

What troubles us most about the current 'romance with epistemology' is that it seems more concerned with attempting to convince the predominantly male academy that a privileged status should be accorded to 'women's ways of knowing' than with enabling us to better discover and understand what is happening in women's lives, and how we might change it.

Questioning some Orthodoxies

Much of our research has not been exclusively 'on' nor 'with' women, since it has involved men and focused on institutions. The issues we have researched, however, are 'feminist issues' – primarily domestic violence and child sexual abuse. We have throughout attempted to 'do' our research as feminists and to ask feminist questions.[12] The issues we wrestle with are different from those which tend to dominate most discussions of feminist research. We have written elsewhere about how our practice has led us to reflect on constructions of 'feminist method', in particular the view that no self-respecting feminist would use quantitative methods.[13] This section extends that discussion through a critical examination of what have become key 'definers' of feminist research, which we present as 'statements', linked in a connected logic. We use our own work, and that of other feminists, to point out the limitations of each, and to suggest routes through which we can extend what counts as feminist research.

Statement One: Feminist research is research on and with women

Implicit in this statement are presumptions about the conduct and content of feminist research: that it involves direct contact with women; that information is gathered directly from women. This sets up a number of intended and unintended exclusions – documents and texts; male participants and institutions – which are in fact the basis for much feminist research. Sophie Laws in *Issues of Blood*[14] records her discomfort with these exclusions, which if accepted would define her research on menstruation – based on interviews with men, recording of discussions in men's groups and analysis of medical texts – as using 'non-feminist' methods and sources. She provides a rigorous justification of her approach, and a strong challenge to the 'comfortableness' implicit in this construction of feminist research.

The work we have conducted in CASU does not all fit the 'on and with women' injunction. We have studied social work,[15] and are currently studying police practice; institutions employing women and men. A project on local policy and practice in relation to domestic violence encompassed a range of institutions and included as one part of a multi-methodological strategy a short survey completed by 240 women.[16] Our ESRC-funded prevalence study of sexual abuse,[17] and a recently funded qualitative follow-up study include both female and male participants. Our decision-making in the sexual abuse studies was the outcome of assessing that our ability to engage in debates within and without academia about the prevalence of sexual abuse in the lives of male and female children, the relative proportion of male and female abusers, and how gender influences the meaning and impact of experiences of abuse necessitated the involvement of both men and women in the projects.

Whilst much feminist research rightly focuses on women, on creating knowledge about women's experiences, if our concern is to understand women's oppression we need to target our attention on the ways it is structured and reproduced. Feminist research focuses on how women's lives are constrained by the actions of men individually and collectively and the strategies girls and women find to resist, challenge and subvert. Studying women's lives as a feminist means that male dominance, masculinity and men are always part of the research. Women's accounts cannot provide us with everything we need to know, since we (individually or collectively) do not necessarily 'know' either the extent or the content of the deliberate strategies men and male-dominated institutions use to maintain their power, nor how the responses we encounter from professionals are connected to theoretical discourses and/or institutional/national policies. Feminist research should map these connections – either within a particular study, or by linking a study to others which provide a broader context. Cynthia Cockburn's recent study of 'men's resistance to sex equality in organizations'[18] is an example of research which explores the perspectives of men and women, and connects them to institutional and government policy.

One of the strongest arguments made for 'men's studies' has been that feminist research has neglected the study of men and masculinity, and that these areas can be studied more effectively by men. We have already noted our view that feminist research has addressed these issues, albeit most frequently through women's experience. We also cautiously welcome critical studies by men of men and masculinity. Sophie Laws notes that a much neglected issue is 'the relationship between individual men's behaviour and beliefs and the social system of patriarchy. In much of the literature men as men disappear altogether – we have only "society" and "women"'.[19] She proceeds to ask a disturbing question: is the implication of making women visible through recording their experiences simply 'informing the powerful about an oppressed group'? Why are feminists so chary about 'studying up'? Why is there so little debate about how we might approach studying men? We are anxious that our 'leaving the field' makes it even more possible for 'men's studies' to become a 'male preserve', a form of academic colonization where feminist scholarship is raided for ideas and concepts and transformed into cultural capital benefiting male academics. Whilst studying the construction of masculinity is of key importance, what needs to be explored is not so much how men 'experience' this, or explicating different 'masculinities', but, as Sophie Laws has pointed out, the connections between the construction and practice of masculinity and women's (and children's) oppression. There are revealing parallels here outside the academy, where work with abusive men has received attention and levels of funding seldom paid to or for work with women and children, and where the framework underpinning the work frequently fails to take the safety of women and children as its starting point.

These deliberations led us to the somewhat contentious conclusion that we would be willing to design and conduct an evaluation of a 'men's programme'. Both the failure to evaluate many such programmes and the simplistic design of the few systematic evaluations of the content, process and impacts of such programmes influenced our thinking. A stern test of attempts to change men's behaviour, which is informed by what we already know about women and children's experiences of abuse, is in the interests of the women and children who will bear the consequences if these forms of intervention are prematurely deemed 'successful'. Although our evaluation outline has not, as yet, been funded, we have used the preparatory thinking and writing[20] in training, consultancy and discussion with women's organizations struggling with the complex issues such programmes have raised.

Statement Two: Feminist research uses qualitative methods

Whilst several brave women in the 1980s defended quantitative methods, it is nonetheless still the case that not just qualitative methods, but the in-depth face-to-face interview has become the paradigmatic 'feminist method'.[21] Although the feminist position connects to broader debates within social science about the accuracy, complexity, depth and integrity of data, this is not the principal ground on which the claim is based. Rather it connects to and builds on the view that feminist research is 'on' and 'with' women. Interviews are seen to provide the route through which inter-subjectivity and non-hierarchical relationships between women researchers and women participants can be developed.

An implicit set of presumptions underpins this position, some of which we have only come to question relatively recently: that women want to share their experiences with another woman; that this is always of personal benefit; that the sharing of gender will enable any difficult or painful accounts to be dealt with sympathetically and effectively. Where our research is based on voluntary samples, the first presumption might hold true, although even here there are problematic issues of who chooses to participate and why. Neither of the other presumptions can be made in advance of actually doing the research. Sophie Laws has also suggested the notion of the 'therapeutic' interview as an 'exemplary feminist practice'[22] is based on a liberal revision of the practice of consciousness-raising (see earlier discussion).

In conducting our prevalence study, which used a questionnaire, we began to ponder on the presumed willingness to reveal experience. The range and depth of what the young people participating chose to tell us varied between only answering simple yes/no questions about forms of sexual abuse through briefly answering in-depth questions on them to detailed and personalized accounts. Since they did not volunteer for the study (although they were given explicit permission to not participate) we are not convinced that some of them would have mentioned experiences in a context where they were obliged to answer follow-up questions. Whatever our topic of investigation individuals will be at different stages in their willingness and ability to discuss it. It means something different to disclose information anonymously on paper or computer than to speak/communicate it interactively with another person. Whilst it is not necessarily the case that matching interviewers with interviewees in terms of race, class, age and gender creates more 'ease' and 'disclosure',[23] these interactional dynamics are part of the interview process and play a lesser role in surveys. We need to explore these issues in our research, rather than presume we know what their implications and consequences are in general and in particular.

Our increasing use of the self-report questionnaire, in a range of studies, has led to other questions and insights. Ann Oakley's classic essay on interviewing[24] is an account of how its traditional form was adapted in relation to her feminist practice – the classic social science interview had to be transformed. We ought to at least explore the possibility of transforming the survey/questionnaire. The problem for feminists is not necessarily the form of surveys, or the creation of numeric data, but 'the ways in which research participants are treated and the care with which researchers attempt to represent the lived experience of research participants'.[25] Surveys can include open-ended questions, and need not be designed with ease of analysis as the primary criterion.[26] In the prevalence study the design of the questionnaire and our modes of analysis allow us to move between generalized numerical data, direct quotations and individual experiences.

Rather than assert the primacy of any method, we are now working with a flexible position: our choice of method(s) depends on the topic and scale of the study in question. Wherever possible we would combine and compare methods, in order to discover the limitations and possibilities of each. But where we are bound by contracts that is a luxury we are seldom in a position to afford.

We have also come to question the presumed benefits of qualitative methods to participants. Whilst most feminists have taken the potential unintended consequences of participation in research seriously, many of our accounts are self-justifying descriptions of how we ensured that participation was neither damaging or exploitative. Few of these refer to explicit attempts to 'research' the meaning and impact of participation, as an integral part of methodology. We need to take much more seriously the potential for harm, that participation may be more of an intrusion/imposition/irritation/responsibility than a benefit. Several feminists have noted recently that the fact that in-depth, ethnographic methods reduce distance means that the potential for harm increases.[27] Fonow and Cook suggest that 'A well crafted quantitative study may be more useful to policy makers and cause less harm to women than a poorly crafted qualitative one'.[28] It may be that participation is positive, but our practice of 'reflexivity' ought to extend to our participants, asking them to comment on the research process from their experience of it. We are now committed to self-consciously studying the impact of participation in research, which includes inviting feedback from participants on our research design. In two current projects we are adapting the conventional practice of piloting: instead of asking individuals or groups to 'pretend' they are participants we are using a more interactive mode in which we ask them to tell us what they think the questions mean, and to suggest ways of rewriting them if they are unclear or too complex. We also include a question at the end of every questionnaire we design where participants can record any additional questions they think we should have included.

Statement Three: Feminist research should be empowering for participants

Two levels of problem arise here; precisely what researchers are claiming in research with women and the relevance of this aim where the study involves institutions and/or includes men. The failure to explore the latter stems, in our view, from an acceptance of statements one and two.

Given the concern amongst feminists to 'democratize' the research process it is surprising how little published work conducted in the West involves the use of 'action' or 'participatory' methods (there is some small-scale community research which draws on this tradition, but these studies are seldom made available to broad audiences). These forms of research were designed precisely for that purpose, and their relative absence (in contrast to the practice of feminists in developing countries) is both surprising and revealing.

Some of the glib ways in which 'empowerment' is used in discussions of feminist research with women concern us greatly. They reflect either an arrogance of viewpoint or a failure to think through what our 'power' consists of. A well designed and carefully constructed study can result in reflecting differently on experience, and where researchers have 'done their homework' it is often possible to refer participants to resources which they may benefit from. But participating in a research project is unlikely, in the vast majority of cases, to transform the conditions of women's lives. We cannot, for example, provide access to alternative housing options, childcare places or a reasonable income. Nor are the women's services to which we may refer women, especially in the resource-starved voluntary sector, always able to meet their needs.

Even participatory research methods are based on research as a way of politicizing participants in order that they can subsequently engage in actions which will challenge the conditions of their oppression. In this context a distinction needs to be made between not exploiting participants, offering them feedback and more grandiose ambitions. We would also benefit from information from participants about precisely how, and in what ways, participation did or did not benefit them. We would then be in a much stronger position to develop appropriate conceptions of what kinds of empowerment are possible through research.

Simplistic notions of participation and empowerment also mask other aspects of the power and responsibility of the researcher. It is we who have the time, resources and skills to conduct methodical work, to make sense of experience and locate individuals in historic and social contexts. One group of feminist researchers has provided us with a remarkably honest account of their attempts to democratize research.[29] An integral part of their methodology was to include the participants in the analysis phase, and they were surprised by women's resistance: what the women participating wanted was for the researchers to 'be' researchers – locate their individual experiences in relation to those of the other participants, and the research team's developing analysis. This contextualizing and comparing of personal experience is what many research participants want 'back', and some – but by no means all – are interested in more general discussions. There is no doubt that this feedback and dialogue enriches research, but it is an illusion to think that, in anything short of a participatory research project, participants can have anything approaching 'equal' knowledge to the researcher.

The women in this research team also raise the troubling issue of what we do when our understandings and interpretations of women's accounts would either not be shared by some of them, and/or represent a form of challenge or threat to their perceptions, choices and coping strategies. Reliance on simplistic models of 'empowerment' disguises and denies these complexities. It is entirely possible, not to mention probable, that some women participating in research hold anti-feminist viewpoints. What does 'empowerment' mean when women express overtly racist, homophobic and/or classist opinions in a research context? Not only do these realities problematize the 'empathy' which shared gender is frequently deemed to embody, they also raise complex issues about whether we simply treat such responses as 'data', and whether some of 'us' are more able to do this than others – our own identities/biographies/politics affect our reactions.

Extending the range of what we research and how produces complex dilemmas, which simple definitions of feminist research cannot accommodate. We cannot presume common experience or perspective with women participants. Extending this discussion to men and institutions raises additional issues, but also presents a possible alternative model.

Where our research involves studying men or institutions, how we think about power, and the 'power' of the researcher, shift dramatically. Rather than 'sharing' it, our concerns are how to limit its potential use against us, and how to conduct a study which reveals its surface and hidden forms in relation to the research question/topic. In this context the 'empowerment' of research participants is not and indeed should not be our goal. If that concept has any meaning it must relate to the groups over which these individuals and institutions exercise power. One position, taken by many radical researchers, is that the end results of a project will be a contribution to challenging the power relationships exposed by the study. But is this sufficient? What are the implications for feminists of collecting data which documents the reproduction of inequality, and presenting no challenge to those beliefs/attitudes/behaviours when they are expressed? If we see our feminism as constructing our methods what kinds of practices are appropriate here?

We want to propose a concept of research practice which is seldom addressed in the literature, and which perhaps departs even further from traditional 'objective' formulations, which draws on aspects of action and participatory research. Part of our task is to develop 'challenging methods', by which we mean ways of conducting research which not only create knowledge, but are designed to question oppressive attitudes and behaviour. The topic of study, who the participants are and the methods used will affect the form of challenge and how direct or indirect it can be. But we believe that it is possible, even in questionnaires, to ask questions in such a way that they encourage different ways of thinking. We also know there are ways of interacting with others, even where you are dependent on maintaining access, which at best problematize and at worst refuse to support/collude with particular attitudes and actions.

In the research commissioned by Hammersmith and Fulham to study local responses to domestic violence we constructed both interviews and questionnaires to be used with workers in a range of institutions to address responses to different groups of women. These questions were intended to serve a dual function – to assess whether additional needs are understood and responded to, and to raise these as issues which need thinking about. In an interview context we were able to record the initial responses and, where the response indicated a lack of awareness, use probe questions to raise these directly. The probes were directed towards exploring an individual's ignorance or prejudices, by encouraging reflection on how women's circumstances and needs may not be the same. We used open and general questions rather than leading questions (such as 'is that always the case?' or 'what about the issue of immigration status?' or 'do you think elderly women might find it harder to talk about these things?' or 'why do you think you've never dealt with a lesbian experiencing abuse?') because our intention was not simply to demonstrate bad practice (a relatively easy thing to do in most large institutions), but to encourage within the research process a questioning in the participants of their suppositions. Both the discussions which took place within and after some interviews and comments which were made in relation to others suggested that we had indeed raised consciousness to some degree. We did not have the time or resources to follow through the impact of the interviews on individuals' practice, and we see this as an important area for future research; not simply what institutions do with research reports, but whether the practice of those who directly participate is, or is not, affected.

A somewhat more contentious area in which challenging methods can be explored is in research with women, and there are strong parallels here with practice in support services such as refuges or crisis lines. Whilst one version of feminist practice recommends listening, recording and a non-judgmental stance, there is another possibility which is to raise/offer different ways of understanding experience. In our support work with individuals, both in CASU and outside it, we see this latter version as feminist practice. For example, in both support work and research, where women attribute the reasons for an assault to ethnicity or class, it is possible to use further questions to explore the root of this view, and to use other evidence to question its validity as a general explanation for sexual violence whilst exploring its relevance in a particular instance. Conversely, where women are clearly blaming themselves for abuse, exploring their reasoning in more depth and linking this to the intention and behaviour of the perpetrator(s) can open up different ways of understanding for both researcher and participant, support worker and woman seeking support.

The most basic, yet fundamental feminist question has always been 'why?' Exploring with individuals why they think and act as they do enriches our understanding, and is a far stronger base from which to explore potential change than knowing only what they think and do. The context and content of the issue in question will affect whether feminist researchers choose to offer alternative possibilities for understanding and/or action. This offering of other possibilities leaves open whether the research participant chooses to accept or reject, ignore or explore further these options in the research or any other context.

If we accept that conducting and participating in research is an interactive process, what participants get or take from it should concern us. Whilst we are not claiming that researchers have the 'power' to change individuals' attitudes, behaviour or perceptions, we do have the power to construct research which involves questioning dominant/oppressive discourses; this can occur within the process of 'doing' research, and need not be limited to the analysis and writing-up stages. The potential of research to create change can become an aspect of our methodology, which will in turn create more complex understandings of resistances to social/individual change.

Statement Four: Feminist research is directed towards social change

This statement is implicit in the 'for' women component of the simple definition – that feminists do research with the intention of being of use in the struggle for women's liberation. There is, however, a marked absence of discussion of how this occurs. Our earlier discussion of consciousness-raising and the importance of 'useful knowledge' is relevant here, with implications for both how we conduct our research and how we present and use our findings.

In CASU we are in frequent contact with practitioners – through both consultancy and training. We do not offer 'skills-based' training, but rather time to think and rethink perspectives. We have had to learn how to work with theory and research in ways which are 'of use' in the complexity, messiness and highly pressurised context of professional practice. What has become increasingly obvious is how frequently work which should and could be 'of use' is not, since the authors are speaking to their peers in academia rather than those who are in a position to put the knowledge and insights to practical use. Who we envisage ourselves addressing, and the purpose for which we are writing, affects what we produce. One of the peer reviewers of our first final report to the ESRC[30] commented that 'as it stands this is of more use to practitioners than academics'. They regarded this as a criticism, we took it as a compliment – as we had hoped that the work we had done would be 'of use' to those who have responsibility for child protection.

Most of the projects we have worked on have been directed towards informing change, and hence have been written with those who are in a position to make change in mind. The domestic violence project was influenced by a belief that there are things we do not know which influence how women make sense of their situations, what options they feel are open to them in seeking support, and what informs the responses of others to them. The project combined exploring what a wide range of women had done/thought they would do with an assessment of all facets of local provision. The primary aim was to improve both our understanding of women's needs and the services available to them. Because of our commitment to 'using' knowledge we were asked to produce an information pack on domestic violence and conduct a training for trainers programme in the borough.[31] Both used the research directly. The research and its applications has been cited, and used, as a model of innovative practice for local authority initiatives in relation to domestic violence.[32]

Not every research project offers such obvious possibilities for making it 'useful'. But as feminist researchers we should be assessing from the outset and throughout each project, how the knowledge created could be made useful outside the academy.

The Conditions and Relationships in which Feminist Research is Produced

In a previous paper we noted the lack of attention to feminist practice in research teams.[33] We have found only one paper which explores this issue,[34] and this does not address the issues we have found most difficult. What is seldom discussed is the status and location of researchers (as opposed to 'research') within academia; what Liz Stanley has called the 'academic division of labour'.[35] Although a period of training, learning one's craft, is necessary, the position of researchers as employees, rather than students, in higher education, continues to afford less financial reward, status and security than teaching positions. The traditional model of research involves tenured academics being grant-holders, with the majority of the work being done by over-qualified female research 'assistants' – the title itself is revealing.[36] Seldom noted is the fact that the invisible work in research – data-punching, coding, transcribing and typing – is also done by women who have even less status (although their jobs may be relatively more secure than those of research assistants). The use of information technology means that this work can increasingly be done through variants of 'homeworking'. These contributions to research may be referred to in acknowledgments, but are seldom considered core contributions. There are also assumed conventions (which are not always rigidly adhered to) about who is cited as primary author and who presents the work publicly. What interests us is the absence of discussion of these issues from a feminist perspective.

Feminist concerns to not conduct 'exploitative' research seldom refer to the hidden aspects of knowledge production which may be extremely exploitative. For example, how many of us talk to women who transcribe or data-punch about what it is we are asking them to do? Whilst skilled typists and coders can 'switch off', disengage from content, they may also engage – either to shift some of the tedium or because the subject matter is relevant to or interests them. By seeing what they do as simply 'technical', we treat them in the ways we have been so critical of in the treatment of research participants; as processors (rather than providers) of data. Our practice in this respect has developed over time, and possibly connects to the particular subjects we study. Where women are transcribing interviews we have discussed the content, and ensured that they are comfortable with it and will talk about any difficulties they encounter. We have also spent time discussing their reactions and responses to the content – some of which were insightful and challenging. We made sure the data-punchers who worked on 1,244 prevalence study questionnaires knew the subject matter and felt comfortable with it and we offered to talk through any issues or difficulties which emerged.

In terms of relationships between researchers, and within research teams, we suspect that many of us work from the presumption that what matters is relative status, that our role if we are more experienced/established is to provide recognition for those who are not yet 'known', in order to enhance their future career development. We have yet to read accounts which explore the meaning of this model from the perspective of those who have less status. What does it mean to know that you have conducted much of the 'research', but that the words on paper are not your words, nor necessarily how you would conceptualize or prioritize the 'results'? How do we work with one another when our knowledge, experience and confidences are not 'equal'? How do the concepts of 'power', 'empowerment' and challenge relate to our practice as colleagues/co-workers? These issues have underpinned our working together, with our biographies and different formal positions being the point from which we have struggled with the contradictions.

When we began working together, Liz Kelly had already been working for fifteen months in CASU and had got an ESRC award to conduct an exploratory prevalence study. Linda Regan was appointed full-time research fellow and Sheila Burton part-time administrative assistant for the project. (After the project was completed Sheila was 'promoted' to research fellow, and is now a full-time member of the CASU team – for as long as we are able to employ ourselves.) Both full-time staff were on the same grade to avoid a three-layered hierarchy in basic status, pay and conditions of work. At this point Liz had a history of doing research, a PhD and a published book; Linda and Sheila had both graduated, having done first degrees as mature students. They shared employment histories in secretarial and administrative work. Alongside these differences, however, was an interesting similarity – class backgrounds and female socialization which had left powerful legacies of insecurity and uncomfortableness with the positions we now inhabited. We quickly discovered that each of us lived with a lurking fear that some day, someone would 'find us out', that we were in some indefinable way 'impostors' or 'squatters' in a place we were not entitled to occupy.

We were all daunted by the prospect of conducting a large-scale survey research project, and each had a sense of responsibility and connection to the topic. Liz was particularly conscious of responsibility, as holder of an ESRC award, few of which have been awarded to feminists or for feminist research. From the outset we agreed, in principle, that we wanted to limit hierarchical and status distinctions between us. But neither good intentions nor feminist practice change differential wage scales, formal status or the ways we were constructed by others. In retrospect our shared desire to construct equality, whilst not ignoring differences between us, led us to underestimate some of the difficulties. It is not possible to 'equalize' detailed knowledge which has been acquired over time, and skills such as writing and speaking in public develop through practice. Some of Liz's concern to share the publicly recognized skills had the unintentional consequence of reinforcing the hierarchical devaluation of more invisible skills which both Linda and Sheila possessed –

typing/word-processing, organization, computing. Taking account of the relative uncertainties and insecurities, of identities, biographies and experiences of each member of the team can result either in accepting a status quo, or in pushing someone to take on areas of work which terrify and undermine the confidences which are developing.

What follows is an edited extract of a taped discussion which we conducted for two purposes – for this chapter, and as an assessment for ourselves of what we had achieved, and what we still needed to work on in the future. We reproduce it in this format, although it does not easily 'fit' with the rest of the chapter, in order that our particular positions and concerns are not 'rounded out' by collective prose (SB is Sheila Burton, LK is Liz Kelly and LR is Linda Regan).

SB: For me what dominates is not feeling confident or able – and I know that is my perception of confidence and ability – which prevents me from positioning myself as a 'researcher'. Because I see it as a very powerful thing to do, to take people's stories and put them 'out there', whether as a written piece or a lecture. Never having had power in any real form, not liking it, being frightened of what I could do with that power – I have always actively run away from power. I don't know whether I could handle that power in a positive way. Getting people to tell their stories is different from what you then do with those stories.

LK: But when that work was invisible – like constructing the stories for the TV feature, which you could see as being more 'out there' in terms of how many people saw it – you had no problem doing that.

SB: ... but that was different.

LK: Well, it exposes a contradiction where distinctions are being made between 'doing' and 'doing', where one is visible and the other invisible. And our problem is that recognition always goes to the visible.

SB: That's good!

LK: It's good from where you sit, because you want to be invisible. But from where I sit it reinforces some of the things I wanted us to change. When I speak about the research I can say your names, acknowledge the collective work, but what is visible is me. And that means something in how we are seen and how we see each other.

SB: Yes, it's not just people ringing in asking for you which imposes that hierarchy, I also impose it because it is in my interests to do so ... Of all of us I think I'm the most intimidated by that group/public process ... and I was quite happy to let you do that. That may not be very sisterly, but I knew you would do it and do it well. It's easy to leave things to someone else in those circumstances, especially when I know you're more likely to be listened to. I would like there to be an acknowledgment of my contribution – but ultimately I don't care. I know, we know, if it's valued inside it's valued where it matters.

LK: What I still don't know the answer to, is knowing that, but also knowing where your lack of confidence comes from, whether we should accept that or keep struggling with it.

SB: If we recognize the input that each of us has made – and that has been there in every piece of writing and presentation – then that's okay for me. But if you are not happy being the 'front person' – and I know you're not – then maybe it needs adaptation. But we do have to acknowledge different levels of knowledge and security.

LR: But three years ago I would never have envisioned being able to do what we, and I, have done, of being terrified and intimidated, thrown by situations and still being capable of carrying on. What brought that home to me was that day when I'd forgotten about a lecture for the first years, and the tutor came up to see where I was. And I was apologizing, thinking I couldn't possibly do it and Liz said 'go on do it – you know enough to do it easily'. I went taking one of our papers with me, but I didn't read it, and I realized that I had absorbed an incredible amount not just through the research, but in simply working in this office.

LK: The fundamental question for me is how we work with that difference of knowledge, without it being a barrier to you both feeling confident in what you do know, and that what you know is a lot, especially about the project we worked on together. Another part of what we've wrestled with is hierarchies of skills, and whether we have reproduced that. The laying out of the questionnaire for example, so that it was as accessible as possible – that was an incredibly important contribution. It's those details which are never mentioned in accounts of research. We are so concerned with not exploiting participants, that we have ignored that we can do precisely those things to people we work with.

SB: That has never been at issue between us in terms of the way we work – it's how it's perceived from the outside, the phone calls, including from feminists and Women's Studies teachers for whom 'Dr Kelly' is the only one who can help ... What I was unhappy about was being promoted above what I took as my own ability. That devalued for me some of what I did do, because the expectation was there that now I do something else.

LK: But don't we end up with a vicious circle, where although on one level it doesn't matter what people 'out there' acknowledge, on another it matters extraordinarily, because that's why they ring up and ask for x person. They are actually part of the same process. If our concern as feminists is that participation in research might be a route through to other options – and we did everything we knew how to make that a possibility – then shouldn't that also be taking place in how we work with each other?

SB: I think it was – we all gained in doing this project, we learnt enormously from each other and the young people. For me it's important that other people know that it's possible to do that ... My lack of security has decreased.

LK: We walked a tightrope in this project which had two edges to it. One was that we had to do this piece of work in a given time, and some parts took far far longer than we had planned. The other was my knowing it wasn't fair or practical to expect the same of each of you as of me – and writing was one of the things I took more responsibility for. So on the one hand there was the question of how do I do this so that it enabled you both to get a sense that 'yes, I can do bits of this too', and on the other was deadlines and having to find money so that we'd still have jobs. That context makes developing a 'feminist process' extremely difficult, since planning in the extra time which is needed becomes increasingly impossible.

SB: That time simply doesn't exist, and also we never had the physical equipment – more than one computer – to use it in that way either.

LK: I wonder, if teams include members with secure jobs, if it's easier to plan in that time than when you are simultaneously having to generate all your own income.

LR: That was also affected by our taking time to deal with each other's responses to what we were told by the young people. It's easy to forget how painful and intense a time that was. I wonder what other feminist research teams do, but I know we paid attention in an incredible way, we took responsibility for each other. My suspicion is that that doesn't happen very often. If you take time out to pay attention to those things then you take time away from writing and other things.

LK: I've also wondered whether if we had not been doing the activist work – organizing conferences, networking, supporting isolated workers, mothers and survivors who phoned here – whether there would have been time to do more writing collectively. But then those things both fed into the research and to emerging confidences. It never felt like we were just doing an isolated piece of research, but that it was in conversation with these other strands of the issues.

SB: It was much more like working in women's groups than the academy, but without some of the angst! The angst there was came from the outside and we dealt with it together. Which was why that comment in the *Daily Mail* when the results were published, 'loony left academics', was such an insult!

The central theme in our discussion is what 'equality' and 'empowerment' mean in context of research teams. Is it empowerment to push someone to do certain kinds of work, when they are neither confident nor excited by the possibility of learning how to do it? Are there ways we could develop which give due credit and regard to contributions which are not accorded status? How challenging of each other's 'unconfidences' and 'uncomfortableness' should we be, when we know that at least some of this is constructed through biographies of unequal opportunities? Again we have no solutions, only questions which need to be asked, and explored in our practice and our accounts of doing research as feminists.

Concluding Thoughts

Feminists have been stern critics of 'hygienic research'; the censoring out of the mess, confusion and complexity of doing research, so that the accounts bear little or no relation to the real events. But many of our accounts are full of silences too. These are not simply the outcome of personal choice, but of publishers' insistence that 'methodology' is boring and should be relegated to a short appendix. The most honest accounts are published in books like this one, or limited-distribution publications like Manchester University's Studies in Sexual Politics. Whilst of particular interest and immense value to researchers, they are unlikely to be seen as relevant to many outside the research/academic world. One way of making these accounts relevant is to make explicit the connections between feminist concerns in other settings and contexts. Our taped discussion contains echoes and resonances for anyone who has worked in women's groups, or in any context where challenging hierarchies was a goal.

Whilst there are now some feminists who argue that we need to explore the use of a range of methods, this is far from being accepted and is not a position which sits easily with some of the writings on feminist epistemology. Liz Stanley, in the introduction to *Feminist Praxis*, notes her own movement from arguing for a feminist epistemology to a feminist ontology which she defines as 'a way of being in the world ... the experience of and acting against perceived oppression'.[37]

Most of the methods which have been endorsed as 'feminist' were not created by feminism: in-depth interviews, ethnography, grounded theory and action research all have non-feminist origins and histories. Even reflexivity, reflecting on the process of doing research, is not specific to feminism, and locating oneself within both question and topic, whilst relatively unusual, is not unknown in the history of social research. This suggests that what makes research 'feminist' is not the methods as such, but the framework within which they are located, and the particular ways in which they are deployed. As Sophie Laws says, 'unless the word "feminism" means nothing, feminist research can only be defined by its theory'.[38] What we now talk of is developing 'feminist research practice', where all aspects of how the research is conducted are involved. Accepting this definition of feminist research involves recognizing that the knowledge we create, and the process of its creation, will always be contested, since it begins from theoretical assumptions and has intended practical applications about which there is unlikely to be a consensus.

Notes

1 Kelly (1988).
2 Stanley (1990b), p. 12.
3 See, for example, Bunch (1987); Sarachild (1970).
4 See, for example, Schecter (1982).
5 D. Steinberg (1992), personal communication.
6 Roberts (1981).
7 See, for one clear example, Duelli Klein (1983).
8 See, for example, Harding (1986, 1991); Smith (1988a).
9 Stanley (1990b); Reinharz (1992).
10 Kelly (1992).
11 See, for example, Levett (1991).
12 Laws (1990).
13 Kelly (1990); Kelly *et al.* (1992a).
14 Laws (1990).
15 Kelly and Regan (1990).
16 McGibbon *et al.* (1989).
17 Kelly *et al.* (1991).
18 Cockburn (1991).
19 Laws (1990), p. 6.
20 Kelly *et al.* (1992b).
21 Kelly (1990).
22 Laws (1990).
23 In many discussions of interviewing, matching interviewer and interviewee in terms of gender, race and class is recommended as a way of increasing rapport, and encouraging disclosure and honesty. For many individuals and issues this is likely to hold true. But there is also the possibility, seldom discussed, that similarity may limit disclosure, since it may incur judgment from 'insider' knowledge or that there is a presumption of similarity which may not be experienced as such by the individuals concerned. As with the other issues we have raised, this is an area we ought to explore as part of our research – by asking participants what difference matching and not matching made.
24 Oakley (1981).
25 Jayaratne and Stewart (1991).
26 Kelly *et al.* (1992a).
27 Fonow and Cook (1991b); Stacey (1988).
28 Fonow and Cook (1991b), p. 8.
29 Acker *et al.* (1983).
30 Our initial final report was written according to ESRC guidelines which specified 5,000 words. We checked whether this limitation was variable, since summarizing the project in this number of words gave minimal space for any of our results. We were told that it was non-negotiable. Following the peer reviews we were asked

to rewrite it – the rewriting involved putting back in the data and discussion we had previously had to cut out!

31 McGibbon and Kelly (1989); Holder *et al.* (1992).
32 For example, the research and the ways it was taken up in the borough were used in a 1990 report on best practice by the National Association of Local Government Women's Committees, and Hammersmith and Fulham Community Safety Unit are currently (March 1993) lead agency in an EC-wide Urban Safety initiative on domestic violence.
33 Kelly *et al.* (1992a).
34 Ramazanoglu (1990).
35 Stanley (1990b), p. 7.
36 Scott and Porter (1983).
37 Stanley (1990b), p. 14.
38 Laws (1990), p. 13.

Chapter 3

Practising Feminist Research: The Intersection of Gender and 'Race' in the Research Process

Ann Phoenix

Introduction

An increasing number of feminists have written about their experiences of conducting research and what it means to be a feminist researcher.[1] The complex relationships to be negotiated at each stage of the research process (obtaining funding; negotiating access to respondents; data collecting; analysis and dissemination) are now more clearly recognized than formerly. However, there are still a number of themes that have been neglected. For example, most published material has discussed projects over which the researcher had some control rather than the more common experience where the feminist researcher has no control over the research process. Another gap in the literature on feminist methodology relates to the ways in which the gender, 'race' and social class positions of respondents intersect with those of the researcher.

This chapter will touch on the first issue, but will focus on the second. It will use two studies – one of Mothers Under Twenty and one of Social Identities in young people – to explore aspects of racialized and gendered relationships in the practice of feminist research.[2] It will focus particularly on interviewers' contact with respondents and participants' feelings about taking part in the studies. It will be argued that 'race' and gender positions, and hence the power positions they entail, enter into the interview situation but that they do not so in any unitary or essential way. As a result the impact of 'race' and gender within particular pieces of research cannot easily be predicted. Prescriptions for matching the 'race' and/or gender of interviewers and respondents are thus too simplistic.

Contact with Respondents

Feminist writing on the place of the 'subject' within feminist research has tended to concentrate on what it means for women to interview other women.[3]

In the 1980s the focus o much of this writing was on the contradiction between the differential power status of researchers and interviewees and the
fact that women respondents often enjoyed talking to women interviewers
without apparently recognizing or minding the differential power positions
inherent in the interview situation. This body of writing conveyed a feeling
of feminist interviewing as a cosy enterprise where women enjoy talking
intimately to other women. More recently it has been recognized that, while
it is sometimes very comfortable to be a feminist researcher interviewing
women, that cosiness does not simply come from shared gender but is often
partly the result of shared social class[4] and/or shared colour.[5] The interview
relationship is partly dependent on the relative positions of investigators and
informants in the social formation.[6] Simply being women discussing 'women's
issues' in the context of a research interview is not sufficient for the establishment of rapport and the seamless flow of an interview.

It is easy to see why the emotional dynamics of the interview situation
are potentially important to feminist researchers. Firstly, the establishing of
friendly relations and the willingness of the researcher to give of herself by
answering any questions the respondent poses can create a situation of easy
intimacy which feels (and perhaps is) less exploitative and more equally
balanced in power terms.[7] Secondly, and more instrumentally, rapport established in the interview situation may well have a direct impact on how forthcoming respondents are and hence the quantity (if not the quality) of the
data collected.

Friendly relations between interviewers and researchers are, of course,
not only established in the interview itself. Researchers generally have contact with respondents both before and after interviews. At the very least
there is some discussion of appointments (either for the researcher to discuss
the study or to do the interview). In addition, prior to the interview and after
its conclusion, there is often preamble and informal talk, sometimes over
refreshment and at the end of the research there may also be contact when
the results of the study are disseminated.

While a fair amount has now been published about relationships in the
actual interview situation, much less has been written about researcher negotiations with people that they want to be in a study and about how participants themselves feel about being involved in particular pieces of research.[8]
The first part of this paper will consider factors that have an impact on
researchers' negotiation of respondents' participation in research and the
ways in which this negotiation is affected by gender, 'race' and social class.

Negotiating Participation

When it comes to negotiating respondents' participation, it is often difficult
to gain insights into what potential respondents think about a particular study.

This is because it is rare for respondents to refuse to take par
when faced with a researcher. However, some of those who initial
participate in research do not eventually take part and some who
part may do so reluctantly or for motives other than simply wanting to
a study.

In the study of Mothers Under Twenty, only 25 of 182 possible women
who were approached and who fitted the study criteria for the in-depth study
actually refused to take part. A further 25 were doubtful that they would be
at home predictably enough ever to be interviewed. In-depth interviews were
eventually undertaken with 79 women. The other women who had agreed to
take part in the study and made (sometimes repeated) appointments to be
seen were either not at home or too busy to be interviewed.

However, it was not the case that all those women who were repeatedly
out for appointments or who said that they were too busy at the appointed
times were simply unwilling to take part. In one case a woman who was
interviewed after twenty-seven unsuccessful visits was very enthusiastic about
the study and said that she had really enjoyed being interviewed. In other,
less protracted cases, women were equally unapologetic about broken
appointments but also expressed enthusiasm about being interviewed. The
reasons for such high rates of broken appointments included the circumstances in which the women lived, which in many cases consisted of cramped
or poorly furnished council accommodation where they did not choose to
spend much time. As a result they went to visit their families and friends or
did window-shopping, returning home only when they felt it was necessary to
do so.

The fact that many were not necessarily making a tacit statement that
they did not want to be involved in the study when they broke appointments
did not mean that none were. For example, one respondent who gave a
lengthy (three-hour), frank and friendly interview during pregnancy proved
elusive for the second interview (six months after birth) and, at the sixteenth
visit, said 'I don't want to see you' and refused to explain further. Two other
women refused to continue with the longitudinal element of the study after
the first visit. Although they gave no clear explanation, it was easier to understand why this was the case and they did not require repeated visiting.

The first was a woman who lived at home with her parents and was very
keen to continue doing so. During the first interview we sat in the kitchen
while her parents (both unemployed) sat in the sitting room which was separated from the kitchen by a partition wall and serving hatch. I had not got very
far into the interview when her father came in, told me to turn off the tape
recorder and enquired why I was asking questions about him and his wife.[9]
My explanations about getting background information fell on deaf ears and
he forbade me from asking questions about the rest of the family on the
grounds that they were a happy family with nothing wrong with them. This
naturally created some tensions in the interview situation since some questions required the disclosure of personal information. Having not previously

overheard, I then conducted much of the rest of
...hisper. Nonetheless, the interview seemed to go
...t seemed to be genuinely pleased to see me and
...nths after birth. However, she said that she did
...study any more on the grounds that they were
...d to'. This incident underlined the need to be
...al questions if other people were potentially
...study discussed in this chapter it was always
...private space in which to interview respondents, but
...s was sometimes not possible in the study of Mothers Under Twenty.
Interviewers became adept at asking particular questions when people were
temporarily out of the room.

In the second case, the (white) respondent was the only woman in the
study who said that she did not know who was the father of her child (having
been drunk at the time of conception). At the second interview it seemed
clear to me that her daughter's father was black and I asked her whether she
had ever experienced discrimination because her baby was black. She replied
indignantly 'She's not black. She's Italian. My grandmother is part Italian and
she's dark'. I could only fit in half of the interview at that visit because I had
agreed with the participant that I would stop the interview in time for her to
get to the post office in order to collect her child benefit. She subsequently
refused to see me to complete the interview. Difficulties of this sort cannot
easily be foreseen. In this instance I felt responsible for the potentially negative impact of the research on that particular household and worried about
how the child involved would fare in the future. For while she was clearly
adored and well looked after at six months of age, it was not so evident how
her mother and grandparents would react once other people also made
explicit the assumption that I had, that she was black.[10] I did call again at this
household, hoping to re-establish contact and negotiate further access for the
third interview, but the respondent had moved.

The population of mothers who give birth in their teenage years is an
extremely mobile one since they are mainly dependent on council housing
and seek to make moves from unsatisfactory housing to better accommodation. Flat exchanges or council offers came up unpredictably. Moves out of
and into bed-and-breakfast accommodation were similarly unpredictable. Not
surprisingly, some women were lost to the study if they moved and we could
not contact them.

With such difficulties in recruiting a sample and the added problems of
maintaining them for the longitudinal aspect of the study it would have been
easy to see the sample as a 'difficult one' and simply reinstate negative social
constructions of the women that we had sought to avoid reproducing un-
thinkingly. However, it was obvious that the circumstances in which the women
lived and the ways in which they were positioned meant that we were simply
not as important in their lives as they were in ours. Unlike women in many
other studies, most did not consider that the study merited being given

sufficient priority to make it worth their while to wait in for us when there were competing demands on their time and opportunities to get out of less than pleasant surroundings. These difficulties meant that, as a research team, we spent a lot of time thinking about ways of maintaining contact with the sample. For example, we requested from them the names and addresses of parents and other relatives or friends who would know where they had moved to, we gave housing departments letters to send out to women who had moved to different council accommodation and we gave the women them-selves freepost change of address cards to return to us if they moved (only a handful of these were ever returned).

It is rare to be given insights into any ideological reasons respondents might have for not taking part in a study. However, issues of 'race' and racism tend to evoke these where other issues (such as gender and sexism) may not. The few respondents in our study who gave ideological reasons for non-participation illuminate the potential dilemmas that specific pieces of research raise for some people. In the Mothers Under Twenty study the only woman who refused to participate who gave ideological reasons for doing so was a black 16-year-old who, when approached, expressed doubts about 'what research has done to black people'. Nevertheless, she wrote down details of the study and said that she would consider taking part. She refused at her next ante-natal visit on the grounds that she did not know how her account would be used. In making a statement about why she did not want to be included in the study, this non-respondent clearly showed political conscious-ness. It has been well documented that much social science research on black people has rendered them pathological.[11] Her response is even more sophis-ticated in that, faced with a black researcher in a hospital ante-natal clinic, she did not make the essentialist assumption that this necessarily exempted the research I was doing from the exploitative production and reproduction of negative constructions of black people. Other black respondents in the Mothers Under Twenty study did not raise similar objections.

In her study of mothers returning to education, Rosalind Edwards found that the black women she approached were much more suspicious and more reluctant to take part than were the white women.[12] This may partly be be-cause the educational institutions in which the women were studying passed their names to the researcher without asking their consent to do so. This is likely to have seemed more threatening than being approached by someone waiting around in an ante-natal clinic who does not have your name and is simply being told when any woman in the correct age group enters the clinic.

Much published research on mothers under 20 reproduces stigmatizing discourses about them, some publicized in the media. It was, therefore, potentially possible for the women approached in this study to refuse to take part on the grounds that the research might be damaging, rather than bene-ficial, to them. None of the women approached in the Mothers Under Twenty study expressed such concern.

In the 'Social Identities' study we asked the young people we interviewed for permission to approach their parents and got the addresses and telephone numbers from them. This method produced disproportionately more mothers than fathers and more middle-class than working-class black and white parents. However, sometimes there were indications that the issue of 'race' had a negative impact on young people's and some of their parents' views of the study. The following example comes from the end of an interview with a white mother whose daughter is of mixed parentage. One of the mother's reasons for taking part in the study seems to have been curiosity because her daughter (who did not express this during or after her interview and who did give her mother's name and telephone number) felt that the interviewer's line of questioning suggested that her family was racist:

> *Q*: Is there anything that you would like to ask me?
> *A*: Not really – only I mean – what will you get out of it? It's like a survey really so what are you going to get out of this survey?
> *Q*: (Long explanation about the aims of the study)
> *A*: Well I just wondered what it was really you know. What was the point of the survey itself – which you just told me so. Because Julia says to me they are coming round asking questions about this. She says, 'They think we are racist you know'. She says, 'They want to come and interview you'. She says, 'Don't do it mum, don't do it.' So I says, 'Well I've got nothing to hide. I am not racist anyway'. I says, 'If I was racist – well apart from me and dad arguing and you telling me I am racist, I don't think anybody else tells me that'.

A few black mothers did not necessarily like the questions that they were asked and were sceptical that the research would produce anything worthwhile for black people, but took part in the study because they considered that black viewpoints should be heard:

> *A*: People that I allow in my home are very privileged and therefore you have been allowed into my home and you are actually taking out some information to people that I don't even know and I don't particularly like that, but I have done it.
> *Q*: Why did you do it?
> *A*: I did it because I felt it needed to be done in terms of talking about the issues that are around with black parents, with young black people, cos I think often that is not heard. White people are very good at doing things for us, on behalf of us and even sometimes when they ask us, they still don't listen, but I think it was important, you know, that you do this.

Clearly, respondents have their own, varied reasons for taking part in studies. These include simple curiosity; desire to talk and to be listened to; to help with the researcher's training or the aims of the study; to complain about the aims of the study or about specific kinds of research. They differ in the extent of their knowledge about research and its impact on the lives of people like themselves. How they define people who are 'like themselves' is likely to shift and cannot necessarily be predicted in advance. So, while one black woman (cited above) was concerned about the impact of research on black people, others might well have been more concerned with the impact research might have on other groups to which they belonged. 'Race', gender and social class all, therefore, sometimes play a part in interviewers' contacts with some respondents. It is not, however, possible to be certain which of these social relations will have an impact, when it will do so and what the impact will be.

The complexity and range of respondents' reasons for taking part in a study means that the woman interviewer–woman interviewee situation does not always produce rapport through gender identification. Nor are the power positions between researcher and researched fixed dichotomies; the balance of power between interviewers and interviewees shifts over the course of a study. For example, at recruitment, respondents have the ultimate power to refuse to be involved in a study. In the interview situation power does not only lie with researchers but shifts and varies, while during the analysis of the data and writing-up of the study, researchers are almost always more powerful than their respondents.

Doing Interviews

The above discussion has already touched on situations that challenge the notion of women interviewing women as necessarily relatively easy and pleasurable. Such interviews *are* frequently enjoyable. However, the dynamics of 'race', social class, the issue being researched, and the intersection of the agendas of interviewers and interviewees all have as much impact as gender on the interview situation.[13] Instances where the interview situation becomes uncomfortable and where rapport is disrupted (however slightly or temporarily) all help to identify, by contrast, the elements that make woman–woman interviews comfortable. The following section identifies some of these issues.

Negative reaction to oneself

It has sometimes been obvious that following appointments made on the telephone, a minority of white interviewees are visibly shocked to see me when I turn up on the doorstep. Since I am expected, known by name and not wearing anything unusual, it seems reasonable to assume that it is my colour that is unexpected. It is not unusual for black researchers and academics to encounter reactions of surprise[14] and it is not a novel experience for me. The temporary consternation that I engender seems to have little impact on the conduct of interviews because people recover themselves fairly quickly and it is generally easy to establish rapport. However, I cannot rule out the possibility that for some white interviewees having a black woman in their home, perhaps for the first time, has an impact on how forthcoming they are. That impact is not necessarily inhibitory. For it is possible that some white respondents may feel more disinhibited than they otherwise would when talking to someone of a different colour from themselves. For black respondents who are surprised (although less visibly so) that the university researcher who has turned up to see them is black, the reasons for surprise and their subsequent reactions are likely to differ from those of white respondents but to be equally complex and multi-faceted.

Kum-Kum Bhavnani argues that the inversion of the more usual balance of power in research studies when a black woman interviews white respondents is interesting in itself and that its subversion of traditional power relations can help make explicit the power relations within the research situation.[15] While this is undoubtedly true, the simultaneity of 'race', social class, gender, (assumed) sexuality and age make it extremely difficult to tease apart the aspects of the interviewer which are having an impact on the interviewee or on the power dynamics between interviewer and interviewee.[16]

Negative feelings evoked by respondents accounts
One of the standard textbook notions of interviewing is that the interviewer absorbs all that the interviewee says; reflecting some statements back for clarification or expansion but always accepting it, rather in the style of client-centred therapy. However, depending on the characteristics of the two people in the interviewer/interviewee relationship and the topic being explored, the interviewer can obviously sometimes have negative reactions to the interviewee or to some aspect of their accounts (just as interviewees can to interviewers – see below). This can happen when interviewees rail against a category that the interviewer fits into (e.g. employed mothers; feminists; black people) or make sexist or racist comments. Since the whole point of interviews is to evoke respondents' accounts rather than to hear one's own discourses reflected back, I would argue that this is usually interesting data rather than upsetting and that it is manageable within the interview context. However, I would like to cite examples of two situations in which it can be more difficult to be dispassionate about what respondents say.

If, as a feminist researcher, one has established a warm, intimate interview relationship with a woman, it can be more difficult to have no personal reaction to accounts one does not like. For example, the occasion I most minded what an interviewee said to me was outside the interview situation. I had interviewed this particular woman three times over a period of two years. At the third interview she was very upset about her husband's behaviour (she had just allowed him back into the home having excluded him for a while). When the tape recorder was turned off at the end of the interview, she explained that she was worried about being pregnant by someone other than her husband and that her husband would 'kill her' if she was. She did not want to go to her general practitioner and could not afford to pay for a pregnancy test and yet was worried and wanted to know one way or another. I paid for her to have a pregnancy test. Over a cup of tea she began talking graphically about her distaste for black people (mainly men) in the area in which I live without ever seeming to become aware that she, a white woman, was talking to me, a black woman. She may, of course, have considered that I was not implicated in her account since most of her venom was directed at black young men. Alternatively, since she clearly liked me, she may have made the more usual 'exception' for me.[17] In retrospect, the incident seems relatively trivial and is certainly not unique in the study of Mothers Under Twenty in that other respondents had also expressed racist ideas.

The fact that I found this particular incident upsetting is probably because I had established a warm feminist interviewing relationship with this woman and gone beyond the interviewee/interviewer relationship in attempting to help her begin to sort out a potential predicament. It is more difficult to deal with instances of racism in situations where one has begun to empathize (rather than simply sympathize) with respondents. Researchers are able to listen dispassionately in the interview situation to views which they usually find distasteful because, however warm and reciprocal the interview relationship, it is not a relationship that requires involvement on the part of either participant. Furthermore, the accounts that respondents give are not unitary and there are generally parts of their accounts with which researchers can feel in sympathy.

The other case in which it may be difficult for researchers to deal with respondents' comments is when respondents are critical of a research study on which interviewers are employed to collect data, but to which they have had minimal input at the design stage (a situation not generally explored in writing on feminist methodology, but one that can and does divide women researchers depending on their position in the research hierarchy). At the end of both studies described here, interviewees were asked to discuss their feelings about the interview. In the Social Identities study there were generally no complaints about the ways in which social class or gender were discussed, but some respondents (white and black) did not like the emphasis on 'race' and racism. A few black mothers were hostile to the study design and this was uncomfortable for the black woman interviewer who was not the grant holder:[18]

Q: How did you feel about the interview?

A: Pretty boring. I don't personally think that is quite necessary.

Q: What's not necessary?

A: The whole interview.

Q: And why don't you think it's necessary?

A: Well because you know all these questions about asking people about colour and you know your race and racism and you know. I mean to say what does it really matter? . . . I look at everybody as the

same human being as myself . . . (Black mother whose account made
it clear that she considered there to be a great deal of racism in Britain, that it does matter to her and that she is entirely opposed to it)

The following comment is extracted from pages of largely negative comment
about the study from another black mother:

Some of the questions you could actually feel was a white person
asking them, and some of them were so stupid that you could get the
feeling that somebody was trying to get inside black people to find
out what it is like . . . (Black mother)

Equally some white mothers who were interviewed by a black researcher
expressed hostility to some of the questions on racism (sometimes because
they considered the answers to questions to be self-evident):

Q: Do you think there is much racism in Britain at the moment?
A: Well that's a bloody stupid question. Of course there is. (White
mother of mixed-parentage daughter)

The white interviewer on the project also had to deal with reluctance from
some white young people to discussing issues of 'race' at all since they considered them irrelevant to their lives. She did not like hearing expressions of
racism from young white people and found them difficult to deal with.

Janet Finch[19] suggests that feminist researchers side with the subject when
doing interviews with women and that she (the researcher) shares the powerless position of the women that she interviews. Arguably, however, this is an
instance where lack of recognition of differences between women is not helpful
for, in many ways, women who are interviewers are relatively powerful in
comparison with many other women.[20] The intersection of 'race' and social
class with gender leads to a dynamic situation of shifting similarities and
differences and hence shifting sympathies. Furthermore, the women participants in a study are not equally powerless[21] and some can oppress others.
Thus, the feminist aim of empowering *all* women cannot mean the taking of
sides with women in general.

Offending the respondent
It is often unpredictable which issues will irritate or offend a particular
respondent since most interviewees will readily answer questions about the
most personal issues while a few will bridle at being asked what seem to
be fairly innocuous questions on one occasion but not another. The example
given on p. 52 of the white woman who was offended by the suggestion that
her baby was black is an extreme example in that interviews are usually
repaired rather than curtailed when an interviewee is offended by a question.
It may have been that if there had not been a necessary break in the interview
the respondent would not have opted out of the study.

Less than ideal circumstances

There are various ways in which the circumstances in which an interview is done can make the interview difficult. I would like to consider three of these. The first is where it is not possible to have sufficient privacy in order to conduct a confidential interview (see the example above on pp. 51–2). This is not always stressful, but can have unrealized consequences. For example, in one interview in the Mothers Under Twenty study a respondent spoke very openly about her feelings about her husband's lack of help with child-care and housework in his presence and he appeared not to mind. However, at the next interview he got ready to leave their small flat when I arrived. When the respondent asked him where he was going, he replied that he was not going to stay around to hear her talk about him and wind him up again. Interestingly, he did not attempt to prevent her from taking part in the study.

The second example is where the circumstances in which the respondents live are distressing in themselves. Of the two studies discussed in this chapter, this was only the case in the study of Mothers Under Twenty. Many of the respondents in that study lived in obvious poverty. The emptiness of food cupboards, the absence of meals at lunch time in many households, lack of milk for tea and sometimes the wintry cold in a flat all underlined the fact that the comfort of being women together in an interview situation is partly dependent on comfortable material circumstances. A warm, private space with adequate seating and the provision of a drink every few hours together with an attentive and forthcoming respondent clearly constitute ideal working conditions for interviewers!

The final way in which less than ideal circumstances can have an impact on interviews relates to situations in which researchers feel threatened. In the study of Mothers Under Twenty, some interviewers felt unsafe on some of the council housing estates on which the women lived and hence did not really want to be in interview situations on those estates at all, and certainly not for very long. More direct feelings of threat were experienced in one instance where a Jewish interviewer conducted an interview in a flat decor-ated with swastikas and in another instance where the managers of a bed-and-breakfast hostel suddenly rushed into the room which the interviewee had borrowed for the interview and removed a bread knife from under the mattress. Threats from reportedly friendly dogs (familiar to many interviewers) seem tame by comparison.

Interactions between respondents and others

Occasionally a woman who is the subject of the research asks her male part-ner to stay with her during the interview and, unusually, he answers some of the questions. This is awkward in that it is the woman's constructions that are being sought. For while feminist research may well focus on men as respond-ents it does not encompass men speaking *for* women in studies where it is women's views that are being sought. Nasty interactions between women and their male partners during the period of the interview (particularly where the couple actually scream and shout at each other) are uncomfortable situations for researchers. In both these situations, researchers are likely to feel powerless (which is not to suggest that the respondents are more powerful in these circumstances). Both situations are ones that require analysis rather than to be treated as incidental.

Respondents' Views of and Responses to the Research

It has been well documented that many women enjoy being interviewed by women interviewers.[22] In the studies reported here, many women also said that they had enjoyed taking part in the research. For example, when asked what they felt about the first interview in the study of Mothers Under Twenty, half of the sample said that they had enjoyed it and that it was good. More than a third (36 per cent) said that it had been 'all right'; 11 per cent had both good and bad things to say about the interview and only two women said that they had not liked it. The majority of the women reported that they had welcomed the opportunity to be listened to with interest and without interruption, even apparently deriving some therapeutic benefit from this:

Q: How did you feel about taking part in the study?
A: Interesting.
Q: What was interesting about it?
A: Well it's not every day you get to sit down and tell people your problems ... Makes you feel quite interested you know – I'm an interesting person.

Those who mentioned bad things about the interview generally mentioned the intrusiveness of some questions and the length of time that interviews had taken:

Q: How did you feel about the questions you were asked?
A: Very nosey they are ... About your housing and how much money you earn and things like that.
Q: Did you mind being asked those questions?
A: Well, I didn't really mind, but I think they are a bit personal.

Q: How did you feel about taking part in the study?
A: Um I think the last interview was a bit tiring. It seemed to go on for ever and ever and ever. But um – I thought 'Oh God, when's it gonna get to the end of it?' you know.
Q: What about this interview?
A: No this one's all right. Weren't as long as the middle one. It seemed to go on for ever.

In the above example, the second interview which the respondent claimed had gone on 'for ever' had lasted two hours while the third interview which she said was 'all right' had lasted three hours.

Young people of both sexes in the Social Identities study were also asked about how they had found the interview. They gave similar responses to the women in the Mothers Under Twenty study. Four per cent were negative about the interview; 42 per cent were positive about it; two-fifths said that it was 'all right' or they 'didn't mind it' and 11 per cent gave mixed responses. White respondents were slightly more likely to give negative responses than black or mixed-parentage respondents (8 per cent, 0 and 4 per cent respectively). The same was true of middle-class respondents in comparison with working-class respondents (6 per cent as against 3 per cent) and young men in comparison with young women (6 per cent as against 3 per cent).

In the Social Identities study, a few of those interviewees who did not like the interview said that they found it boring and 'too long' but some disliked it because it asked too many questions about colour. A couple of the black mothers interviewed were sceptical that the study was worth doing because they considered that it would not change anything for black people and so was pointless.

Their reasons for liking the interview were similar to those generally reported to be given by women respondents:[23]

Q: How did you feel about being interviewed in the end, having been nervous to start with?
A: I liked it. I had a chance to explain about how I feel about certain things and I don't really get the opportunity to do that much. (Black young woman)

Q: How did you feel about the interview?
A: It was a good interview. I have never talked so much about myself for a long time, too busy talking about kids and their problems. (Black mother of young woman in the study)

Many parents and young people who liked, or did not mind, being interviewed were concerned about what we would do with the data that we had collected:

A: Didn't mind doing it. Just curious to know what it is for, what it's going to be used for. It is a survey? (White male)

A: What do you do with this now? /. . ./ [three more questions from interviewee and answers from interviewer]
A: Right, and is this tape with my voice go – you know what I am saying about these poor white people? (Black mother with black interviewee)

Lack of certainty about what the study was about and what we were going to do with the data may have been because respondents in the Social Identities study were recruited from schools where initial permission was given by headteachers, and students were selected and then asked whether they wanted to take part. It may be that in some schools the students were not as informed about the study as they should ideally have been. However, in the Mothers Under Twenty study women were recruited directly by researchers who explained the study to them and gave them handouts about the research at each interview. Nonetheless, at the end of the study it was apparent that some interviewees had not understood what the study was about, and so could not be said to have given informed consent:

> *Q*: Do you feel that you were given enough information about the study?
> *A*: I don't know why I'm being interviewed or – you know – maybe I was told, but I can't remember (laughs). Why did you pick on me?

Julia Brannen suggests that 'participants respond favourably to some methods especially where there is overlap between the concerns of researchers and those of participants, and where both parties are in search of similar explanations'.[24] While this is true, it is also the case that the overlap is itself complex in that some respondents are really not sure what explanations they should give in answer to specific questions and are discomfited by the fear (at least when 'race' is being discussed) that there is a 'politically correct' answer that they are ignorant of. The quote above from a black mother indicates the felt vulnerability of respondents who have said potentially compromising things to interviewers they have trusted.

Interviewee Questions to Interviewer

One of the important contributions made by feminist researchers to thinking about the interview situation is the recognition that it is not 'bad science' to allow the balance of power within interviews to be shifted by giving respondents opportunities to ask questions which the researcher answers rather than parries.[25] Yet, even this important innovation has different meaning and impact depending on the positioning of the two people in the interview and the topic being investigated. For example, three-quarters of pregnant women's questions to Ann Oakley in her study of the transition to motherhood were requests for clarification of the process of birth. Such questions are probably more likely to be made to sympathetic women researchers than to men (and indeed most of the personal questions asked to Ann Oakley were about her own experiences of childbirth and motherhood).[26] In this instance gender as a shared characteristic is of prime importance.

In neither the study of Mothers Under Twenty nor the Social Identities study was the style of interviewing a conversational one. This may be because the composition of the samples differed across the studies. Julia Brannen suggests that a conversational style is more likely with middle-class women who feel status equivalence with the women interviewing them.[27] The women in the study of Mothers Under Twenty were almost all from the working classes, while in the Social Identities study most respondents were much younger than the interviewers. However, the parents interviewed in the Social Identities study (who were mainly middle-class) also did not engage in conversational exchanges during the course of interviews.

In the Social Identities study 44 per cent of the young people in the study asked questions when invited to do so by interviewers at the end of their interviews. Questions were asked by almost equal percentages of black and white, but slightly more by mixed-parentage young people; by more middle-class than working-class young people (53 per cent as against 38 per cent), and by more young women than young men (50 per cent as against 35 per cent). The most frequent questions asked were about what the study was really about, what was going to be done with the data and where the study would be published. However, both black and white respondents were more likely to ask general and personal questions about racism to the black re-searchers than to the white researcher who had asked the same things.[28] It is interesting to speculate to what extent this would have occurred if black men had been conducting the interviews. However, the fact that all the interviewers were women and not men may have accounted for the readiness of young women respondents to ask questions.

It would appear that respondents asked questions for four main types of reasons which differed both within as well as between colour groupings. These reasons are as follows.

Curiosity about how their peers had responded
General curiosity (and sometimes anxiety) about the interviewers' views, what the interviewers think about how the respondents themselves have performed in the interview and how they compare with other people was evident in some responses.

Respondent: Can I ask you about the other girls?
Interviewer: I can't tell you what anybody else said at all because otherwise it wouldn't be confidential.
Respondent: What do you think of us here in [girls' school]? Your overall impression?
Interviewer: . . . Everyone seems very nice . . . (Black young woman/ black woman interviewer)

Respondent: It's nice to have the opportunity of asking you these questions. Did you get good results from other people? (8 more questions follow.) (White young woman/black woman interviewer)

Ann Phoenix

Curiosity about the black interviewers
Both white and black young people expressed curiosity about the life and experiences of an adult black stranger whom they expected to have views on the issue of racism and on what they had said:

Q: How did you feel about the interview?
A: (Pause) It was a nice interview. I think it probably got me to talk about things more than I would have otherwise, and yes, I think it covered a lot. I think it was quite good.
Q: Is there anything you would like to ask me?
A1:   What do you feel as a black person? About living in Britain? /. . ./
A2:   Do you have problems? Do you get racism thrown at you? /. . ./
A3:   What do you think about social backgrounds? . . ./. . ./ (Black young woman/black woman interviewer)

Q: Okay, well we are at the end of the interview. How did you feel about it?
A: Quite enjoyed it. At first I thought 'Oh no. I don't want to do this!' But I quite enjoyed it.
Q: Well I am really grateful that you spent, well almost the entire lunch break with me. That's been really nice. Are there any questions you would like to ask me?
A: What is your background?
Q: What do you mean?
A: Well where do your parents come from? (Black young man/ black interviewer)

Seeking approval for their views
Some young people (both black and white) also sought reassurance that what they said was 'right' by either gaining evidence that they were not racist (white young people); that racism is a diminishing problem in Britain (mainly white young people); or that they were correct to view racism as an important social problem (black and mixed-parentage young people).

It was sometimes also evident from white young people's post-interview talk that they had found it anxiety-provoking to be asked questions by a black woman interviewer. This anxiety was exacerbated if respondents felt a general lack of confidence:

Q: Right. Well, is there anything that you would like to ask me?
A: Yes, what do you think about – I mean we're going on about racism. What do you think my attitude is, personally I mean.
Q: How do you mean?
A: Do you think I have a good attitude about racism?
Q: Yes I do.

A: You do? It's just I was very conscious because obviously you're black. You know I think – because I've never talked about it much, I'm very mixed up in my own ideas. So, and it's something that I think I'd probably have to have a little more time to think about.
Q: Would it have been easier to talk to someone white . . .?
A: No. I don't think so, because I think you were very neutral . . . It was quite difficult, but I'm not sure really . . ./. . ./ So I mean what do you think? It's quite – I mean I'd quite like to listen to the other interviewers, interviewees just to compare myself with other people.
Q: . . . How did you find being interviewed?
A: Well I don't think I'm extremely good talking about myself because I don't know myself very well at all, so it's very hard and I think I'm not a very easy person, a bit of a closed book really rather than an open one. So I'm sort of sorting ideas out in my head rather than ready just to put them over. So it's – I probably came over very vague . . . (White young woman/black woman interviewer)

In the above extract the interviewee/interviewer colour difference seems to be more salient for this respondent than their shared gender.

Retribution for having been asked questions about racism
There were a few white respondents whose tone of questioning appeared partly to be exacting revenge from a black person who had subjected them to questions they found awkward while perhaps secretly sitting in judgment on them. A few others were impatient with being asked a lot of questions about 'race' and racism by a white interviewer when they did not consider that these issues were relevant to them. Such retributive questioning or demonstrated impatience may, to some extent, shift the balance of power from the interviewer to the interviewee, but it does not necessarily make either for a comfortable situation or for an equal relationship between them.

It must also be remembered that interviewing in a school is very different from interviewing in people's homes in that information shared in a respondent's home is not likely to be passed around other members of the sample nor to officials in the institution which granted permission to contact respondents. In schools, it was not uncommon for students who had been interviewed to tell others what they had been asked and, unlike the interviewers, respondents are not bound by ethical guidelines on confidentiality.

That 'race' is a particularly controversial and thought-provoking issue is demonstrated by the fact that neither gender and sexism nor social class (which were asked about in the same interview) produced much interviewee questioning of black or white interviewers. It also demonstrates that, despite attending schools with black people, many white young people do not have an easy familiarity either with issues of racism or with black people. Although Ann Oakley was also asked a fair number of personal questions in her study of 'becoming a mother', the differences between her subject matter (motherhood) and ours ('race' and racism, gender and social class) made many of our respondents' responses more emotionally marked.

'Race'/Gender Matching of Interviewees and Interviewers

The argument that black interviewers are best used for black interviewees is sometimes rooted in a realist epistemology, the central tenet of which is that there is a unitary truth about respondents and their lives which interviewers need to obtain. Black interviewers are considered to 'blend in' better with black interviewees and thus to be more likely than white interviewers to get data which is 'good' because it captures 'the truth'. Some studies have found that the colour of the interviewer does have an impact on the data collected. For example, black people have been found to express more radical opinions about their lives when interviewed by a black interviewer than when interviewed by a white one.[29]

Constructivist theories of knowledge differ from realist ones in that they treat accounts as constructions rather than repositories of a unitary truth. They thus argue that it is not possible to 'read off' attitudes from talk.[30] As a result accounts have to be analyzed within the context of the interview itself. This necessitates analysis of the interview situation as the site where specific accounts are produced, rather than the taking for granted of interviews as productive of 'truths'. Even the narrative form of the story produced in an interview is considered to require analysis.[31]

The discussion above has explored some ways in which the intersection of the 'race'/gender positions of interviewers and interviewees can have an impact on the interview itself and on respondents' reactions to it. The complexity of this impact, however, makes it difficult to be clear whether the matching of interviewees with interviewers on particular characteristics will produce 'better' or 'richer' data than not matching. If different types of accounts about 'race' and racism are produced with black and with white interviewers this is in itself important data and may be good reason for using interviewers of both colours whenever possible since it illustrates the ways in which knowledges are 'situated'.[32] It is, therefore, not methodologically 'better' *always* to have black interviewers interviewing black interviewees. Politically, this strategy may also lead to the marginalization of research on black people and of black researchers since it is then easy for white researchers to consider that black interviewers can only contribute to research on black informants.[33] In addition it renders invisible any contributions they make to research which is not only on black samples or on 'race'. It is potentially exploitative in that some black respondents may believe that the research for which they have been recruited is genuinely in the control of black researchers or forget that this may not be the case when, in fact, the black interviewer has little control over the trajectory of the research or the analysis of the data.

The employment of women only to interview women informants is a comparable situation. The very notion of conducting feminist research pre-supposes that the feminists doing the research have some power in and hence control over the research process. Yet the majority of women working within research are at the bottom of research hierarchies where, as interviewers, their input to the research process is limited. The use of women only as interviewers of women respondents can be a cynical and exploitative ploy simply to get the 'best' possible data by encouraging respondents to speak rather than being an attempt to empower women.

It is, of course, helpful in the issue of control of the research process for women (black and white) to move up research hierarchies. However, the employment of a minority of women and black people in senior research positions does not necessarily change the status quo with regard to control of the research process. Nor does it ensure that research is *for* women or black people and hence the empowering of them. However, women at the top of research hierarchies are differentially positioned with regard to research from the women employed to conduct the interviews.

Preference for interviewers of particular gender and colour
Whatever the theoretical debates about the impact of the colour of interviewers, respondents' expressed preferences for colour of interviewers are important in themselves. In the study of 16-to-19-year-old first-time mothers there was no attempt to match the colour of the respondent with the colour of the participant although (since I am black and there were white interviewers) this happened sometimes. We therefore asked the young women what they felt about the colour, age and gender of interviewers. Age of interviewer produced no clear-cut preference in that the biggest response (44 per cent) was for 'no preference', while a quarter of the women said that they preferred interviewers not to be their own age and 30 per cent said that they did prefer to be interviewed by someone nearer their age, that is, younger than their interviewers had been.

Sixty-four per cent of the women said that they preferred to be interviewed by women:

I don't know. I find it hard to talk to men I suppose. They don't seem to see things the way women do.

A further 19 per cent said that they had no preference while the remaining 17 per cent said that they would have preferred to be interviewed by a man.

With regard to colour and ethnicity, most of the women (71 per cent) said that they had no preference for the colour of their interviewers; a fifth said that they preferred to be interviewed by someone of their own colour (they were mainly black) and three women (all black) said that they would prefer to be interviewed by someone who was not their colour.

The less common answers with regard to gender and colour of interviewer are worth exploring. In both cases, the reason for this seems to be that respondents did not wish to be judged by people like themselves and felt that they would get less disapproval and a more dispassionate hearing if the people who interviewed them were clearly different from themselves and not in the same social groups. In addition, some of those women who said that they would have preferred to talk to men as interviewers reported that this was because they considered women to be 'catty' or 'bitchy'.

Expressed preferences for interviewers of particular colour or gender do not necessarily mean that respondents will not readily talk to interviewers who do not fit those characteristics. In the study of Mothers Under Twenty, for example, one black woman said at the final interview:

If — [white interviewer] had been doing the interview I would have had to tell her that the questions were too nosey because white people don't understand what a typical black family is like . . .

However, the transcript of her previous interview with a white interviewer did not appear different in quality from the two interviews with a black interviewer. The colour of interviewer may have made a difference to how she felt, but that difference was not analytically discernible. A study by Michael Rutter and his colleagues done twenty years ago also found no differences in black interviewee/interviewer rapport according to whether the interviewer was white or black.[34] In a similar way, the only two respondents in the study to be interviewed by men (at the first interview) expressed no preference for gender of interviewer and seemed to answer the most personal questions readily. In the study of Mothers Under Twenty, all the interviewers were themselves mothers and some interviewees said that they wished to be interviewed by women who were mothers. However, they only asked (and hence learned) that we were mothers after at least one interview. It is thus questionable whether it would have made any difference to their responses if we had not been.

This does not rule out the possibility that respondents are more comfortable with interviewers of particular colour or gender and that they may even consciously alter their accounts depending on interviewer gender and colour. Some of the spontaneous remarks of black young people in the Social Identities study would seem to indicate that this might be the case.

In the Social Identities study, participants were not specifically asked about preferences for colour and gender of interviewer. This was partly because the aim was to match colour of interviewer and interviewee (although this did not always happen) and partly due to time constraints in some schools. However, a few young people (more young women than young men) spontaneously expressed the view that it was good to be interviewed by someone of the colour of the interviewer. This was mostly, but not always, expressed by black respondents with black interviewers but was sometimes also expressed by white respondents who had been interviewed by black interviewers:

Q: How did you feel about being interviewed?
A: I thought it was good, sort of like you can talk, say what you want to say about what you think about other people, other races. I mean it is good, sort of like a black person interviewing a white person, because then they can share their feelings between each other, what they feel about other colours and things like that.
Q: So you didn't mind answering those questions with a black interviewer?
A: No.
Q: Anything you would like to ask me?
A: Have you ever been picked on because of your colour? (White young man)

Q: Well thank you very much. How did you find being interviewed?
A: I found it comfortable cos you're a black person I can talk to you like more easily than I could talk to a white person. (Black young man)

Q: How did you feel about being interviewed?
A: Well she [teacher] told me I was going to be interviewed and she said there is going to be a white person here and a black person and when she said today that we would be talking to a black person I thought well that is much better because if you was a white person I wouldn't have talked about half the things that I did ... I mean I wouldn't have said that I didn't like white people or that I think that some white people are racist, you know, because I wouldn't like the reaction ... (Black young woman)

Continuity of Interviewers

In the Social Identities study there was only one interview while in the Mothers Under Twenty study there were three contact points. The logistics of finding and interviewing the women in the Mothers Under Twenty study were such that some respondents had the same interviewers throughout the study while others did not. After the third interview, when the women were asked whether they would have preferred the same interviewer throughout, the consensus was that they would have done because continuity enhances rapport and relaxation:

I mean I'm getting to know the person that's been coming and ...
I mean it's easier today than what it was on the first visit.

The fact that rapport increased with increased contact was occasionally demonstrated by respondents who confided something at the second or third interview that they had not mentioned in answer to questioning at the first interview.

Conclusion

This chapter has explored interviewer/interviewee relationships within the research process. It has argued that while contact between women participants and women researchers is frequently pleasurable for both, it is important not to mistake shared enjoyment of conversational exchanges with gender identification through shared positioning. Instances where positive, warm relationships in interviews are disrupted or fail to be established illustrate the ways in which factors beyond the interview relationship enter into interviewer/interviewee relationships as well as into the negotiation of researcher access to respondents. Thus, there are a number of factors which may have an impact on whether potential respondents participate in a study and, if they do, how they feel about their participation. These include other people, women's living circumstances, the topic of the research, their concerns about what the research will mean for the groups to which they belong as well as the colour, gender, social class and age of interviewers in comparison with those of interviewees. However, the strategy of matching interviewers and respondents on particular characteristics (such as gender and 'race') does not produce 'better' data. Indeed, since respondents are not positioned in any unitary way, it does not avoid the necessity for analysis of the ways in which wider social relations enter into the interview relationship.

The chapter has further argued that issues of 'race' and racism are particularly uncomfortable or thought-provoking for many respondents and that, as a result, colour differences may be more salient than shared gender for some young women respondents. However, respondents who are of the same colour and gender can have very different reactions to being asked the same questions. It is, therefore, important to recognize differences and commonalities between people who are socially constructed as belonging to the same group as well as across groups, a project which is consonant with feminist concerns over the last decade.[35]

Notes

1 For a recent account see Reinharz (with Davidman) (1992).
2 The first study included a sample of seventy-nine 16-to-19-year-old women who gave birth in the mid 1980s. The women were given in-depth interviews in late pregnancy and as many as possible were followed up six months and twenty-one months after birth. It is written up most fully in Phoenix (1991). The second study was completed in the early 1990s. It explored the social identities of 'race', gender and social class in a sample of 248 mixed-parentage, black and white 14–18-year-olds and seventy of their parents. See Tizard and Phoenix (1993); Phoenix and Tizard (in prep.).
3 See, for example, Oakley (1981); Finch (1984). The conduct of feminist research with men as respondents has not been subjected to the same scrutiny.
4 See Brannen (1988); Reid (1983); Malseed (1987).

5 For a discussion of how black women reacted less favourably to being approached to be in a study of women returning to education, see Edwards (1990).

6 Burgos (1989).

7 See Oakley (1981).

8 For examples see Brannen (1993) and Phoenix (1990a).

9 I was at the time asking about the employment status of household members.

10 Women who had children of mixed parentage in this sample (all of whom were white women) were among those who experienced most disapproval from their parents.

11 Jones and Nelson-Le Gall (1986); Lawrence (1982); Phoenix (1986, 1990b).

12 Edwards (1990).

13 See, for example, Brannen (1988, 1993); Edwards (1990); Phoenix (1990a).

14 See Jacquelyn Mitchell (1982); de la luz Reyes and Halcon (1988); Centre for Staff Development in Higher Education (1985).

15 Kum-Kum Bhavnani (1990).

16 For example, three black respondents in the Mothers Under Twenty study reported, to the white interviewers who asked them, that they preferred to be interviewed by white people. The reason they gave for this preference was that they wanted to avoid having people who are black like themselves making judgments about whether or not their behaviour is appropriate for black people.

17 See Michael Billig (1982) for discussion of how white people can be close friends with black people while expressing racist views about black people in general.

18 There were two black women and one white woman who did interviews on this project.

19 Janet Finch (1984).

20 See Cook and Fonow (1986).

21 For example, in the study of 16-to-19-year-old first-time mothers, there were a minority who were more economically powerful than the majority. Two, who came from middle-class backgrounds, also had some advantages which other members of the study did not have.

22 Ann Oakley (1981); Ann Phoenix (1990a).

23 See, for example, Finch (1984).

24 Julia Brannen (1993), p. 329.

25 Ann Oakley (1981, 1993).

26 See Ann Oakley (1979).

27 Julia Brannen (1988).

28 The aim in the study had been to colour-match interviewers and interviewees but this was sometimes not possible.

29 See Tim May (1993) and Reese *et al.* (1986).

30 Jonathan Potter and Margaret Wetherell (1987); Margaret Wetherell and Jonathan Potter (1992).

31 Martine Burgos (1989).

32 Donna Haraway (1988).

33 Penny Rhode (in prep.); M. de la luz Reyes and J. Halcon (1988).

34 Michael Rutter *et al.* (1974).

35 See, for example, Avtar Brah (1992).

Chapter 4

Situating the Production of Feminist Ethnography

Beverley Skeggs

Introduction

In 1980, to supplement my PGCE grant, I was teaching sociology to a group of 16-to-18-year-old, white, working-class women in a northern further education college as part of their 'Community Care' course. Part of the work I did with them involved an analysis of media images of femininity. Their responses were fascinating. They were far more critical and discriminating then the contemporary theories of ideology and femininity suggested.[1] At the same time I was starting my PhD and these responses, along with the reading of Paul Willis, profoundly affected the direction it would take. It was to be a study in hegemony and practice:[2] i.e. I wanted to know if, how and why women consented to positions of subordination and what this meant for the construction of their own identities. The research question was 'why do young women, who are clearly not just passive victims of some ideological conspiracy, consent to a system of class and gender oppression, which appears to offer few rewards and little benefit?' It was not long before I asked myself: what alternatives do they have? The students I was teaching consented to participate in the research. In 1981 I was offered more teaching in three other caring courses and consequently the research group grew in total to 83 women (see table 4.1).[3]

Over a period of three years I did the research by spending as much time as I could with the young women. I also spent time working on details of the national and local economy, housing, poverty and education statistics. I used such information to map out the general economic and cultural framework in which the young women were located. It was a geography of their positioning and possibilities. I used cultural information to build up a picture of what Berger describes as a plausibility structure, i.e. what they see to be possible and plausible.[4] To understand their movement through this mapping I traced the trajectories of the young women through the education system and asked them for biographical details,[5] constructing a 'case-study' file of each student. I also conducted formal and informal interviews and meetings with family members, friends, partners and college teachers.

Table 4.1   Time scale and contact

	Main Group		Also contact with	
1980 Initial contact			CC (11)*	First Year
1980–1981 PhD Year One	CC (13) PHS (13)	PCSC (15)	CC PCSC	Second Year
1981–1982 PhD Year Two			CC PCSC	First Year
1982–1983 PhD Year Three	CC (15)	PCSC (16)		

* numbers are provided for the groups I had main contact with.
PCSC is the Preliminary Social Care course, PHS is the Pre-Health Service course and CC is the Community Care course (now renamed as Family and Community Care).

When I left the college in 1984, I followed the young women's progress through further interviews and questionnaires in 1985, 1989 and 1992. Obviously it was physically impossible to do intensive participant observation with all eighty-three of them all of the time, so during the three years, I concentrated on different groups at different times. It was the length and intensity of the research that helped me to define it as ethnographic (I now find it odd when people claim research that rests on a few months and some interviews to be ethnographic). I had entry to different parts of the young women's lives in different ways. With some it was very social, with others it was a quiet chat; the different relationships elicited different types of information. The time spent doing the ethnography was so intense that the boundary between my life inside and outside of the research dissolved.

Situating the Research

This chapter comprises a retrospective, reflexive account which relies on memory and sporadic field-notes.[6] It shows how knowledge is produced but also how ethnographies are the outcome of continual theorizing and research practice. It begins by situating the research, then enters into feminist debates about ontology, epistemology and methodology. An examination of the specificities of ethnographic analysis and writing shows how ethnography is a theory of the research process.

When I began I did not know what ethnography really was or how to do it.[7] I had not followed a methodology training course, and I was so carried away with the initial responses to questions that it was about a year before I began to reflect on what I was doing. This needs to be historically located. Methodology was not such an issue then as it is now.[8] The educational work on which to draw was limited.[9] Participant observation studies were part of a tradition which focused on male deviance and sub-cultures and had little applicability for the study of young women.[10] My readings of early-twentieth-century anthropological work, which often involved ethnography, had convinced me of its imperialism and sexism.[11] I did not even know that there was

73

a long tradition of feminist ethnography, starting in 1837 with Harriet Martineau's *Society in America*.[12] Nor did I know of Golde's (1970) *Women in the Field*.[13] And then I read Paul Willis' *Learning to Labour: How Working Class Kids Get Working Class Jobs*.[14]

Willis' research was the first I had read on the contemporary experience of the working-class lives of young people that did not patronize them. It gave dignity to the participants and allowed the agency and energy of the researched to surface. Here were young, working-class men fighting back, although, ultimately, with disastrous consequences. I wanted to do similar research that demonstrated that working-class women were not ideological dupes of both social class and femininity. Willis' work locates itself within a Marxist tradition that uses participant observation and theoretical analysis of structures to show how people make history but not in conditions of their own choosing.

I thus entered into ethnography by default. I wanted a method of analysis which would make the links between structure and practice, between the macro and the micro; a method which could link everyday interaction to history, economics, politics and wider cultural formations. Althusserian theories which suggested that people were ideological dupes were prevalent at the time the research began.[15] I felt that it was important to see if there was any possibility of resisting dominant ideologies, especially as my early experiences with the students suggested that this might be happening. Thus, my study was concerned to show how young women's experience of structure (their class and gender positioning) and institutions (education and the media) framed and informed their responses and how this process informed constructions of their own subjectivity. Ethnography, according to Willis, is concerned to see how structures are lived, reproduced and challenged on a daily basis:

> The role of ethnography is to show the cultural viewpoint of the oppressed, their 'hidden' knowledges and resistances as well as the basis on which their entrapping 'decisions' are taken in some sense of liberty, but which nevertheless help to produce 'structure'. This is, in part, the project of showing the capacities of the working class to generate, albeit ambiguous, complex and often ironic, collective and cultural forms of knowledge not reducible to the bourgeois forms – and the importance of this as one of the bases for political change.[16]

It is what bell hooks calls a 'view from below'.[17] Initially, I used Willis' study as a model of good practice, bringing to it a realization that femininity was constructed very differently from his account of masculinity.[18] One important outcome of the pressure from my supervisor to study the participation of the young women in their further education courses was that I was forced to develop an understanding of institutional power and the role of the state. State policy was at the time attempting to reformulate the social relationships of young people (by enforced staying on in education and increased surveillance; by the movement from real jobs to training).[19] Willis had also claimed a new and powerful authenticity for works of cultural criticism, what Marcus describes as 'ethnographer as midwife' – who delivers and articulates what is vernacularly expressed in working-class lives.[20]

My initial intervention into the lives of the young women was based upon naturalistic assumptions. I believed that if I went into the young women's 'natural' context I would find and deliver their 'real' (even 'true') experiences; if I spent enough time with the young women, I was sure, they would eventually reveal themselves to me. The opposite, in fact, happened; the longer I spent with them the more confused I became. I had to find a framework which could account for the contradictory thoughts, words and actions of the young women. The process of doing ethnography led me from a position of certainty to one of doubt. Doubt is a healthy theoretical position but it does not help much when trying to construct coherence out of many disparate empirical experiences.

Marcus makes a distinction between realist and modernist ethnographers.[21] Realist ethnographers believe in coherence, community, historical determination and structure. By contrast, modernist ethnographers concentrate on the complex formation of identity across a range of different sites in relation to wider global issues. The modernist problematic, as defined by Marcus, is the question of who or what controls and defines the identity of individuals, social groups, nations and cultures.[22] This was also the basic problematic that I pursued in order to understand how consent to subordination occurs.

This analysis of distinctions between ethnographic theories enabled me (only recently) to realize why I had so many difficulties when trying to relate my empirical observations to my theoretical framework. My theoretical analyses had generated particular questions in contradiction with naturalistic assumptions. The theories developed from readings of cultural analysis suggested a multiple subjectivity constructed across a range of sites (in many ways similar to Marcus' modernist question), yet I had been operating with a methodology which suggested that community was the site of identity production. The knowledge I finally produced was a product of the struggle between naturalistic methods and the modernist theoretical frameworks. My doing of ethnography implicated me in a naturalist framework for studying the 'other',[23] whilst my reading and theory construction suggested that naturalism is not possible nor politically desirable. My research was and my theorizing still is underpinned by a belief in critical realism.[24] That is, I did not construct the worlds of the young women; their worlds are still there now that I am not. Rather, I constructed a discursive representation of it. I discovered elements of their world through the discursively/socially constructed concepts that were available to me. Whenever we speak or write about a reality, the language we use is not the reality to which it is supposed to refer.[25] We also have to deal with the possibility of tacit knowledge, knowledge which is non-discursive.[26] This will always be a problem for ethnography.

I also experienced the same problems that Marcus identifies in Willis' ethnographic account. I, too, began with strategically situated ethnography, in the further education college, yet realized that the young women's responses to education were influenced by a variety of other locales such as their family, their positioning, negotiations and resistances to the media. Moreover, their class and gender positioning operated in different ways in response to each different locale; and some sites could engender resistances to other sites. The final product emerged out of this struggle. I was under pressure to produce an account of educational responses yet the ethnography indicated that these were only a small part of their responses to the wider discourses of femininity and caring.

I tried to focus their responses to different locales by using theories of subject positioning: that is, whilst education offered particular subject positions for the young women to occupy, this had to be seen alongside the other subject positions that were available and which predisposed them towards others.[27] Walkerdine, for instance, argues that young women's exposure to romance predisposes them towards caring.[28]

Through much struggle, learning by doing, moments of complete incomprehension and doubt, I came to realize that ethnography is not a method, rather it is a theory of the research process. It is a methodology which involves certain features in specific ways. For instance, the characteristics that most ethnographies will encompass are: some account of context, of fieldwork that will be conducted over a prolonged period of time;[29] being conducted within the settings of the participants; involving the researcher in participation and observation; involving an account of the development of relationships between the researcher and the researched; involving study of the 'other'; focusing on experience and practice; having culture as the central focus; treating participants as microcosms of wider structural processes. Ethnography provides interpretation and explanation by strategies of contextualization. Once we see how something exists by being embedded in a set of relationships we more easily understand it. Because ethnography is a methodology it means that many types of methods can be employed. So all the different methods I used (interviews, questionnaires, participant observation, statistical analysis, historical documentation etc.) were part of a more general framework which put all these fragments together in ways that related practice to theories.

Whilst ethnography is a theory of the research process, ethnography itself is defined by its relationship to theoretical positions, hence feminist ethnography. These theoretical positions are not clear-cut. My ethnography began with a theoretical home in historical materialism, developed through Gramscian marxism and marxist feminism; when I had problems theorizing the everyday workings of power and powerlessness these theoretical positions shifted into post-structuralism. Jaggar argues that every method entails at least an implicit commitment to a certain theoretical understanding of the social world and to particular criteria for empirical and theoretical adequacy.[30]

This is why feminist ethnography is different from other ethnographies which normalize their theoretical positions.

Ethnography also comes to be defined through theoretical pragmatics: the problem or area on which you decide to focus – 'the field'; the questions that you ask; the amount of time you consider necessary and how you use your time; the type of relationships that you develop with the participants; the way you decide to select and write ethnography. These are all theoretically informed positions.

Three fundamental research questions structure any research project.[31]

1 What is there that can be known – what is knowable? This is the *ontological* question; it deals with the assumptions one is willing to make about the *nature* of reality.

2 What is the relationship of the knower to the known? This is the *epistemological* question. The assumptions that one makes about this process depend on how one conceives of reality (ontology). Epistemologies are theories of knowledge.

3 How do we find things out? This is the *methodological* question. How this is answered depends on what decisions have been made about ontology and epistemology. The ways in which these different questions are answered or ignored in the research process will demonstrate the different theoretical positions held by ethnographers.

Feminist Ontology

I began with the belief that there was a specific reality to working-class women's lives which had been made invisible through the production of a sexual division of knowledge. I relied on the cultural theories generated by Chris Griffin[32] and Paul Willis to provide a model for understanding that reality:

> Social reproduction and contradiction must be shown not as abstract entities, but as embedded dynamically within the real lives of people in a way that is not simple 'correspondence' or 'reflection' of unchanged, somehow 'deeper' structures. Agents' intentions do not proceed from themselves, but are bound up in the complex way in which structures are inhabited through 'cultural forms'.[33]

This position is not dissimilar to what has been defined as feminist standpoint theory.[34] Flax has criticized standpoint theories for assuming that the oppressed have a privileged relation and ability to comprehend a reality that is 'out there' waiting for representation.[35] However, by showing how structures are inhabited through cultural forms emphasis is placed on how structures are lived as well as spoken about. For instance, the sexual division of labour and the sexual division of knowledge in my research were partially lived through cultural concepts of glamour. The young women 'chose' courses at college and future occupations on the basis of the amount of glamour that they contained, as well as the use to which they could put their resources of female cultural capital. By focusing on the cultural forms which young women occupied I could sketch the subject positions to which they had access and how these worked across a range of sites.

This feminist ontology also maintains that the knowledge produced by feminists will be different. The researcher and the researched have different discursive resources to draw on, making different discursive configurations – the way ideas and arguments are given shape.[36] This is overlayered, and mediated, through access to other positions in discourse, such as 'race' and class. This is not an empirical argument, such as that suggested by Stanley and Wise who argue that the similarities in women's experience enable research to be feminist.[37] This would deny all the power relations and differences between women. Nor would my argument support a spurious dichotomy between experience and method, which ignores how both experience and method are a product of discursive positioning.[38] Rather, it suggests that any feminist ontology needs to take into account the access to, and discursive positions available to, different groups that are likely to produce different knowledge. This applies just as much to the researcher as to those being researched.

Feminist Epistemology

This point can be developed in relation to epistemological questions which ask, what is the relationship of the knower to the known? Many male researchers are normalized in the process of research; they are able to leave their gender, and its accompanying institutionalized power positions, unquestioned. It is more difficult for the female researcher researching young women not to be seen as feminist. In my case it would have been impossible. The young women visited my flat and had contact with me through teaching. However, I did occupy normalized positions of race and heterosexual privilege. My lack of recognition of race in the research is a major shortcoming. Heterosexuality worked to my advantage. The establishment of friendships requires reciprocity, time, confidence, intimacy and disclosure. When I began asking the young women about personal matters, such as attitudes to partners, the confident ones forced me to disclose similar information. I was very honest with them. I think their responses might have been different if they had known that I was not heterosexual, especially as one of their major topics of conversation was boys. We had similar knowledge to trade which restricted the differences to overcome. However, we occupied and drew upon different discursive knowledge and resources.

The awareness of access to different discursive positioning, normalization

and objectification suggests that we can only ever produce partial k
Because experience is shaped by social relations, just as is writing
Harding argues that women's experiences in themselves or the thing
say do not provide reliable grounds for knowledge claims about social relationships, culture and structure.[39] We, therefore, need to know about the
locations of different knowledge. This has led to an argument for feminist
objectivity.[40] This challenges previous feminist thinking, which dismissed
objectivity as the mechanism by which men are able to ignore the gendered
production of their work. Haraway and Harding, however, argue that objectivity has always been about a particular and specific embodiment.[41] 'It is about
limited location and situated knowledge – only partial perspective promises
objective vision'.[42] Awareness of several partial perspectives could be combined so that the result is less partial but no less objective, indeed more
objective. Therefore there can never be an unmediated account. Unlocatable
knowledge, Haraway argues, is irresponsible knowledge. Irresponsibility
necessitates being called to account.

Mies set forth methodological guidelines for feminist research that proposed that the hypocritical 'postulate of *value free research*, of neutrality and
indifference toward the research objects, has to be replaced by *conscious
partiality*' towards the oppressed, engagement in their struggles for change
and the creation of a form of research that fosters conscientization.[43] We have
to be careful that this does not lead to condescension. Why should we assume
that the women whom we research desire or are in need of conscientization?[44]
This may stop us listening to them. The young women I researched had a
pragmatic approach to feminism. They responded to it from their location as
young, white, working-class women; they evaluated its usefulness for their
lives. In many instances it was detrimental to their aspirations. Rollins found
a similar situation with the domestics that she interviewed who knew the
importance of knowledge of the powerful to those without power.[45] What the
young women I researched really needed was access to money, power and
authority to change the structures of inequality that made up their lives. It
was those who taught, employed and housed them who seemed in greater
need of conscientization. This is not to argue that raising feminist awareness
should be abandoned. After a variety of disappointments by 1992 a substantial
number of the young women no longer have investments in things such as
marriage which once offered cultural and economic reward. Time, experience
and access to different knowledges has made feminism seem more appropriate
for explaining their circumstances.

Feminist Methodology

Feminist research places emphasis on power relations. Early feminist research
suggested that the power relations between the researcher and the researched
should be non-hierarchical. This is now dismissed as naive by most feminist

researchers, who argue for an acknowledgment of power and differences between women. I experienced both similarities and differences with the young women, all informed by power. When I first met the young women I was 21; they were 16. I was a student and, according to them, looked like one. I was younger than their other teachers at the college by at least ten years. My age enabled me to engage comfortably in their social activities.

Though there were similarities in class background – I had, earlier in my life, signed up for a caring course at a further education college, I had occupied similar restricting cultural and economic positions – I had also escaped. By the time of the research I was highly educated and most of my accent had gone. I also came from a large city in the north-east and they were from a small town in the north-west which meant that many of our cultural experiences were dissimilar. Ann Game argues that it is often through identification with the other of the research that the autobiographical is not realized.[46] Yet it was precisely because of my autobiography that I began the research and I constantly moved between an awareness of similarities and of our acute differences. They had become 'others' through the process of doing research; so had I. I was constantly reminded of my changed history. For instance, one of the most pertinent comments of the whole research suggests their awareness of difference:

> It's all right for you not to get married, you can afford things by yourself, you're dead well paid, you've got your own flat and all your clothes, we'll never have that, where would we find a job as well paid as yours ... nursing if we're really lucky and everyone knows how badly nurses are paid, you can't live on them wages ... you don't realise how bloody lucky you are ... you don't take no shit cos you can, we can't, where would we end up if we were as stroppy as you, nobody'd talk to us ... On the shelf.

I also had the power to access their lives. The initial willingness of the young women to participate in research interviews was to some extent an index of their powerlessness. Remember I was a part-time teacher in the 'caring' department when I first asked the young women if they were interested in discussions. It would have been difficult for them to refuse, although some did. I also had functions of which they could make use, as Michelle succinctly notes:

> At first we thought who is this idiot, you know we were wary, didn't know what you wanted, didn't know whether you'd creep back, like you're not used to teachers treating you like humans, you know like adults ... then when you flashed the fags, I were gobstruck, we all nudged each other, did you see? Then when Trisha and Mandy went to your place for that party, they said it were a riot and everyone were really pissed ... we knew then you were all right ... mind you

> I think we talked to you for the fags and coffee at first ... you know,
> we used to say, oh Bev'll give you one you just have to sit there ...
> Trisha said you knew loads of fit fellas.

Golde argues that all fieldwork should encompass some form of reciprocity;
that researchers should offer services or materials in exchange for the privilege of studying and disrupting other people's lives.[47] I do think this is particularly hard for doctoral students who are also struggling to make ends
meet. However, I knew that I was building my future out of these women; I
therefore justified my overdraft as an investment. They liked coming to visit
the university; it reinforced their sense of self-worth. They had learnt that
students were meant to be clever, but they could never find much evidence
of it. It also opened horizons (three went to polytechnic after spending an
extra year at further education college doing 'A' levels).

Reciprocity occurs in other ways. Vision is always a question of the
power to see.[48] The male gaze is institutionalized through the media, arts,
film, literature etc. and it gives men the legitimacy to look publicly at women.
Valerie Walkerdine suggests that the power of the researcher to objectify and
scrutinize the 'subject' of research is a process similar to that of the male
gaze.[49] However, I would argue that the process of objectification can have
more positive outcomes. Many of the young women confirmed Ann Oakley's
observations that they could not believe they were interesting enough to be
of any use to a study.[50] The student's sense of self-worth was enhanced by
being given an opportunity to be valued, knowledgeable and interesting. In
the follow-up studies this continues to be important. To be seen as a worthy
object of study has a value to these women. This challenges the idea that the
researched are *just* objects of a voyeuristic bourgeois gaze. Also, do working-
class feminist researchers automatically inhabit the position of the traditional,
masculine, bourgeois gaze?

I was also able to reciprocate in a more positive way by providing support and a mouthpiece against injustices. Whilst student confessions can give
the researcher a great deal of power, for, as Foucault notes, the technology
of the confessional is an effective form of control, confessions can also provide
a space for support. Rarely were these women given much listening space or
taken seriously. I listened to disclosures of violence, child abuse and sexual
harassment. To some extent this jeopardized the research as a great amount
of time was spent counselling rather than interviewing. But what else can you
do? This is an ethical dilemma of feminist research.

The power of the researcher is not unidimensional. I had to face the
same spatial limitations as the young women. Access to space is gendered.
When meeting we had to make sure that, as women, we were safe to walk out
at night. Research in provincial night-clubs exposes you to aggressive male
pursuit. Hanging around in city centre pubs by yourself makes you a target
for sexual hassle. It is also difficult not to be offensive to a persistent cousin
or the best mate of a student's boyfriend when they will just not go away. The

female ethnographer has to deal with many social situations she would normally copiously avoid. Other female researchers have reported overt sexual propositions, the over-sexualization of interaction and the covert sexual hustle that is called research cooperation.[51] I am sure that this rarely happens to male researchers.

Oakley suggests that researchers should productively use their power by giving any information and knowledge which they have that may be useful to the researched.[2] In the process of the research the young women asked for advice and interpretations.[53] (They would also offer it.) How could I refuse? To concoct some vague response (as the research textbooks suggest) would have been to insult them. As a feminist, with a belief in providing frameworks for understanding that can lessen exploitation, I provided feminist critiques. At first I worried about this and overestimated my power, but I then learnt that the young women always set my explanations against their own beliefs – their cultural capital – so I had a relatively minor impact. To believe that you can spend three years of your life with *anyone* and not have any impact is downright naive. The young women knew where my ideas were coming from and could make assessments accordingly. The information given is weighed up by the researched against their history and cultural background (after all, this is how hegemony works).

Ethnographic Analysis

I constantly analyzed what I was hearing from the young women throughout the research process. I did not just work from the ground up, using theories as examples of empirical experience, as suggested by Glaser and Strauss.[54] Nor did I use the ethnography to improve specific pre-existent theories, as suggested by Burawoy *et al.*[55] Rather, different theoretical readings at different times sensitized me to look for particular issues. I continually modified theories constructed from reading in the light of responses and observation of experiences. In the beginning my insecurity led me to the safety of other people's theories, furiously searching for something that would make sense of the empirical experience. Now that I feel more confident I try to work out my own from a variety of appropriations. I usually concoct a multitude of different theories, using them when appropriate, ditching them when not, reworking them to construct explanatory frameworks. I always ask: 'could this theory say anything to me about my life or about the lives of the young women?' Strathern identifies this as routine reflexivity where there is constant discovery that analytical concepts are context-dependent.[56]

This means that some theories are prioritized because their fundamental structures have more in common with the explanation of ethnographic material. My readings of psychoanalytic film theory seemed to have little bearing on these young women's lives. Yet cultural theories on audience research seemed more appropriate and were duly reworked. Only later did I find out that I had been using the psychoanalytic concept of investment. My major influences have been Valerie Walkerdine, Angela McRobbie and Paul Willis. Appropriations of Marx, Althusser, Gramsci, Genovese, Bourdieu and Foucault were made for feminist purposes. My friends have also been important for discussing the analysis. As few educational theories worked to explain how wider cultural forms affect women outside the institution of education, and as my initial and continuing interest was in the media, I appropriated and reworked media theories. Morley's work on cultural codes enabled me to explore how ideological messages were encoded and decoded by the young women.[57] In this sense the research was a product of its time (1981–6). When post-structuralism emerged in academic discourse, I was able to use it to explain the operations of differential power. At a later stage I questioned this, asking myself whether these young women really had power (they were very effective at humiliating others) or just strategies to overcome powerlessness? At a later stage (1990), after reading de Certeau, I was able to modify analysis of their strategies into tactics.[58] A more detailed example of the process of theoretical modification may help to outline the process.

The dominant feminist attitude to romance in 1981 was that it was a great ideological con that tricked those who believed in it. I thought it was too, until after a long discussion with Ann (PCSC) about why she ditched her boyfriend of two years after he became unemployed. Ann stressed right from the start of the research how much he was the 'right one', how much she believed in romance, and how much she was in love. In a clear state of distress she told me:

> What's the point, Bev, OK he was a nice bloke but we could never go anywhere, never do anything not like we used to, he was dead miserable, he used to drive me mad, so depressing, but he wouldn't get up off his arse and do anything, he seemed to lose interest, like he didn't care anymore, about nothing, it got to the stage where I used to think what's the point in seeing him, but Bev you can't go on like that, you know there's no point to it, imagine being married to that, stuck like that for the rest of your life. I know I shouldn't have stuck the boot in when he was down, like it wasn't his fault or any-thing, but there just didn't seem any point anymore, you'd have done the same, it was just pointless, he was never going to make anything of his life and that got on my nerves and made it worse.

Ann's emotional investment had not paid off. The rejection was not based on a straightforward financial appraisal but a thorough consideration of the negative aspects produced by unemployment. The negative aspects are considered to be insurmountable, the boyfriend changes from the 'right one' to the wrong one because 'right ones' are not associated with major problems that cannot be overcome. The romantic notion of the 'right one' is imbued with realistic economic expectations, illustrating how romantic ideology has a basis in material practice. Moreover, Ann was unable to motivate him into doing anything, suggesting that she had little power against the ravages of unemployment. This contradicts the ideology of romance that suggests that women have the power to emotionally manage relationships. In this sense unemployed boyfriends not only are a poor economic prospect but also confirm powerlessness against structural features – features which are not recognized within the culture of romance in which all problems are solvable with the 'right one'. Ann still believed in romance; her definition, however, was economic, not just ideological. Ann could not be tricked into believing that the 'right man' could be separated from economics. Romance, for the young women, is about the desire for something better, freed from the constraints of the economic.

This example shows how theories are modified to account for ethnographic responses (Ann's was not the only one). In the process of this modification other areas for investigation are highlighted, for example emotional management and the future of marriage in areas of high unemployment. Other theories were generated such as how the structural is individualized and how different subjectivities are constructed.

Having the privilege to study so intensely over a long time enabled an awareness of how responses changed over time. Repeated listening to tapes is often a neglected area of analysis and yet one of the most essential. I dutifully transcribed my first set of tapes – it took ages, and was useful, but now I selectively transcribe tapes for what seems appropriate at the time. Re-listening to tapes is a lot more inspiring than re-reading transcripts.

One group of young women asked if they could re-listen to their tapes, so they came, as a group, to my flat. It turned into a regular social event.[59] This was a really useful and informative time. They would often question what they had said, denying comments and changing their mind. This was pursued to find out how the responses were context-specific. The parts of the tape where emotional confessions had been made, or intimate details had been given, were enjoyed. It also put the whole process of the validity of my theories under scrutiny. I was able to ask why they had responded in particular ways at particular times. This also led me to pursue contradictions as part of the analysis. Contradictions were not used to refute previously collected evidence, as suggested by Hargreaves,[60] but rather, to provide a basis for further enquiry about how contradictions are experienced and lived.

Femininity, for instance, was rarely responded to in a straightforward way. It certainly was not taken on board uncritically and intact as previous theories suggested; it was used tactically, when appropriate, and often in contradictory ways. One of the most dismaying features of this finding was that many of the young women who displayed quite feminist sensibilities in the confines of the single-sex classroom, or in safe public spaces, purposefully forgot their feminism when interacting with any boys or men whom they could use as future investments. This was not dissimilar to other research that shows how young women measure the prospects of the men with whom they come into contact and accordingly moderate their responses.[61] By searching for feminist transformation in this process I was led to conclude, pessimistically, that as long as women are forced to be economically dependent on men it is unlikely that they will display behaviour likely to jeopardize their future economic security.

There were times in the process of analysis where I became completely blocked. In 1986 I was so pleased to read James Donald on educational subject positioning.[62] I had modified the work of Denis Gleeson, by accounting for gender, to show how further education performed an allocative function by preparing students for different vocational routes *and* routes out of the labour market into private and voluntary domestic labour. However, I could not work out exactly how the students became willing participants in this allocative process. Donald's reworking of Foucault showed how the curriculum provided different subject positions for students to take up which provided an occupation identity. From this I could see how the young women would willingly take up subject positions which defined them as responsible caring women with occupational potential. Had I finished my research before reading Donald it would have looked very different and a great deal more naive. This new reading made me rework three other chapters and now, having encountered new theories, I would write the research quite differently. Doing ethnography is a constant process of revealment. There are still many angles which I would like to pursue further. As Geertz notes:

> Cultural analysis is intrinsically incomplete. And, worse than that, the more deeply it goes the less complete it is. It is a strange science whose most telling assertions are its most tremulously based, in which to get somewhere with the matter at hand is to intensify the suspicion, both your own and that of others, that you are not quite getting it right.[63]

This shows just how much history and access to theory informs the interpretation that is given to ethnographic research. The research can be made to look different depending on which theoretical frameworks are chosen. I now suspect that my attempt to frame some of the young women's actions within rational-choice theory was my own fantasy of control over chaotic everyday ethnographic events.[64]

The process continues. I struggled with the first draft of this chapter until discussing it with a friend[65] who suggested that I read Marcus. This helped me (as noted earlier) to identify some of the problems which beset the whole research. Now, having read the anthropologists who have deconstructed the writing of ethnography,[66] I move to apply their analysis realizing that ethnography is not just a methodology informed by theory but is also a form of writing.

Writing Ethnography

All writing occurs within particular histories and within an academic mode of production. This presupposes that we are writing for a particular audience.

My initial concerns to give space and validity to the voices of young working-class women meant that I was writing against all the academic work in which they had been silenced in the past. I realized that I was not just writing for them but about them. I wanted them to be taken seriously (because I wanted to be taken seriously). But the audience to which I was speaking required a language that would make my work inaccessible to the young women. I was writing for an entry ticket into academia. The doctorate was my apprenticeship. On completion I wrote for a wider academic audience to gain academic respectability, and hopefully a job. Doctoral style does not square with accountability to those outside the academic establishment. This is one of the ethical dilemmas that feminist researchers have to deal with. Who do we do research for? I became aware of how, when interspersing the young women's spoken comments into my academic writing, they were made to sound authentic and simple. This juxtaposition, which is about the distinction between written and oral communication, reproduced the divisions between us. The distinction between my positioning within the academic division of labour and theirs within the unpaid and unskilled sectors of the labour market is a structural problem which informs all research with the powerless. For research is nearly always written for the (relatively) powerful. The whole process of systematizing everyday events, which is the work of ethnographers, has to draw upon concepts which were developed for theorists to speak to each other.

I did try to make the research accountable to the young women by giving them chapters and articles to read. 'Can't understand a bloody word it says' was the most common response. They were especially upset by pseudonyms, wanting to see their names with their comments in print. Yet, I also know that they are proud to be written about in such a way. They say it makes them feel important. I was faced continually with divided loyalties: action versus writing; challenge versus acquiescence. The research often had to be secondary to the problems it generated.

Ethnography requires the researcher/writer to adopt stylistic techniques usually associated with literature. It relies upon particular narrative and constructive methods. It defines topics, shifts from one locale to another, juxtaposes other perspectives and thus decides which context, at what level and from whose perspective the reader will see.[67] It uses the label of authentic voice to give weight to the shifts. This becomes a question of internal composition, of the organization of the analysis, the sequence in which the reader is introduced to the concepts, the way categories are constructed.[68] So the reader not only holds together the theoretical analysis and the information that is being presented but also needs to be aware of how it is being presented. When writing up, the researcher becomes conscious of how conventions of text and rhetoric are among the ways in which reality is represented.[69] Ethnography is automatically placed within the genre of realism as it relies on 'authentic' voices. The selection and organization of the transcripts makes the process of representation explicit, although in reading this process may remain implicit. After much deliberation and for purposes of col chose accounts and transcripts which operated as theoretical dram. cators[70] to exemplify the structural relations as they were lived at th everydayness.[71] The accounts were considered to be a product of the particular moment in which they were made. Social construction theorists – in the field of the sociology of knowledge – would argue that I constructed the world of the participants through my representations.[72] I did not. I partially represented their social productions.[73] For that is all that can be achieved – how can you encapsulate three years of your life, eleven years of contact and thousands of interviews and observations into limited wordage? I do not have the power (nor do any individuals) to socially produce the lives of young women. This is why ethnographies are more than just narratives. They relate to a reality that exists before and after the research.

The recent emphasis in ethnographic anthropology on style needs to be kept in perspective. Ethnographers may end up communicating and competing with each other for the development of sophisticated styles in which the politics of their research becomes obscured. Those of us not born into the privilege of literary cultural capital may find the language and the confidence to play operating as yet another exclusionary device. For as Rabinow notes, groups long excluded from positions of institutional power have less concrete freedom to indulge in textual experimentation.[74] Strathern argues that the ironic re-reading of some of the 'new' ethnographers (in anthropology) seems in danger of becoming cultural self-reference. Similarly when the anthropological ethnographers deconstruct the authority of ethnography,[75] which raises important questions about representation and who speaks for whom and how, they may also be referring to their own institutional authority, which is very different from the authority of the doctoral female ethnographer.

Conclusions

Putting my own actions and intentions under scrutiny in retrospect has been a difficult process (I recommend that anyone doing ethnography keeps a research diary on their reflexivity right from the start). It has been useful in giving me a clearer picture of how knowledge is produced. I have shown that feminist ethnography is a theory of the research process, which draws upon different methods and is defined by its location within feminist epistemologies and ontologies, whilst simultaneously constructing these ontologies and epistemologies. By showing how ethnography is also a style of writing, questions of reality, representation and accountability have also been raised. Ultimately, I would argue that feminist research should elicit and analyze knowledge in a way that can be used by women to alter the oppressive and exploitative conditions in their society.[76] Bhavnani suggests that the crucial question for all (feminist) researchers is to ask, does the analysis reinscribe the researched into powerlessness, pathologized, without agency?[77]

Feminist ethnography can contribute to a wider feminist project by giving knowledge a practical relevance and by exposing the constructions of knowledge as a form of control and categorization. Feminist ethnography can account for the practice of different women, at different times, in different places. It can increase the specificity of analysis by providing an economic, institutional, social and discursive context. It can bring into question universalistic or homogeneous theories which speak from a position of privilege. Feminist ethnography shows how women make history but not in the conditions of their own choosing. It can show how feminist ethnographers do the same. The longevity and intensity of ethnography enables the feminist researcher to gain greater insights into the contradictory behaviour of the everyday in which women are located. It can show how subjectivities are constructed and changed over a period of time. The modification of theories in relation to the empirical enables the construction of frameworks and explanations that would have everyday applicability. The prolonged contact with young women made accountable my constructions of feminism; I could not theorize or practice solely in an ivory tower or a vacuum. The young women are still firmly lodged in my consciousness. It is difficult not to be reflexive about my positioning vis-à-vis power. It should also be difficult for a feminist ethnographer to produce obscure, irrelevant, pretentious and ungrounded feminist theories.

It is for these reasons that I would take issue with Judith Stacey who argues that the involvement and intensity of ethnography make it *the* most exploitative method because ethnographic methods subject the researched to greater risks of exploitation, betrayal and abandonment by the researcher than does much positivistic research.[78] Yes, the women were used in constructing my career; that is a debt that can never be repaid. However, I also think that Stacey overstates the power of the researcher and places the researched into a victim category. The young women were not prepared to be exploited; just as they were able to resist most things which did not promise economic or cultural reward, they were able to resist me. This is the counterhegemonic approach to research. They enjoyed the research. It provided resources for developing their sense of self-worth. More importantly, the feminism of the research has provided a framework which they use to explain that their individual problems are part of a wider structure and not their personal fault. This is not inconsiderable when one thinks of the enormity of ideological materials devoted to encouraging women to take responsibility for emotional management. Overall, however, the research was just too small a part of their lives to concretely position them. They made the most of it. To assume that they were exploited confines them to a category of passivity that most feminists are at pains *not* to reproduce.

However, what Stacey does is to draw attention to the many difficult ethical dilemmas involved in feminist research in general[79] – often amplified through the intensity of ethnographic relationships. Issues of principles and power will inform any research project. Feminist ethnography forces the researcher to confront these issues, rather than – as other methodologies allow

– ignore them. If we take on board the arguments for a feminist objectivity then we will become more accountable and open to scrutiny, for as Deem and Brehony argue, accountability is best regarded as something which is to be worked towards rather than fully achieved.[80] However, such reflexive goals often remain at the level of desire rather than competent enactment.[81] Ethnography is always limited by the context and mode of production. Maybe doing feminist ethnography corresponds to much of daily life. We use the cultural resources available to us in the most beneficially feminist way possible, with an accompanying knowledge of the dangers, constraints and limitations in which we are located.

Notes

Thanks to Mary (who has been an inspiration since my undergraduate years), June, Amos and Andrew Sayer, for their constructive comments. Thanks also to my colleagues at the Centre for Women's Studies, Lancaster University, for such a supportive and stimulating research environment.

1 Althusserian theories of ideology (if used to explain gender) suggested that women were interpellated (hailed) to a position of femininity. It was assumed that they acquiesced in femininity without resistance.
2 Gramsci argues that for power to operate successfully consent to its operations needs to be won. I wanted to see how the everyday activities of the young women would involve them in giving consent to oppressive conditions. See Gramsci (1971); Bourdieu (1977).
3 For more details see Skeggs (1986).
4 Berger and Luckmann (1971).
5 It was important to keep details of these biographical responses, because they changed often in the process of the research. This led me to analyze the importance of memory and how we construct narratives of our own lives. It also leads me to question what it was about our relationship that made them want to provide me with specific narratives.
6 Woolgar and Ashmore (1988, pp. 1–12) argue that reflexivity is only successful when it is closely tied to the specific occasion of the knowledge occurrence. Reflexivity, they argue, is a specific local accomplishment. I disagree. This unnecessarily limits any reflexive activity. Reflexivity occurs over different times in different places. It should be a continual process that we are involved in rather than a singular process tied to specific events.
7 Most of the debates on ethnography have been in anthropology. My ethnography differs from traditional anthropological fieldwork in that I did not leave the country, I did not study the 'other' in the traditional sense of the term and I was not isolated in my fieldwork. My ethnography is part of the British cultural studies tradition from CCCS, Birmingham. See Hall and Jefferson (1976).
8 Roberts (1981) and Bell and Encel (1978) were the only books recommended.
9 Research such as that by D.H. Hargreaves (1967) and Lacey (1970) focused on interaction in the school without any awareness of wider structural issues.

10 For example, Whyte (1955); Patrick (1976). See McRobbie (1980) and Skeggs (1992).

11 The history of ethnography in the early twentieth century was part of a colonial project to know, measure and control the 'other'. The method of participant observation was seen to be the most effective way to collect knowledge on other cultures which were potentially disruptive to the English rule. Ethnographers and colonial administrators worked together to maintain the status quo. This gave the early ethnographers both status and authority, what Clifford (1983) calls the professionalization of synthetic cultural description and the professionalization of representing otherness. Another legacy from the history of ethnography is what Gellner (1970) defines as 'contextual charity'. To react against the ethnocentric and colonialist beginnings of anthropology some ethnographers adopted cultural relativism, according to which the knowledge of other cultures was to be treated as beyond the scope of external criticism. All of this occurred within the discourse of rationality i.e. what looks irrational in one culture can be seen to be rational if one looks far enough.

12 See Reinharz (1992) for more details. Reinharz argues that early feminist ethnography is rooted in the travel literature of nineteenth-century radical feminists.

13 Golde (1970/1986).

14 Willis (1981).

15 Althusser (1971).

16 Willis (1981).

17 See hooks (1984).

18 See Skeggs (1992).

19 Gleeson (1983).

20 See G.E. Marcus (1986).

21 G.E. Marcus (1992) distinguishes between modernity as a mode of analysis and modernism as a historical epoch. However, there are many semantic differences and slippages in the terms modern/ism/ity/ist and postmodern/ism/ity/ist when used by ethnographers located in anthropology (as in other areas). For the most ferocious of these debates see *Current Anthropology*, vol. 29, no. 3 (June 1988).

22 However, Marcus' definition may prove to be confusing. Andrew Sayer suggests that Marcus appropriates Raymond Williams' arguments about literary realism which is not the same as the philosophical realism which is usually referenced in methodological debates. Modernism and philosophical (critical) realism are equally compatible with literary realist and modernist ontologies (discussion with Andrew Sayer, April 1993). See also Sayer (1992). I retain the dichotomy to point to useful differences.

23 Clifford (1983) argues that all fieldwork is structured on a narrative of self and others.

24 Realism assumes that events can be read off from and back to external forms. However, I would rather operate with economics as a framework into which people are unequally distributed, but from which there is a small amount of space in which they can move. The young women from similar economic backgrounds moved differently into economic positions within and outside the labour market.

25 Strohmayer and Hannah (1992).

26 See Winch (1958).

27 Donald (1985).

28 Walkerdine (1984).

29 This makes the concept of compressed ethnography rather dubious. Many researchers have called their interviews ethnographic even though they were conducted in a short space of time with little observation to substantiate them.
30 Jaggar (1983).
31 Guba (1990).
32 Chris Griffin's theories were circulated in papers presented to seminar groups at the CCCS (Centre for Contemporary Cultural Studies) in Birmingham University. They were finally written into book form with *Typical Girls* (1985).
33 Willis (1981), p. 201.
34 See Hartsock (1983); Harding (1990, 1991).
35 Flax (1987).
36 See Rattansi (1992).
37 Stanley and Wise (1983).
38 See Hammersley (1992).
39 Harding (1991).
40 See Haraway (1988).
41 *Ibid.*; Harding (1991).
42 Haraway (1988).
43 Mies (1983).
44 Walkerdine suggests that it is fear of change and resistance to it that keeps many working-class women in their 'place': see Walkerdine (1990a).
45 Rollins (1985).
46 Game (1991).
47 Golde (1970/1986).
48 Haraway (1988).
49 See Walkerdine (1986). Fernando (1992) argues that black people have also been divested of subjecthood, as objects of white scrutiny and classification. So the process of objectification needs to be carefully set against sexism and racism.
50 Oakley (1981).
51 Warren (1988).
52 Oakley (1981).
53 Acker *et al.* (1983) noted a similar tendency in their research.
54 Glaser and Strauss (1967).
55 Burawoy *et al.* (1991).
56 Strathern (1987a).
57 Morley (1979).
58 De Certeau (1988) distinguishes between strategies and tactics. Strategies, he argues, have institutional positioning and are able to conceal the connections with power. Tactics have no institutional location and cannot capitalize on the advantages of such positioning. Rather, tactics constantly manipulate events to turn them into opportunities. Tactical options have more to do with constraints than possibilities. They are determined by the absence of power just as strategies are organized by the postulation of power.
59 There were demands by the students to listen to other groups' interviews, but I resisted those pressures.
60 A. Hargreaves (1982) suggests this.
61 Leonard (1980).
62 Donald (1985).
63 Geertz (1973), p. 29.

64 Walkerdine (1990b).
65 Celia Lury, University of Lancaster.
66 See Clifford and Marcus (1986) for an edited collection of the debates within anthropology. The journal *Current Anthropology* provides the most recent states of play. Other significant references are: Marcus and Cushman (1982); Clifford (1981, 1983); Van Maanen (1988); Atkinson (1990), which outlines the arguments for sociologists.
67 Clifford (1983).
68 Strathern (1987b).
69 Atkinson (1990).
70 Collins (1983).
71 Cf. Apple (1982).
72 See the collections in Steier (1991) and Woolgar (1988).
73 Clifford (1986).
74 See Rabinow (1986). Footnote 11 in Clifford (1986) debates this point in more detail.
75 Clifford (1983).
76 Cook and Fonow (1986).
77 Bhavnani (in prep.). Elsewhere I have suggested a detailed plan for changing the caring courses: see Skeggs (1990).
78 Stacey (1988). Although I take issue with some of Stacey's arguments, any ethnographer should be aware of the dilemmas she details. It is a very reflexive account, although we come to different conclusions from similar problems.
79 See Cole and Coultrap-McQuin (1992) and Frazer *et al.* (1992) for a general debate on ethics.
80 See Deem and Brehony (1992).
81 Harding (1991), p. 163.

Chapter 5

Dancing with Denial: Researching Women and Questioning Men

Elizabeth A. Stanko

In the context of researching women's lives over the past fifteen years, I have become accustomed to dancing with denial, my description of traditional criminology's myopia when it comes to gender and crime. The purpose of this chapter is to reflect upon my own development as a researcher, and to acknowledge the power of the research process in forming and formulating my view of criminology from a feminist perspective. Researching women's lives forces me now to question men about their lives, and leads me to directly challenge masculinity and its underpinning of the dominant perspectives in criminology. I conclude by encouraging others to contest the imagery of gender in criminology (and any other discipline), an imagery which persists in contradictory portrayals of women, whether as crime victims or offenders, as heartless, helpless, hopeless, and/or in need of protection or isolation by the father-state, and of men, as altruistic protectors of women, savage violators, or themselves untouched by violence. Such imagery can be exposed through research on women's lives, consistently uncovered by feminist research, and can be challenged though a feminist approach to the study of men and crime.[1]

I proceed in this chapter by tracing my personal efforts to come to terms with how women create apparently irreconcilable discourses within my chosen field of criminology. I am not the only one to confront the frustrations accompanying engagement with this especially intractable discipline.[2] Carol Smart, for instance, goes so far as to observe: 'I see criminology as something of a siding for feminist thought, with feminist criminologists risking something of a marginalized existence – marginal to criminology and to feminism' (1990, p. 71). Although I agree with Smart that feminist criminologists are on the fringes of criminology and feminism, I still choose to remain a truculent, but engaged, outsider to both feminism and criminology. It is the research on women's lives which keeps me here.

All of my over twenty years of professional life have been spent working in criminology. I have been employed as a research fellow on two American, state-financed research programmes, and have been a university lecturer for seventeen years. I am actively involved in campaigns against men's violence towards women: as part of a team, I founded a refuge for battered women, and in my various research projects, I attempt to articulate how women cope and manage various forms of violence in our everyday lives. I was also engaged in my own struggle through a prolonged lawsuit alleging sexual harassment, an experience which has undoubtedly left its scars. I have little doubt that this personal experience has fuelled my passionate confrontation with men's violence. My work now explores how men feel about the violence they experience at the hands of other men.[3]

Some Background

For the readers unfamiliar with criminology, it is necessary to provide some background. In their capacity as offenders, theorists, practitioners, university teachers, the judiciary, legal advocates, victims, and policy-makers, men dominate the crime business. The cult of masculinity, a common description of one fundamental tenet of police and policing, can be readily found amongst all players in the criminology game. Women, it seems, are a problem – albeit a marginalized one[4] – in and for criminology, regardless of whether they be offender, victim or professional. Theoretical explanations of women's crime and criminal indiscretions, as many commentators note,[5] embrace historically a biological determinism: women offenders are, constitutionally, somehow more masculine than their law-abiding sisters. This thinking can be found in traditional reasoning about women and sexual assault: women victims, potentially sexually insatiable or confused about how to accept male attentions, ask for sexual violence. Such determinism even lies at the root of women's entry into the all-male police: they were recruited for their special skills *as women*,[6] because, it was assumed, they could better handle the needs of women and children coming into contact with the criminal justice system. Once recruited, despite their supposedly specially-valued skills in dealing with women and children, women police are subjected to sustained sexual harassment and abuse by their male colleagues.[7] Even today, in other capacities in the criminal justice system, women rarely walk the halls of the judiciary establishment. There has never been a woman chief constable in the UK. Uniquely, three women occupy top positions in the UK: in England and Wales, as Director of Public Prosecutions, MI5 and HM Customs and Excise. By and large, however, in virtually every capacity, women are amongst the minority in criminology.[8]

Beginning in the mid 1970s, a cohort of women, inspired by the second wave of the Women's Movement, began to study criminology. What we found was the poverty of information, in quality as well as in quantity, about women in any capacity in criminology. Biological or psychological explanations for women's crime predominated; women victims were characterized as enticing their assailants. These women criminologists set out to document women's involvement with the criminal justice system, as victims, offenders and professionals, with the goal of making women visible.[9] The study of female criminality took prominence. Not surprisingly, research reveals that women's relationship to femininity,[10] rather than their criminality, heavily influences women's treatment by criminal justice decision-makers. Mary Eaton's work suggests that convicted women are ultimately sentenced through a lens of women's role in the family.[11] Pat Carlen summarizes 'what is already known' about women law-breakers:

1   that women's crimes are predominantly the crimes of the powerless (for example, women are more likely to engage in petty theft, low-level fraud, and prostitution);
2   that disproportionate numbers of women from ethnic minority groups are imprisoned;
3   that typifications of conventional femininity (such as those noted by Eaton above) play a major role in the decision whether or not to imprison women;
4   that the majority of women appear to be law-abiding and when in trouble are much more likely to be in receipt of medical, psychiatric or welfare regulation than caught up in the machinery of criminal justice.[12]

Astute critiques of theory and practice exist. They are largely, as Smart, Gelsthorpe and Morris, Heidensohn and others continue to observe, peripheral to the criminology game.

R.W. Connell suggests that the exclusion of women from public discourse is a part of the homogenizing process within masculinities.[13] The exclusion of women, who continue to be associated with affairs of the private, not the public world of crime, is reproduced in maintaining women's marginalization in the field of criminology. Criminology, as Jefferson recently observed, perpetuates 'woman as problem' by its total reliance on notions of appropriate masculinity as its explanation for all crime.[14] The celebration or condemnation of bad boys, often to the exclusion of women, is sustained by the assumption that male law-breakers or deviants are only acting their part.[15] The four common features noted by Carlen (see above) have an invisibility in the discipline, overshadowed by the concern for male law-breakers, with a simultaneous failure to examine masculinity. Whilst Carlen's work, and that of others, unmasks this characterization, the abhorrence of the female criminal is often unquestioned, either by criminology's intentional neglect or by its failure to confront the very real issues of female offenders' lives which the research continues to document: poverty, confusions about sexuality, the very real effects of abuse, violence and neglect, the damaging and destructive effects of substance abuse and, I would also argue, the strength of gender as a mediator of life experience.[16]

In many ways, I hoped to avoid the angst of theoretical criminology by not engaging in the primary debates around the nature and explanations of offending. Instead, I found myself focusing upon violence against women, only to find a similar myopia. So much violence, threat and criminality that penetrates women's lives was, and largely remains, hidden.[17] As feminist researchers ripped open and made public the issue of men's physical and sexual abuse of women, we did not initially intend (I think) to challenge the foundation of criminology, only its neglect of these issues. Many of the studies of rape and domestic violence, influenced by radical feminism, have been excluded from mainstream criminology.[18] It could be that they have been considered exclusively 'women's issues', thus not of major concern to the study of 'real' crime. As such issues are not central to the crime question (recorded violence, sexual and physical, comprises such a small proportion of official crime), they are virtually ignored. Whatever the reason, however, when conventional criminologists do include these issues within textbooks on crime, women are still portrayed as 'teases' and 'flirts', inviting their abuse.[19] In particular, the insights of radical feminist research often remain outside the traditional criminological text.

Theorizing about women and violence exposes problems for criminology, for, as it turns out, men known to women, not the vilified strangers found within criminological theorizing, pose the greatest danger. It is feminist research that uncovers this contradiction within criminological discourse. I must pause here to define what I mean by feminist research. Debates about feminism and its impact on social science methodology and approaches are lively and ongoing. I do not believe there is 'a' feminist research perspective. I personally rely upon intensive interviews and ethnography as my methodological mainstays. I work from a perspective which asserts that women's voices, as different as they are from each other, converge into some common themes. My work has focused largely on one of these common themes: violence, its impact on women, and women's strategies for minimizing and avoiding it. I call my approach feminist because I believe women's experiences of the world, their knowledge base and their interpretations are fused within a gendered context. And this context is one of subordination, by and large, to men and men's needs. Of course, I am not naive enough to deny the very real and powerful contributions of economic standing, race, ethnicity, being disabled, sexual orientation and so forth to women's lives. But the collective voice of 'women' does tell us a great deal about personal safety, the issue I choose to study.

The voices of 'women' lay bare the hypocrisy of the criminal justice system, the state's apparatus in the ideological and practical protection of citizens. Feminist research on women whose lives have been touched in some way by their encounters with violent men and with the institutions which mediate that violence does not depict a system of justice designed to protect. Battered women, and their advocates, angrily and regularly demand better treatment by the police, the courts and social services.[20] Raped and sexually abused women, few of whom even bother to complain to the justice system, typically meet the contempt of a legal process which can find no way of proving rape and sexual abuse without routinely humiliating the complainant.

What is interesting is that much of the humiliation is now a recognized and largely uncontested part of legal enquiry. As Helena Kennedy shows, even in situations involving defendants unknown to victims defence strategies can be built upon allegations that the woman consented to rape.[21]

In sum, what has developed for me is a perspective about crime carved from a feminist viewpoint about women's oppression. Whilst the debates amongst women criminologists are lively, the commonality lies in the observation about oppression, and that research (whether it be described as 'feminist' or not[22]) on women, crime and violence will *display* oppression. I would like now to turn to my own journey, and draw on the lessons I have learnt from studying women's lives.

Criminology from Within: Documenting Women's Harm

Let me begin by exploring how researching women became the avenue for my collision with conventional approaches of criminology. My work with battered, raped and abused women and my own personal experience combined to question why, and how, violence acquires a sense of ordinariness within women's lives. Criminologists' fascination with violence embraces an underlying anxiety about public danger.[23] But it is the violence of the public, not the private, that occupies the forefront of criminological theorizing. Yeatman[24] offers us an explanation by suggesting that 'the ruling paradigms or theoretical frameworks in social science are flawed by a masculinist bias which is indicated in an arbitrary privileging of the public aspect of social existence'. Because criminologists equate crime with public life, much of women's experience of violence has been obscured because of its largely private, hidden nature.

Women's voices challenge the focus on the public and require an examination of the so-called private sphere of violence. Throughout my research career, women themselves have described the process of the silencing of their understanding about violence more eloquently than I have. One battered women commented:

> The feeling of helplessness [when in a violent relationship are] due to the fact that it was my fault that I got battered, which I think is common that a woman is blamed because she provoked him. Certainly my husband immediately blamed me. 'If you had done so and so; if you hadn't done so and so.' And the fact that he did almost kill me and threatened if I said anything to the police he *would* kill me and the destruction of confidence or any way out. I had no money, I had kids. I couldn't for years see my way out of this situation, in myself I didn't have any sense of it. If I left, he'd follow me. He'd take my kids away. He threatened to do that. I believed all that.[25]

In the early 1980s, feminist researchers asked women to reflect about their lives vis-à-vis men's violence. The extensive and pervasive impact of serious sexual and physical violence on women's lives could hardly be denied. The often quoted figure that derives from the work of Diana Russell[26] in the United States is that one in three women experience a serious sexual assault in their lifetimes. This illustrates the normality of serious sexual assault.

The more I spoke to women, the more I began to see how the fact of rape, as observed by Brownmiller[27] in the mid 1970s, and the experiences of physical violence in childhood and adult relationships, documented by a number of feminist researchers, keep women alert to men's violence. A common factor in my work on violence against women is the strength of women's voices in the telling of the story of violence. One woman, recalling childhood abuse, said:

> My dad would beat up my Mom, and me or one of my sisters would call the police if it got really bad. Or if my mom told me to call, and they would come. I was really scared, for her and for me, because it was really obvious that if he was going to hurt her, he would hurt us too. I was really concerned about her, trying to figure out how to make it safe for her, to do something. It was frustrating because there was nothing really I could do, because he was so much bigger and things like that. I was frustrated and angry.[28]

A woman recalling rape said:

> I think of my life as pre-rape and post-rape in some ways. I think it altered relationships tremendously. It changed my view of the world and I think it was very difficult with relationships with other women. . . . I feel more vulnerable for whatever reason. . . . You realise there is no safe place.[29]

A woman remembering being fondled in public said:

> It's funny how things come back [while we are talking]. I remember one time walking across the street and this kid who was, I think at that point he wasn't in my class, but he just reached out and grabbed my crotch and I remember being, in some way, more so than some of the ongoing stuff with this man [for whom I babysat], I was just so mortified. I remember almost fainting.[30]

Painful and distressing as these stories may be, they are records of the ever-presence of men's violence. Essentially, the purpose of my feminist research is to make visible these hidden realities.

Ironically, feminist criminology, including my own work, once accused of being unnecessarily alarmist because it suggested that large numbers of women experienced abuse at the hands of men, is now being accused of portraying all women as victims.[31] Penny Green suggests that feminist criminology, through its contemporary work, imposes a 'victim status attributed to women in general'.[32] Jim Messerschmidt, in his treatise on masculinities and crime, also makes this point.[33]

At the same time, with woeful regularity in the media and elsewhere, women's experiences of encountering violence are reduced to simple accounts of 'just being a woman'. For example, since the early 1990s, highly publicized cases of random murder against women have seen sudden speculation that 'no woman is safe in public'.[34] Observations from such feminist commentators as Caputi[35] or Cameron and Frazer,[36] who argue that sexual murder is not just an unfortunate event, but part of systematic violence against women, are not to be found. Raising the *potential* of victimization because one is a woman, it seems, may also raise the dubious biological determinism found within explanations of women's criminality. Women, according to this perspective, are 'naturally' victims. By focusing upon victimization, feminist researchers are sometimes accused of reinforcing the image of women as helpless. I do not agree. If anything, women who survive living with violence demonstrate a creative endurance well beyond many people's imagined strength.

The persistence of the assumption that women are natural victims prompted me to move away from examining the more horrific examples of men's violence, such as rape, incest and battering,[37] to articulating women's daily encounters with unsafety.[38] It is in the making visible of women's daily lives that I can better articulate how so many women structure their lives around the avoidance of men's violence. In a recent article, Marjorie Devault[39] suggests that certain kinds of interview talk, especially women's talk, can provide insight into how we can better translate women's experiences into standard vocabulary. She suggests that 'By speaking in ways that open the boundaries of standard topics, we can create space for respondents to provide accounts rooted in the realities of their lives'.[40]

My own work on women and safety aims to extend the standard criminological analysis of 'fear of crime'. Relying on the survey method to interview victims, conventional criminological approaches to 'fear of crime' use standard questions about perceived danger and likeliness of encountering crime. As the research consistently documents, women's fear of crime is greater than that of men, with women's reported level of fear exceeding men's by a factor of three. This approach seems to capture women's concerns about personal safety, and fails to do so for men.[41] Some researchers even state that macho reticence might be to blame for men's silence, but fail to explore women's willingness or men's reticence to disclose vulnerability. Moreover, concern for what is termed 'fear of crime' focuses upon women's concern about personal danger in public.[42] It is within this criminological framework that it makes sense to engage in the debate about women's safety. What happened to all the research that documents women's harm at the hands of the familial and familiar? Devault's point, that feminist topics go beyond standard (here, traditional disciplinary) labels, applies to the 'discovery' of safety as a major issue for contemporary (and I suspect, past) women. Clearly, feminist enquiry opens up new questions and challenges the disciplinary straightjacket of criminology.

My strategy is simply to ask women what they do to 'make themselves feel safe'. What women describe, in great detail, are the panoply of behavioural and physical devices they call forth to manoeuvre themselves through a world saturated with potential danger. In public, women carry keys in their hands, walk purposively, place men's hats on the seats of their cars, choose routes they are most comfortable with, and so forth. The work of Carol Brooks Gardner[43] in the United States also shows how women's lives are permeated by the intrusions of men. While she is concerned solely with the use of public space, women, she shows, actively construct 'presentational strategies' in public to protect themselves from men's potential violence. She states that 'The felt obligation to behave in a crime-conscious manner can undermine subtly or not so subtly, women's trust in the majority of quite innocent men whom women observe or with whom they come into contact in public places'.[44]

My work links the strategies used by women in public with those they use in private. Women avoiding violence from known men display skills similar to those used in public: some women allow men to choose the television programmes to watch, some cook the men's food preferences, some keep children out of the men's way, some refuse to be in the same room on their own with sexual harassers. What is interesting to me is to see how women's knowledge of danger, as documented in the literature, rarely informs the campaigns around domestic violence, rape and women's safety in public in any holistic way. Women who face violence in the home are not assumed to also face violence outside, and vice versa. In the UK, there is currently a flurry of activity on the part of police and local authorities addressing domestic violence. As Radford and I argue elsewhere,[45] whilst institutional responsiveness to women experiencing men's violence is clearly welcomed, confrontation with male power is certainly not part of the police agenda. Yet the picture of helpless women, which often underlines the institutional response to violence against women by agencies such as the police, does not always hold up to empirical scrutiny. Research documenting that women *do* actively seek assistance, advice and alternatives to violence[46] is lost in the practice of many institutional responses to violence against women. What is sometimes hidden is the very real and deep damage such endurance leaves behind. Yet we know that managing public and private violence at the hands of men is clearly part of women's lives. As such, feminist research underscores the structural constraints which shape women's so-called choices to live free of violence, whether it be in the home or elsewhere.

No doubt, as Dobash and Dobash[47] have explored recently, women's own stories of abuse and violence serve as the foundation for feminist campaigns around violence against women, and as the starting point for radical feminist researchers. (There is, of course, a history of how the ideas about battering are contested by research and researchers.[48]) But what women are saying about men continues to be denied. The majority of abusers are regular guys: ordinary men. Yet abuse of women is blamed on men's drink, drugs, violent childhoods, job stress, unemployment, even tension caused by women's (so-called) liberation. Rarely do we find the portrayal of women's assailants found within accounts of the ordinary men who are middle-class and work in banks, universities, the civil service; violence is usually associated with working-class or criminal men, and here, only a few men are cast as woman-abusers. The resistance to the explicit and implicit lesson about men is virulently ignored: distinguishing between the dangerous and not so dangerous men is extremely difficult.

Despite the volumes of evidence accumulating about women's experiences, however, criminology's discourses about harm, evil and danger continue to spotlight the evil stranger, the menace to the seemingly tranquil social order of contemporary life. The work of radical feminists who have researched violence against women has exposed the fallacy of this image.[49] As I have suggested elsewhere,

> We gather our knowledge of danger and of violence in private, yet it is in the public domain that the thinking about crime and violence takes place. The public debate about crime, in too many respects, wrongly silences our private understandings about personal danger. And the way in which anxiety about safety is publicly expressed serves to separate the fear of crime from our private knowledge about danger. For despite the clear evidence that the risk of interpersonal violence is overwhelmingly from those near and dear to us, we all seem to worry more about threats from strangers.[50]

The work on sexual violence, pioneered in the UK by the work of Hanmer and Saunders,[51] Kelly[52] and Stanko,[53] demonstrates that women's primary danger comes from known men. While it may now seem odd that such a 'fact' was not commonly accepted by (or for that matter, acceptable to) criminologists, and, for that matter, police,[54] barristers and judges,[55] and the media,[56] they all retain theoretical, policy and practical stances about danger which place the stranger in the spotlight. These perspectives deny women's knowledge about danger: known men hurt them more than strangers.

Central to government crime prevention and police advice to women about personal safety is the dangerous stranger. In an examination of safety advice to women, I explored the ways in which the police approach emphasizes that it is women's behaviour in public, and guarding against stranger intrusion at home, that needs to be altered to avoid danger.[57] In reminding women to have petrol in their car, avoid dimly lit alleyways, and keep their handbags grasped tightly to their bodies, the police advice assumes adult women have somehow never considered such precautions to avoid crime. My own research on women's attention to personal safety, on the other hand, shows me that women already use the common sense the Home Office presents as a new approach to safety.

The lesson I have learnt from my work and campaigning around the issue of sexual violence, battering and women's safety is that women who live with abuse become experts in the management of men's (too often 'their' men's) violence. Managing sexual and physical danger, and all of the daily efforts women use to accomplish safety,[58] are often overlooked by criminologists. This can be seen by contrasting what women say with criminology's dominant discourse about danger. The fact that the potential for violence from known men has been recognized by many institutions and individuals does not mean that the image of the dangerous stranger has been removed from centre stage. On the contrary, the acknowledgment of men's violence has only come by pushing into the limelight those hapless and unsuspecting 'victims' of such violence. Thus the focus remains on men's so-called aberrant sexual and physical violence, not its mundane, but nonetheless controlling, forms. Yet the whole structure of criminology inhibits me from engaging with the most important determinant of women's safety – men. Men vary in enormous ways as do their masculinities. One thing they share, however, is an aggressively dominant and frequently violent relationship with women.

Challenging Masculinity through Research on Women's Lives

For me, explanations of what happens to women and the inadequate approach of conventional criminology to account for this treatment soon becomes apparent: women are almost always harmed by 'ordinary' men, who, because these men seldom come to the attention of the criminal justice system, are not characterized as presenting a criminal threat to women. 'Criminals', at least those who attack women whose complaints are sometimes upheld in court, are portrayed as savage beasts, not the guy next door.

Criminology's preoccupation – shoring up what Connell terms hegemonic masculinity[59] – reinforces the denial of the overwhelming danger to women. The resistance to *this* message of feminist research on violence against women was, and is, formidable. Curiously though, today, few deny women's widespread experience of sexual and physical violence. Yet despite this, criminological discourses about gender, femininity and masculinity tend to overlook abuse of women by men. Not just 'sick', 'deranged', lurking strangers, but the seemingly safe men who harm women, often the epitome of appropriate masculinity, escape scrutiny.

Explorations of how men account for violence against women suggest that there is a tendency, even amongst convicted rapists,[60] to downplay the amount of violence used and to fail to acknowledge the damage of the rape. Women are blamed for 'asking for it' whenever violence befalls them. Or men plead diminished responsibility for their violence, due to drugs, drink, stress or whatever. At the same time, man-to-man violence has justifications which sound similar to those used to explain men's violence to women: drugs, drink or violent theft. 'Character contests' is one term used by Lonnie Athens[61] to explain men's violent confrontations with each other. Overlooked is the fact that these violent negotiations are about hierarchies of masculinities, excused, for example, as 'teaching someone a lesson', 'saving face', 'disciplining a sissy' or 'controlling territory'. There is a tendency to treat fights amongst men as mechanisms for resolving disputes,[62] and also as a method of preserving and reinforcing status, or perhaps resolving insecurity about status.

My latest strategy for confronting the denial of men's experiences of violence is to examine how men cope with being victims of violence themselves. For me, it is a search for how men come to understand violence in their own lives, which might present clues to how to understand how men characterize violence in women's lives. Even in this arena criminology tends to view violence as abnormal, unusual and largely confined to certain classes of men, rather than ubiquitous. What are the implications for uncovering men's private, hidden experiences of violence? How does criminological thinking characterize man-to-man violence? To what extent does the knowledge about gendered violences pave the way for a clearer understanding about the violence women face in their daily lives?

This work is in its preliminary stages, although I have been conducting research about it since 1985. I am reluctant to leave the political arena of *women's* safety, simply because of my personal commitment. I am however compelled to explore the issue of men's victimization. Theoretically, I feel, it holds some keys to how men manage hierarchies within masculinities, and the negotiation of hierarchies is rooted in the potential for, and use of, violence, man to man. The major disadvantage, for me, is that I do not have the personal resources to tap into my own experiences to explore what men say about violence. I am not a man, and do not have the accumulation of gendered knowledge against which to balance what the men are saying and sharing about their lives. This work, I suspect, will have to be done by men. The lesson here about research is that gendered researchers are resources for their work. My work on men, in many ways, will never reach the same depths of understanding as my research on women's lives.

Some Final Thoughts

It is the research on women's lives which motivates me to challenge criminology. One way of handling the dissonance I continue to face is perhaps simply to walk away from the profession. A long-time feminist friend of mine recently wrote to me, saying that she was not attending an upcoming criminology conference, summarizing her discontent: 'No money, no childcare, no interest in criminology'. I do not know how many women have walked away from my discipline (or any discipline) in disgust and with frustration, due to the inability to fit women within a frame (any frame) recognized and recognizable as criminology (or other disciplines). Writing this chapter (and for you, the reader, reading this chapter) helps me face my own angst and doubts about the impact of feminist research on women and on the discipline, criminology. But I cannot deny what I know about women, men, danger, violence and crime, and this knowledge is too often far removed from what is considered creditable criminology. I suppose I shall be dancing with denial for some time to come.

Notes

1 Of course, I know that 'women' as a category is entirely problematical. Throughout this chapter, I will be using the term 'woman' or 'women' despite the fact that I know that there are many women, of various relationships to each other and the state. For a lucid and courageous confrontation of feminism and 'woman', see Ramazanoglu (1989a).

2 See, for example, Cohen (1989) and Smart (1990). See Carlen (1992) for an opposing viewpoint.

3 See Stanko and Hobdell (1993).

4 McDermott (1992).

5 For more extended discussions of how criminology theorizes women as offenders, see Heidensohn (1968); Klein and Kress (1976); Heidensohn (1985); Gelsthorpe and Morris (1988); and Morris (1987).

6 Heidensohn (1992); Radford (1989); Bland (1985).

7 Hilliard and Casey (1993).

8 See Reiner and Rock (in prep.).

9 For summaries of this work, see Heidensohn (1985); Cain (1990); Hudson (1990); Gelsthorpe and Morris (1988); Morris (1987); Smart (1976).

10 R.W. Connell (1987) suggests that there is not hegemonic femininity in the sense that there is a hegemonic form of masculinity among men. He uses the term 'emphasized femininity' to illustrate the way women accommodate to subordination by men. When it comes to women offenders, however, there is a strong emphasis on women being 'appropriately' feminine: carers of children and husband, non-violent, modest and so forth.

11 Eaton (1986).

12 Carlen (1992), p. 65.

13 See Connell (1987), pp. 247–8.

14 Jefferson (1992), pp. 10–12. For a fuller discussion of masculinity and crime, see Newburn and Stanko (in prep.).

15 Observes Tim Newburn (personal communication): 'It is also based on a kind of "bad apple"/"sweet-smelling orchard" model of masculinity. Thus like the police, we [men] are OK really, there are just a few bad boys who let us down'.

16 Chesney-Lind and Shelden (1992).

17 See Stanko (1988).

18 Daly and Chesney-Lind (1989).

19 Wright (1992).

20 See, for an excellent and comprehensive history, Dobash and Dobash (1992).

21 See Kennedy (1992).
22 Carlen (1992).
23 Sparks (1992).
24 Yeatman (1987), p. 159.
25 See Stanko (1985), p. 56.
26 Russell (1975, 1982, 1984, 1986).
27 Brownmiller (1975).
28 Stanko (1990a), p. 31.
29 Stanko (1990a), pp. 70–2.
30 Stanko (1990a), p. 90.
31 For a critique, see Hester *et al.* (in prep.).
32 Green (1993).
33 Messerschmidt (in prep.).
34 This speculation was raised by John Stalker in an article in the *Sun*, 21 January 1993.
35 Caputi (1987); see also Caputi (1993).
36 Cameron and Frazer (1987).
37 Stanko (1985).
38 Stanko (1990a).
39 Devault (1990).
40 *Ibid.*, p. 99.
41 Stanko and Hobdell (1993).
42 Stanko (1992).
43 Gardner (1980, 1988, 1990).
44 Gardner (1990), p. 325.
45 Radford and Stanko (1991).
46 See Hoff (1990) and McGibbon *et al.* (1989).
47 Dobash and Dobash (1992).
48 *Ibid.*, especially ch. 8.
49 Kelly and Radford (1988).
50 Stanko (1990a).
51 Hanmer and Saunders (1984).
52 Kelly (1988).
53 Stanko (1985).
54 Chambers and Miller (1982); Blair (1982).
55 See Kennedy (1992).
56 Soothill and Walby (1990).
57 Stanko (1990b).
58 See Gardner (1990); Stanko (1990b).
59 See Connell (1987).
60 Scully and Marolla (1985); Grubin and Gunn (1991); Beneke (1982).
61 Athens (1980).
62 See Stanko and Hobdell (1993).

Chapter 6

Sensuous Sapphires: A Study of the Social Construction of Black Female Sexuality

Annecka Marshall

How do we create an oppositional worldview, a consciousness, an identity, a standpoint that exists not only as that struggle which also opposes dehumanization but as that movement which enables creative, expansive self-actualization? Opposition is not enough. In that vacant space after one has resisted there is still the necessity to become – to make oneself anew.[1]

This chapter explores the problems of developing a Black feminist methodology and epistemology within dominant models of social research. By consolidating feminist and African-centric politics, my study is essentially a critique of the racist tendency of academia to either distort knowledge about Black womanhood or render it invisible. My research, undertaken for a PhD, explores the resistance of women of African descent to derogatory images about our sexuality. It offers a tool that Black women may utilize so that we can give our own accounts of the impact of racialized sexual imagery upon our identities and our relationships. Advocating a self-reflective approach this paper examines the multiple ways in which my racial identity affects feminist research.

The decision to do a PhD, the search for a supervisor, the choice of an academic institution and the selection of a topic is problematic for everyone who wants to do doctoral work. For the Black feminist, I intend to explain, both racism and sexism contribute to this dilemma. I argue that given the racist and sexist environment that most Black women researchers endure, it is extremely pertinent to create Black feminist paradigms. Constructive criticism of mainstream sociological and feminist research methods that do not sufficiently examine the experiences of Black women is, I will assert, central to my work as a Black feminist researcher. As a pioneering area of investigation, Black feminist research leads to exciting redefinitions of sociological thought. My research examines the ways in which Black female sexuality is stereotyped and the impact of this upon Black women's lives. Under enslavement Black women were defined as animalistic, evil, diseased and lascivious. The icon of the sexually denigrated Black female not only effectively legitimated the maximum exploitation of her reproductive labour but also exonerated white men who abused her from guilt. The rearticulation of this history of racialized sexual subordination is the focus of my work. I discuss the extent to which the representation of Black female sexuality in contemporary British culture reproduces stereotypes that have existed since the sixteenth century.

My interest in the degree to which these myths prevail as well as the effects upon Black women's self-perceptions and interactions influenced my research strategies. These are divided into three areas. First, I tested my hypotheses by formulating them in questionnaires which I distributed to men and women from different racial backgrounds. Secondly, building upon the questionnaire data I conducted a pilot study. Thirdly, I interviewed a number of Black women to discuss the issues that were raised by the literature review, questionnaires and pilot study in more depth. Speaking on their own behalf in in-depth semi-structured interviews, twenty-one Black women explain the effect of racialized sexual images on their lives. Their testimonies challenge the marginalization of Black women as sexual animals.

Black Feminist Subjectivity and Methodology

When addressing the personal, academic and political concerns that have been fundamental to embarking upon Black feminist research it is significant to mention my experiences as an undergraduate student. Motivated by the queries 'Who writes? And for whom?' I suspected that it was predominantly white men who wrote for those who shared their identity and/or ideology.[2] The exclusion of Black women from claims to knowledge was an issue that I was becoming distressingly aware of but I was not at that time quite ready to address. This predicament was exacerbated by my frustration at not having the conceptual tools to 'prove' it. I was outraged by seemingly universal theories that either completely denied the existence of Black people, or just concentrated on the situation of Black men. I was angry that white lecturers perpetuated a racist account of social life and that white students failed to recognize this. Instead of articulating my despair I internalized it. Often I remained silent in seminars. I felt alienated by discussions that excluded my reality. The creative energy to use the pen as a weapon against such racist and sexist misinformation was frequently suppressed by the fear that I needed to conform in order to survive and ultimately to pass my degree.

At that desperate time I believed that it was inappropriate to openly oppose racism and sexism within sociology. Nevertheless I was determined to redress the balance by engaging in studies that put a Black feminist perspective at the forefront. My first refuge was doing an MA in Women's Studies. That year of delving into feminism was crucial in giving me a voice to criticize my subordination. Breaking the silence about the position of Black women in Britain I overcame some of my fears about my ability to do this. As my awareness about the institutionalization of heterosexuality increased, I realized that this was as central to the oppression of Black women as racism, sexism and class oppression.[3] However, it became apparent that I also needed to find a supportive environment that would stimulate me to do feminist, anti-racist, marxist and anti-heterosexist research. I became reconciled to the fact that the feelings of depression, isolation and rage that had characterized most of my scholarly experience would be intensified by the solitary nature of doing a doctorate.

The research process has been inextricably and often painfully linked to my subordination as a Black woman. Traditionally excluded from the creation of sociological and feminist thought, the position of the Black female researcher is unique. She is aware that Black women have been pathologized by sociological and feminist literature that has adopted popular stereotypes that exist in British society: for example, notions of Black matriarchs and Sapphires who emasculate their men have been given academic credibility. This awareness is extremely alienating as the (so-called) 'angry Black woman' struggles to tackle the negation of her experiences by theorizing about the complex reality of Black womanhood.

I want to expand upon Sandra Harding's critique of sociological analyses that attempt to 'add women in' since I wish to explore the specific problems of research with Black women in Britain.[4] Just as traditional methodologies systematically exclude women, as Harding explains, so feminist research that attempts to rectify this problem is based on the circumstances of white Western women. Thus feminist research, whilst rejecting the patriarchal bias of social science, has reproduced its racist paradigms. Since mainstream feminism has generally marginalized the distinct racialization of gender by generalizing from the situation of a minority of white women who are middle-class, middle-aged, heterosexual and able-bodied, there is an urgent need to rectify this. The prevalence of negative images about Black women both in 'common-sense' thinking and in academia is a central concern for Black women researchers. Due to our isolation and the fact that our own training has encouraged us to be disassociated from Black female subjectivity it is very difficult for us to transcend this scenario. The process of conducting research is especially difficult for Black women because we occupy an 'outsider within' status. Patricia Hill Collins asserts that the unique 'insider-outsider' position of the marginalized Black feminist researcher allows her to recognize ramifications that those who are part of the dominant culture are unable to comprehend. Black feminists have the advantage of a special African-centric and feminist insight whereby we can assess the contradictions of the familiar world from the perspective of the unfamiliar because we are outsiders. Black feminist researchers utilize our consciousness of the diversity of Black women's experiences as well as our knowledge of dominant social structures. As Collins observes:

On certain dimensions Black women may more closely resemble Black men; on others, white women; and on still others Black women may stand apart from both groups. Black women's both/and conceptual orientation, the act of being simultaneously a member of a group and yet standing apart from it, forms an integral part of Black women's consciousness.[5]

The double perception of the Black woman researcher is, according to Amina Mama, complicated by the difficulty of trying to both step out of and also draw on one's subjective awareness of the social, economic and political subordination of one's community. Sharing a common experience with other Black people of being objectified by white culture conflicts with her role as a researcher who has been trained by Eurocentric social scientific models. This conflict is resolved by developing research practices that challenge existing knowledge and prioritize the values, issues and problems that are defined by the participants. Thus the Black woman researcher has to deal with her dual status as a researcher in the Western academy and as a member of a community that is marginalized and oppressed by racism. For Amina Mama this necessarily entails a holistic, historical and community-oriented approach that supports the struggles of Black women.[6] Amina Mama developed a methodology that rejected the reproduction of dominant power relations and augmented a greater understanding of Black women's experiences of domestic violence:

> conducting social and policy research on oppressed groups – in this instance – black women, requires that the cultural, social and economic position of both the researchers and the target group be taken into account. This applies to all social groups, but in doing research on oppressed groups it becomes vitally necessary if we are to avoid the tendency of research to reinforce and contribute to the plethora of stereotypes and derogatory myths that prevail in the dominant society.[7]

By placing Black women's ideas at the centre of analysis, Black feminist research negates and replaces dominant definitions that objectify, dehumanize and control Black women. Furthering our understanding of the interlocking nature of racism, sexism, heterosexism and class oppression it contributes to the struggle against internalized and wider oppression. Such research examines how Black women cope with the simultaneity of oppression, resist external definitions and assert our subjectivity as fully human beings. This is more than an academic endeavour since the validation of Black women's self-definitions is necessary for Black women's survival.[8] Amina Mama's research empowers Black women as human subjects:

> This meant treating women who are traditionally treated as 'passive victims' (Asian women) or 'aggressive criminals' (women of Caribbean

descent) and who are often blamed for their situation by institutions and services, as credible informants and whose accounts are valid data. In this research their experiences are given credibility, and as research subjects, black women are given the status of citizens who are assumed to be entitled to basic human rights.[9]

Thus Black feminists have to create new frameworks that refute Western theories, concepts and tools that marginalize our lives, subjugate our intellect and restrict our potential to critically examine our position. It is therefore significant to question how I as a Black feminist researcher reject the denial of my reality. I believe that more than a rejection is required. I need to develop an analysis that moves beyond resisting racist, elitist, heterosexist and sexist frameworks so that I can put forward an alternative epistemology, one that is by Black women, of Black women and for Black women.

Patricia Bell Scott exposes stereotypes of Black women in social science scholarship and advocates anti-racist and anti-sexist research strategies that are action-oriented. She argues that social science either ignores Black women or focuses on their 'problems' and uses them as evidence of their inadequacies. Asserting the necessity for Black men and white people to also be involved in developing radical theoretical frameworks and redefining concepts, Scott maintains that these investigations would be beneficial to implementing public policy that meets the needs of Black communities:

> These research priorities must be coupled with some very practical, action-oriented strategies. These strategies should involve the sensitizing of members of this society to the 'roots' and workings of overt, covert, and institutional racism and sexism. Black men must be made aware of the fact that sexism is not only a white problem, and white feminists must also be made aware of the fact that racism and class bias are not peculiar to white men only.[10]

Elizabeth Higginbotham argues that empirical studies must examine the sources of Black women's oppression and reflect the diversity of their experiences. It is important to explore the multiple roles of Black women as opposed to recreating the notion of the superwoman. A historical and analytic framework which focuses on the varied and complex experiences of Black women not only gives an inclusive view of Black womanhood but also pinpoints areas where change is essential:

> In our eagerness to counteract the negative stereotypes, we must not create a different one, which also fails to reflect accurately the varied lives of Black women. Even though many Black women are able to overcome difficult situations, Black women are not 'superwomen' devoid of needs and emotions.[11]

For all researchers it is vital to find a supervisor who not only is interested in and familiar with your topic but also with whom you can have a fruitful relationship. I maintain that for Black women researchers this is especially relevant since there are few supervisors who meet our criteria. The racist myopia of most white academics, the sexism of the majority of male intellectuals and the limited number of Black women lecturers greatly restricted my options. I had to be extremely careful about choosing a supervisor because it was essential that this person understood the constraints that my structural situation had on my potential to successfully do research. The support of my supervisor has been and continues to be pivotal to counteracting the feelings of inferiority that I often endure as a Black woman in a white institution. However, at times I fear that I suffer particular stress because she, like other white academics, has assigned me to the role of the superwoman.

By opposing the trend in academia to pathologize and dehumanize Black womanhood I support a process of self-actualization whereby the Black woman as the researcher or as 'the researched' is an active subject. She is able to define what is essential to her, she has the ability to articulate her own self-perceptions and she has the power to change her status as the Other. The development of Black feminist standpoints transcends the limitations of sexist and racist research strategies and constitutes a form of empowerment. This is a political process because it necessarily entails a revolutionary challenge to the interface of racism, sexism, heterosexism and class oppression in Black women's lives. Afrocentric feminist knowledge, Patricia Hill Collins contends, generates collective consciousness that transforms social, political and economic relations:

> Afrocentric feminist thought offers two significant contributions toward furthering our understanding of the important connections among knowledge, consciousness, and the politics of empowerment. First, Black feminist thought fosters a fundamental paradigmatic shift in how we think about oppression. By embracing a paradigm of race, class, and gender as interlocking systems of oppression, Black feminist thought reconceptualizes the social relations of domination and resistance. Second, Black feminist thought addresses ongoing epistemological debates in feminist theory and in the sociology of knowledge concerning ways of assessing 'truth.' Offering subordinate groups new knowledge about their own experiences can be empowering. But revealing new ways of knowing that allow subordinate groups to define their own reality has far greater implications.[12]

Examining how the dominant model of Black female sexuality affects Black women's lives I am confronting and transcending the limitations of oppressive white models and concepts. Thereby I am developing new frames of reference that legitimate the defiance of Black women's self-definitions. However, this work is not in isolation. Carol Smart's argument, that because a study is *for* women does not necessarily mean that its entire subject matter has to be women, is pertinent to my research.[13] Thus the next section high-lights the questionnaire data and a pilot study of men and women of different 'ethnic' groups which enabled me to begin to assess the impact of racialized sexual images.

Surpassing Sensuous Slavery

> I have to sort out how to select my sample ... e.g. access as a result of working in a pub or a factory ... I could advertise in a paper or a magazine and then follow up the questionnaires by selective inter-views.... what about geographical location, socio-economic back-ground, gender, 'race' and sexual orientation? ... How do I match up questionnaire and interview schedules with my central research questions? (Research diary, March 1991)

This quotation shows my concerns about the process of designing question-naire and interview schedules as well as finding a 'representative sample'. I have decided to combine qualitative research methods such as participant observation, questionnaire surveys and semi-structured interviews because I believe that this is the best way to test my theoretical hypotheses. Due to the sensitivity of issues of racism and sexuality I think that the use of various techniques is constructive since I maintain that people respond differently to questionnaires and to taped interviews.

Questionnaires

Whilst recognizing that the intimate character of the topic limits the viability of this type of data collection, I also believe that the anonymous question-naire is useful for gaining personal and confidential information that a respondent would be reluctant to tell an interviewer. In terms of my interest in the extent to which people's perceptions of their sexual identity are influenced by racism and heterosexism it is important to consider the problem of bias. For instance the validity of the data would be disputable if my presence as a Black female affected the response to questions about 'race' and sexuality.

The main purpose of this investigation was to assess the interrelationship and social implications of racist and heterosexist images. For this purpose, I designed the questionnaires to address four areas. The first part asked about sexual identification and societal pressures upon sexual behaviour. The sec-ond part addressed the extent to which the issue of 'race' influences sexual identity, and opinions about the sexual proclivity of Black and white people as well as 'mixed race relationships'. This included questions about the existence and significance of media portrayals of Black and white sexuality. Attitudes towards homosexuality, the ways in which it is portrayed by the mass media and how this influences the treatment of bisexuals, homosexuals and lesbians was the third area of focus. The last section considered views about the relevance of changing racial and sexual imagery.

The socio-political nature of my research influenced my sampling techniques in the following manner. Issues of racism and sexuality are very sensitive and respondents need to be assured of anonymity and confidentiality. Subsequently I have chosen a student-based sample for with a fellow student common experiences are shared that facilitate acceptance and trust. Nonetheless I have written to the students to assure them that the information that is given is completely confidential. I have also asked them not to disclose their names. I distributed five hundred questionnaires to students at a university at the beginning of the Spring term of 1991 and I requested they return them as soon as possible. Approximately a third of these were sent to listed members of the African-Caribbean society. The rest were distributed at random to student accommodation on campus.

By the end of that term I had received seventy-eight questionnaires completed by forty-four white students, twenty-three African-Caribbean students, six Indian students and five Chinese students. The low response rate means that the results are illuminative rather than generalizable. Thus the fact that only 15.6 per cent of the potential sample actually returned the questionnaires necessitates an acute awareness that people who did not complete the questionnaires could be substantially different from those who did. Additionally, since this in itself raises the problem of a distortion of results, what I can claim from this data is not general relatability but rather a hypothesis that needs to be elaborated. This is further supported by my awareness that a student sample represents a relatively privileged educational and socio-economic group.

In recognition of these limitations I tentatively argue that the questionnaire data demonstrates that perceptions of sexual identity are influenced by stereotypical notions about 'race' and homosexuality. I explore the connections between racialized and homophobic images of sexuality. Recognizing the importance of theorizing the interdependence of racism and heterosexism I consider the potential to transform images of unbridled sexuality that are attributed to Blacks, homosexuals, lesbians and bisexuals. Further research is needed to analyze these initial insights into the connections between myths of Blacks, lesbians and homosexuals as abnormal, licentious and diseased. It would also be interesting to explore the links between these stereotypes and derogatory ideologies of working-class and female sexualities.

Pilot Study

My interest in further exploring the links between racist and heterosexist stereotypes encouraged me to conduct a pilot study. Due to this being a delicate issue and the potential vulnerability of the interviewees it became imperative to design the interviews as exchanges of ideas. Since this was an exploratory exercise I conducted unstructured interviews with two white

men, two Black men, two white women and two Black women, selected
from people who had filled in the questionnaires and volunteered to give
additional information. I asked them their views about images of 'race' and
sexuality in the media and in British society generally. Then I questioned the
influence of these images upon their own self-concepts and experiences.
Some of the aspects of doing this research, during April 1991, are shown by
the following extract from my research diary:

> I was suffering from an anxiety attack. The interview with a Black
> woman, a Black man and a white man made me wonder to what
> extent there actually were distinct sexual images about Black women.
> As we approached Baker Street I thanked my two male companions
> for taking part in my research. Whilst leaving me on the train the
> Black man jocosely remarked: 'Don't talk to any strange men'.
>
> Moments later a white man, who was unknown to me and who
> seemed to pounce from nowhere, grabbed me and proclaimed: 'I can
> tell that you're warm and friendly. You talk to anyone Black or
> white. You're a very sexy Black girl.'

This example illustrates well the tendency of the researcher to worry about
one's theoretical hypotheses. During that controversial interview I queried
whether my concern about the significance of images of Black female sexuality was indeed relevant. It shows that the researcher's autobiography frequently influences the choice of a research topic as well as the process of
doing research. My own experiences and those of other Black women of
being defined in sexual terms led me to investigate this issue further. It soon
became evident that I was not merely trying to assess the prevalence of these
images but more importantly I wanted to examine how much they impinge
upon Black women's lives. Therefore, while I believe that the opinions of
white people and Black men can significantly contribute to an understanding
of racialized sexual imagery, my primary aim is to understand the socio-
economic and political relevance to Black women's reality.

Such encounters have reinforced my interest in validating Black women's
perceptions of racial and sexual imagery within the wider context of our
experiences of racism, sexism, heterosexism and class oppression. Thereby I
explored the material generated from the questionnaires and the pilot interviews by conducting semi-structured interviews with Black women. Interviewing Black women about the impact of racialized sexual imagery upon their
experiences, I am able to discuss additional questions and unifying themes. I
intend to explain the political significance of my research in documenting
Black women's struggles against these images.

Interviews

Believing that a theoretical account of racialized sexual imagery that is supported by empirical data is central to challenging the oppression of Black

women, I conducted the interviews with the purpose of gaining further information. Whilst the questionnaires and the pilot study had explored views about images of Black female sexuality in British society and in the media, I wanted to examine this in greater depth. I have previously mentioned the emotive nature of my project. It is this feature of my research that made me decide to employ a 'snowball' technique of selecting a sample. In April 1991 I contacted friends, acquaintances, academic colleagues and Black women's organizations. I informed them of my quest to interview Black women about images of 'race' and sexuality. In view of the tendency of academia to either ignore the distinct experiences of Black women or misrepresent them, some women were justifiably cautious. After being persuaded that my study would not be exploitative, twenty-one Black women consented to being interviewed. Undoubtedly my own biographical details have influenced the kinds of women that I could gain access to. Hence I am not claiming that my research provides a representative cross-section of women from whom generalizable data can be gathered.

From June until November 1991 I interviewed women mostly in their own homes, but some came to my parental abode in London or to my student dwelling in a town in the Midlands. Their homelands were Africa, the Caribbean and, especially in the case of the younger women, Britain. In terms of self-definitions of their sexual identity, eighteen were heterosexual, two were bisexual and one was a lesbian. Their ages ranged between 20 and 65. Some were housewives, some students, some nurses and some secretaries, and one woman was unemployed. Among the others were health and housing officers, a machinist, a catering assistant, an office supervisor, a research worker, an artist, a teacher and a solicitor. Through learning from their rich range of experiences my own thoughts about my sexuality and my identity as a Black woman have been challenged in numerous ways. They are not just research subjects but rather they are friends, sisters, mothers and generators of knowledge in their own right.

Since I thought that there could be additional issues that I had not considered I structured the interviews on open-ended probe questions. Semi-structured interviews facilitated exploring the impact of racist and heterosexist images upon Black women's sense of 'race', gender and sexual identity. This allowed the interviewees and myself to enquire about opinions on relationships with Black and white men. We discussed debates in Black communities about bisexuality, homosexuality and lesbianism as well as their own ideas. Through these interviews we became conscious of the potential to resist and to transform the social construction of Black female sexuality. Therefore this method encouraged us to talk about a wider range of issues than if I had relied upon a formal approach. It also incorporates my attempt to minimize the unequal power relationship between the dominant interviewer and the subordinate researched.[14] The interviews were taped and lasted between thirty minutes and four and a half hours. The average time taken was ninety minutes.

Realizing that they would be cautious about 'sex' and 'race' research I had been worried about meeting women who would be offended by what may be interpreted as intimate questions. Thus I had been afraid that it would be difficult to have a good rapport. However, I was pleasantly surprised not only by their willingness to talk but also by the level of trust that we achieved. In view of this I became aware of the potentially exploitative character of the interview situation.[15] I realized that a common racial and gender identity between the interviewees and myself facilitated a greater responsiveness to my research than I had previously envisaged. Although this was beneficial to me it also increased their own vulnerability as they were extremely open about the effects of racialized sexual imagery upon their experiences. Their relatively powerless position as respondents was increased by their willingness to trust me – a trust that could be betrayed. As advocated by many feminists, accountability is especially necessary when the subjects of research are from groups who are in the lower echelons of society.[16] Due to a moral and ethical responsibility to protect their interests I have maintained a promise of confidentiality. This entails anonymity and a commitment to giving as truthful as possible an account of their arguments. Twenty of the sample chose their own pseudonyms whereas one woman insisted that her own name be used.

My efforts to be as unobtrusive and non-threatening as possible led to occasions whereby the supposedly powerful position of the 'detached' researcher was denied. For example, several women felt more at ease in a group interview with friends whom they had asked to accompany them. On one level the solidarity of two or three friends, considering the potentially hierarchical nature of the interview setting, confirms my objective to encourage interviewees to also control the research situation. However, on another more personal level, I felt vulnerable as a lone sociologist encountering unfamiliar territory. Of course my feelings of being defenseless when interviewing are minor in comparison to the general exposure to attack that these women confront daily.

Sharing a similar identity with these women I am able to offer an insider's awareness of the complexity of their conditions. Having documented the historical and contemporary significance of racialized sexual imagery with reference to primary and secondary sources, films, questionnaire data and a pilot study, I am also able to place this awareness within a broader Black feminist framework.

Orgasmic Slavery?
Black Women's Views of Racialized/Sexualized Identities

My respondent-centred analysis of Black women's perceptions of racialized/sexualized identity is still in its early stages. It is possible, however, to signal some preliminary outcomes. The first draws attention to three kinds of images which the women felt reflected on them. A small minority, two women, believe their sexuality to be rendered invisible. For example, one woman argued that it is the invisibility of Black women in British society and in the media which is the primary problem, rather than derogatory sexual images. Tammy, a 24-year-old housewife, said: 'I don't think that Black women are seen full stop really. Not in a sexual way anyway'.

A second recorded imagery defines Black women as asexual mammies. Such a perception was put forward, for instance, by one interviewee who, believing that Black women are viewed as sexual or motherly, sees herself as closest to the latter, due to her physique and gestures. Although Zora, a 29-year-old temp, rejects the stereotypes, she maintains that she would rather be seen as an asexual mother than as a super-sexual whore. She asserted:

> I suppose I do define myself in a kind of mother role because it's safer for me; because if somebody says 'hey Zora you're a sexual being' I just want to tell them to 'piss off'. It's not like anything has happened to me, it's just the way I react. Perhaps I feel threatened by it and I just don't want anything to do with it.

By far the majority of women, however, believed that they were perceived by many Black men and white people as being licentious and lascivious. Eighteen women argued that they were stigmatized as sensuous, promiscuous temptresses who either bewitch and emasculate men or are animalistic breeders. These images reinforce the oppression of Black women and protect people who violate them from punishment. In this context, for instance, one woman argued that for British society the Black woman is a source of eroticism. Melisa, a 26-year-old office supervisor, said:

> Black women are something new and different like an exotic fruit you want to bite. You don't want to try an apple because everyone's had one. Try a kiwi fruit and once one person's tried it and spread the news then others will have a bite; scared at first but will try it.

Caroll, a 21-year-old student, voiced the view that a Black woman is seen only in terms of her posterior: 'A Black woman is a bottom. You measure a Black woman by her bottom'.

With regard to the effect of societal imagery of their sexuality on the identities of the Black women interviewed, two broad trends seemed to emerge. A small number of women suggested that they were not affected by it. For instance, when I asked Marva, who was a 45-year-old housewife with two children, about the significance of racialized sexual images, she replied that it was not an issue that she had previously considered: 'Well, I haven't really thought about it so to me it's not really important in my life'. Fiona, a 25-year-old teacher who is single, articulate and witty also said: 'Not really. I don't think so. I've never really thought about it. You know, sex is sex!' The views of these women were summed up by Susan, a 28-year-old secretary, who argued:

> I don't think colour matters in that respect. I think it's the way the person carries herself and how she respects herself. But colour, I can't see how it can affect a person. I think it's the individual ... Well I haven't really looked deep into myself as a Black woman. I just think neutral. If I do have to look at myself as a Black woman, I don't know, I don't see it as a colour issue. . . . As I'm getting older as well, now I'm getting neutral. I think you can think too much about colour on a day-to-day basis but I don't.

The majority of the women, however, condemned what they saw to be the power of racialized and homophobic sexual myths, which in the words of Fosuwa, a 31-year-old artist, mean 'You're not allowed to just be'. Thirteen women resisted the dominant images and, instead, created strong self-definitions, as the following words from the women themselves show. Tracy, a 32-year-old research worker, stated: 'I certainly don't see myself as being a sexual temptress or a molten volcano'. Beverley, a 47-year-old single nurse, stressed: 'I don't think that what people think of me is important. I think that what is important is what I think of myself'. Hilary, a 54-year-old nurse, maintained: 'There are prejudices but there are certain things that you can ride over as long as you know what angle to take'. Mrs Welltodo, a 65-year-old machinist, argued: 'If I wasn't strong I'd be dead already'. Patricia, a 52-year-old nurse, maintained that 'As a Black woman you have to prove yourself in society, that you are just as good as a white woman'. Rosanne, a 22-year-old student, asserted: 'Race affects how I feel about my sexual experiences in the sense that being a Black woman I have to compete with the challenging myths that exist about my sexuality'.

Yvonne, a 39-year-old legal secretary, explained:

> Maybe it's a bit of a power thing with me, being Black and on top. I think it must be, a bit like Margaret Thatcher actually; the Black Maggie Thatcher. I think maybe that has been what has made me strive so hard although I haven't really thought about it too tough.

A further element which is emerging from my research is the way in which myths about Black female sexuality help to circumscribe relationships, particularly the difficulties this causes for Black women's relationships with Black men. Further, there is the danger of internalizing negative images of Black masculinity, as Sally, a 32-year-old housing officer, describes:

> There's a danger of doing that, and also the danger comes from all this. We're all talking about images and we're all talking about stereotypical ideas and views from the media and all that. And we also fall

into that danger as well because we tend to believe. Or we see a negative portrayal on the television about Black men. We immediately take that up. We suck them into our subconscious and use that.

Another aspect which is emerging is how, given the history of the sexual oppression of Black women by white men, the decision to have a white partner is extremely problematic. This difficulty is voiced in the following quotations. Maria, a 50-year-old catering assistant, draws attention to the racialized regulation of sexuality, whereby relationships between Black and white people are stigmatized:

> Another thing they always put on TV is this 'mixed race' thing but it never works. They never show you one that really could work. They do it to put in your head, especially the younger ones, that you should either stick to your own or forget about this 'mixed race' business.

Yvonne Ayoka, a 20-year-old student, believes as a result of her own experiences that 'mixed race' relationships are positive. She recognizes, however, that this is not a general view within Black communities:

> It's more acceptable in the Black community for Black men to go out with white women than for Black women to go out with white men. It's all about control and power. A Black man is seen as the one who controls the relationship and so his 'race' isn't being downtrodden and trampled. But if a Black woman does the same thing she is being submissive.

From my interviews, I am able to argue that most Black women challenge the stereotypes which are constructed about them. Bombarded by these myths Black women adopt a range of self-perceptions that serve as coping strategies. Nonetheless they argue that for these stereotypes to be radically altered their own defiance needs to also be supported on a collective level. Coalition work with other Black women, Black men and white people in, for instance, Black, feminist and left-wing organizations is also necessary. Furthermore, this process of re-education and liberation has to be taken on board by the mass media, educational establishments, workplaces, the legal system and the welfare state. It is imperative to challenge the sexual denigration of Black women on a political level because it contributes to the institutionalization of racist, capitalist, sexist and heterosexist ideologies and practices.

A Black feminist analysis of the ways in which sexuality is constructed within the institutions of a racist culture indicates that dominant representations of white sexuality (heterosexual and middle-class) take their meaning from the contrast with Black women (and 'under-class', 'ethnic' and sexual 'minority' women). The pathologization of Black women as licentious contributes to an oppositional definition of 'normal' white female sexuality. Feminist research on sexuality thus needs to appreciate the racialization of the social construction of sexuality. Failure to recognize the different experiences of Black women misrepresents not only our lives but also by implication those of white women. A full understanding of the construction of white female sexuality necessitates an awareness of the construction of Black female sexuality. It is not acceptable merely to add the experiences of Black women to mainstream feminist analyses of sexuality. Instead such research needs to be reconceptualized in order to examine the specific experiences of Black women.

Defined by others, Black women are usually the objects of research that fails to seriously defy stereotypes. There is so much ignorance about Black womanhood, ignorance that contributes to our oppression, that it is important to increase knowledge about Black women's conditions. Research that is Black-woman-identified is therefore crucial. By addressing the priorities of Black women, such projects not only increase general awareness but can also have wider implications. Black feminist research, in consulting Black women and documenting their requirements, offers important insights that can be used to improve the position of Black women in Britain. Interviewing other Black women has given me the strength to struggle against scholarship that negates our experiences. By demonstrating that the racist and heterosexist social construction of sexuality is not a natural and inevitable fact I hope that my work contributes to the fight against our subordination. By putting the interviewees' ideas at the centre of my analysis I am providing a progressive platform through which we can strive for realistic recommendations to radically transform our lives.

Stressing Our Power: The Power of Stress

In this final part of this chapter I intend to discuss the importance of my research and the effects of tension on the research process. Self-doubt about my intellectual abilities and the fear that my interpretation of the data does not really do justice to the interviewees' views obstructs my writing. Rather than seeing my uncertainty about the meaning of the transcripts as part of the nature of conducting fieldwork, I worry that I am theoretically deficient. This lack of confidence not only prolongs my work but generates thesis phobia. Unfortunately literature on getting a PhD and debates on methodology fail to address the impact of stress. As a Black feminist I endure the additional problems of dealing with my insider/outsider situation, the denial of my autonomous and womanist sexuality/identity and the pressure to be a Black superwoman.

In this chapter I have concentrated on my desire to use Black feminist research as an empowering process. I believe, however, that it is also necessary to discuss the contradiction between paradigms of Black feminist method-ology and the actual experience of doing research. These issues are not restricted to Black women but I think that they take a distinct form in our lives. Before describing my situation I want to stress, indeed stress is the key issue, that my experience is not necessarily typical. Indeed I have met many Black sisters, 'womanist', 'feminist' and 'ordinary', who practice what they preach. The purpose of this section is to explain some of the less positive personal characteristics of my doctoral research.

I think that it is important to address various contradictions that I am dealing with. The dilemma between my belief in identity politics as a source of strength and my own feelings of weakness is hard to discuss. The difficul-ties that I have with my work are partially a consequence of my examining the relevance of the interviewees' perceptions of their sexuality whilst being unable to really explore my own racialized sexual identity.

Black feminist research, as I have previously shown, not only analyzes the interface of racism, sexism, heterosexism and class oppression in women's lives but offers solutions to our situation. As a Black feminist I have in-corporated this approach when describing the significance of racialized sexual imagery. I have done this on a general level in relation to the Black women I have interviewed so that their resistance is emphasized. I am frustrated by the fact that my own experiences do not reflect their ability to cope with stereotypes of Black female sexuality although I try desperately hard. This brings me to the issue of coping strategies.

Since 1990, when I started my research, I have grappled with the notion of 'success without stress'. Struggling against the self-negation that academia sometimes projects onto those like us who attempt to subvert dominant claims to knowledge is extremely tiring. We rarely talk about the distinct health problems that we share as a result of our battles with the Western patriarchs. My ability to defend my position within a white and male-regulated discourse simultaneously involves euphoria and depression. The joy of amplifying Black herstories is central to my life yet it is also a counterbalance to painful periods of self-doubt.

Theoretically I try to oppose my low self-esteem and lack of confidence by claiming that my work is good. Whilst I try to rationally assess the merits of my research this is often futile. It is agonizing to think clearly when I am distressed by insomnia. I find it strenuous to write because I often suffer acute panic attacks and computer blues. The motivation to study disappears as I worry about my vomiting and difficulty with eating. I really believe that doing research can seriously damage your health. I'm not sure whether this is a widespread tendency or one that is restricted to anti-establishment/pro-Black/women's studies. All that I know is that my bouts of fear, nervousness and anxiety seem to be linked to my 'status' on the margins of intellectual life. I persevere despite misgivings about my potential to complete my thesis.

As a Black woman in academia I share the pressures of other feminists but the extra burden of racism accentuates my repressed rage. The need to move beyond the pain that I have mentioned is, according to Audre Lorde, fundamental to our survival. She urges us to use anger as a site of clarification, mutual empowerment and transformation. I frequently read the following statement by Audre Lorde because it encourages me not only to fight back but also to create my own assertive arena:

> But anger expressed and translated into action in the service of our vision and our future is a liberating and strengthening act of clarification, for it is in the painful process of this translation that we identify who are our allies, with whom we have grave differences, and who are our genuine enemies.[17]

My PhD has cost me so much on monetary, emotional and psychological levels that I am determined to persevere. The financial strain has been alleviated by funding in my last year. Previously I barely supported myself through teaching, clerical and catering work. Traumas are caused by the pressure of challenging racism and sexism in isolation. Aiming to compensate for the fact that there are relatively few Black feminist academics in Britain by delving too prematurely into the realm of publications, lectures and 'progressive' organizations has also been detrimental to my research. This is demonstrated by the fact that I have had to suspend my registration for six months whilst getting professional help to combat these difficulties.

Rather than dealing with these problems on my own I am interested in developing anti-stress strategies with other women. Meanwhile I cope by attempting to realize that although getting my PhD is important it is not the most essential thing in life. I try to meditate, exercise and have saunas regularly. Time management and regular breaks are central to my wish to relax. A vibrant network of supportive women continues to be pivotal to my well-being. However such initiatives are only effective in the long term when linked to feminist activism for radical change.

Conclusion

It is only when the recognition of the origins of racialized sexual imagery is combined with an acute understanding of why it continues to exist that Black women can surpass being stereotyped as sensuous Sapphires. The pervasiveness of these myths is shown by the data that was generated by the questionnaires, the pilot study and the semi-structured interviews. My research demonstrates that derogatory images of Black female sexuality have contributed to the subordination of Black women. I am striking a balance between Black feminist research that supports Black women's struggles against these images and research that meets the academic requirements of a white/male-dominated institution. In my private life, my teaching and my writing identity politics helps me to analyze the political significance of my own individual relationship to systems of oppression. I consider my subordination as a Black woman whilst recognizing my privileged position in relation to other women in regard to class, sexuality, age and ability. Like other feminists I share the common dilemma of reconciling my personal life and political goals. I firmly believe that differences between women, although threatening unity among us, also constitute a source of power. This belief is pivotal to my research.

The purpose of this paper has been to demystify the research process. I am adopting a self-reflective Black feminist methodology which gives primacy to the opinions of the interviewees. Research that challenges negative images of Black femininity is not only the prerogative of Black women and as such needs to be conducted across racial and gender barriers. In other words, the methods that I have been discussing are not exclusive to Black feminism but rather characterize good praxis. Such research incorporates personal and political objectives from a perspective of gender, class, 'race' and sexuality. Further investigations with Black women in areas such as art, social services, education, employment, housing and the legal system are vital.

Ultimately the process of doing Black feminist research has been extremely empowering. I am also woefully aware of the contradictory nature of this empowerment. For me a Black feminist approach moves beyond the dictates of a white feminist elite. The construction of the Black feminist researcher by white feminists is terribly oppressive. Being the token Black female author or explaining your experiences in a manner that is palatable for an audience of predominantly white women fucks you up. If through this limited work those who read it not only try to understand the extra burden that racist sexual stereotypes represent for many Black women but also help us to overcome it I have achieved my goal.

Notes

This chapter is dedicated to the interviewees and to my parents, Marlene and Hammington Marshall, with thanks for their love and support.

I am deeply grateful to Davina Cooper, Rosemarie Mallett and Julia Hallam for reading a first draft of this paper and for being true sisters. 'Respek' to Cecily Vahau, Janice Acquah and Judy Scully for rescuing me from despair when I 'flipped out'. Special thanks to funky fembeaux Andrea Massiah, Joanne Taylore, Valentina Alexander, Didi Herman, Pauline Anderson, my godson Justin Redman, Ozzy and Nigel Rudder for 'being there'.

I owe my life to my 'empowerer' Jennifer Comrie and I am devoted to Eliana Pinto, Sonia Cadon Francis and the other Shanti sistrens who saved me (from suicide or worse) in March.[18]

1   hooks (1991), p. 15.
2   Said (1978).
3   Lorde (1984).

4   Harding (1987).
5   Collins (1990), p. 207.
6   Mama (1987).
7   Mama (1989), p. 28.
8   Collins (1986).
9   Mama (1989), p. 29.
10 Scott (1982), p. 90.
11 Higginbotham (1982), p. 96.
12 Collins (1990), p. 222.
13 Smart (1984).
14 Roberts (1981).
15 Stanley (1990a).
16 *Ibid.*
17 Lorde (1984), p. 127.
18 Shanti is a women's counselling service in Brixton. It is at the leading edge of 'cross-cultural' and 'woman-identified' therapy. Shanti empowers women of different ages, abilities and from a variety of cultural, racial, class and sexual backgrounds.

> We recognise that the difficulties women face in their lives can cause them to break down or become depressed. We want to create a space where all women can make changes, grow, become confident and powerful, and in doing this take control of their own lives. (West Lambeth Health Authority (1993) *SHANTI Women's Counselling Service*, Oval Printshop)

Chapter 7

Coming to Conclusions: Power and Interpretation in Researching Young Women's Sexuality[1]

Janet Holland and Caroline Ramazanoglu

Introduction

Feminist researchers have made a major contribution to critical reflection on the research process, but deciding whether, or how, we can arrive at authoritative conclusions about the nature of other people's experiences remains a problem. Our aim in this chapter is to explore some of the issues involved in taking the accounts that people give in unstructured interviews, and presenting them as feminist sociology. Although we focus here on interviews, interpretation is part of any research that produces data from questionnaires, observation or recordings of other people's talk.

The many possible ways of interpreting interview transcripts face feminists, like other researchers, with a problem of validity. More baldly, we can be questioned about what sort of truth we can attribute to our conclusions. Coming to conclusions is not just a process of following rules of method to the end point of a research project, but a very active and complex process of social construction that raises questions about what we mean when we claim that feminist knowledge should be believed.[2] We have to decide whether feminist conclusions can be in some sense 'better' than those of unreflexive or masculinist research in grasping the nature of relationships, or whether they are simply different. There is a political difference, for example, between claiming to *know* how women experience sexuality, violence or motherhood, and opening up the possibilities of multiple interpretations of the complex diversity of women's lives, all of which may have some validity.

We have approached these issues by reflecting on a feminist research project on young people and sexuality in which we have been engaged with colleagues for some years, the WRAP (Women, Risk and AIDS Project) studies, which we describe below, and trying to make the research process explicit. In these studies we have tried to make it as clear as possible to ourselves what we are doing when we do research: what we are taking for granted and why; what 'findings' we disagree over, and generally what we do to the interview transcripts and field notes that comprise our primary data. To do this we must locate ourselves as researchers and as fallible, subjective people within the research process. More than this, we have to make explicit what the young people who agreed to be interviewed contributed to the research and what we have made of these contributions.

Since no researcher can gain more than a glimpse of other people's lives through accounts given in an interview, much of the 'skill' of interview-based research lies in what sense we make of the interview after the subject is gone – how we interpret our interview texts. Dorothy Smith[3] has warned that feminists face the danger that in turning talk into texts and texts into sociology, we can be drawn into incorporating people's accounts into existing sociological frameworks:

> a moment comes after talk has been inscribed as texts and become data when it must be worked up as sociology . . . as long as we work within the objectifying frame that organises the discursive consciousness, we will find ourselves reinscribing the moment of discovery of women's experiences as women talk with women, into the conceptual order that locates the reader's and writer's consciousness outside the experience of that talk.[4]

Smith argues that sociological discourse embodies a standpoint from 'the relations of ruling' in which relationships of gender, class and race are 'seen' from the standpoint of those in dominant positions, notably white men.[5] When we attempt to write sociology from the standpoint of women's experience 'we are returned to just that way of looking we have tried to avoid'.[6] Patricia Hill Collins notes that even if we incorporate women's experience into our ways of knowing, decisions about 'who to trust, what to believe and why something is true are not benign academic issues. Instead these concerns tap the fundamental question of which versions of truth will prevail and shape thought and action'.[7] Struggles over interpretation can be political struggles between women or between men as well as between masculinist and feminist knowledge.

The WRAP team has not resolved the problems of inheriting both the patriarchal sociological discourses recognized by Smith, and the racist and Eurocentric categories identified by Collins. But we have tried to be conscious and critical of this problem and to avoid the exclusions that are inherent in unacknowledged relations of ruling. This has meant an emphasis on the salience of power relations throughout the research.

While we may start from a feminist standpoint, however, we may end by producing sociology that is little different from other sociologies in making objects of the subjects of research. In the language of ethnomethodology, Dorothy Smith notes that sociology's 'objectifications are always at odds with the lived actuality in which they are accomplished'.[8] Even if the researcher identifies politically *with* women, this does not necessarily give us the methodological tools with which to avoid the conceptual distancing of women from their experiences.

Smith comments that this is not an epistemological issue – it is not one of realism. Coming to conclusions, however, does raise questions about whether we should believe feminist conclusions. Feminists are divided over whether there is some essential or material reality in people's lives of which they may be unaware, or whether the only level of reality accessible to us is the multiple accounts of plural realities given by different informants all of which may be true in their own terms. This contrast between feminist realism and feminist empiricism (overlapping with various postmodern versions of relativism) divides feminist researchers.[9]

These issues were not resolved within our own experience of the research process. Although the project team was constituted as an explicitly feminist and collective effort, we sensed the dangers of exploring too openly the extent of our feminist differences. We embarked upon research without an open exploration of everything that we were taking for granted. Differences have emerged in the course of coming to conclusions, and in adding a male research assistant to the team. We have tried to meet these, however imperfectly, through retrospective reflexivity in handling our selection and interpretation of data, in developing different areas of feminist theory, and in thinking about the policy implications of the research.[10]

The WRAP research on young people and sexuality was intended to be of practical use to policy-makers concerned with sex education, the promotion of safer sex and the transmission of HIV; specific efforts were made by our original funding body, the ESRC, and ourselves, to communicate our conclusions to policy-makers and practitioners.[11] Our conclusions, which we believe to be valid, mattered in terms of their possible effects on people's lives: for example, our claim that the pursuit of conventional femininity by young women encourages unsafe sexual practices. Our interpretations of interview data were available for incorporation into various levels of decision-making.

In this chapter we unpack the research process to show the factors which contribute to modes of interpretation. By treating coming to conclusions as a social process, we can show that interpretation is a political, contested and unstable process between the lives of the researchers and those of the researched. Interpretation needs somehow to unite a passion for 'truth' with explicit rules of research method that can make some conclusions stronger than others. Our lived experience as women does not simply create us as feminists; feminist methodology requires critical theory and critical reflection on women's accounts of their experiences. The different possible ways of knowing what gender is like link theory, experience and our openness to hearing and conceptualizing the diversity of the voices of different women. By treating interviews as social events, we were able to see them as a learning process both for the research team and for our informants.[12] Rules of method are made explicit by clarifying our epistemological position and recognizing our parts in the research process.

Sexuality and Young People: The WRAP Studies[13]

The WRAP research team aimed to work as a feminist collective in generating a large body of qualitative data on sexual knowledge and practice in two studies of young women and young men. We intended to build up a detailed picture of the sexual practices, beliefs and understanding of young people in order to interpret their understanding of HIV and sexually transmitted diseases, their conceptions of risk and danger in sexual activity, their approaches to relationships and responsibility, and their ability to communicate effectively their ideas on safety within sexual relationships. It was also our intention to contribute to the development of the theory of the social construction of sexuality, by identifying some of the complexity of the processes and mechanisms through which young people construct, experience and define their sexuality and sexual practices. Interpretation of interview transcripts was, therefore, central to our data analysis.

It was intended that all members of the research team should contribute to all stages of the research process. In practice this was not possible. Caroline Ramazanoglu did no interviewing, and other members of the team made variable contributions to different stages of conceiving the project, fieldwork, analysis and dissemination. During our regular team meetings, we agreed a division of labour for each stage of the research and attempted to deal with exhaustion, stress, discouragement, resentments, irritation with colleagues, and other negative aspects of the research process.

There are problems for feminists in managing disagreements over values and strategies when these cannot simply be resolved within a research team hierarchy which makes some assertions or positions inherently more valuable than others. Yet these problems can become critical issues in the social process of interpretation, and in balancing the contradictions and compromises of collective interpretation. The WRAP team did not succeed in making all voices heard all of the time, but has tried to retain a critical consciousness of issues of power and control in the research team. This led us to consider explicitly our thinking about interpretation.[14]

The Place of Interpretation in the Research Process

In order to make sense of interviews the feminist researcher, like any other, has to have some conception of the research process. Conventionally sociologists say very little about exactly what happened during the course of their research.[15] The conventions of field research place interviewing at a particular point in a complex research process. Figure 7.1 represents the research process as starting from theory – in our case feminist theories of the social construction of sexuality – and proceeding through the collection and interpretation of data to a logical conclusion.[16]

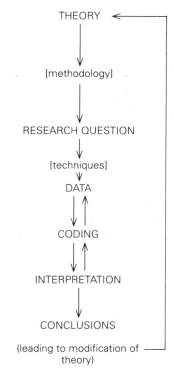

Figure 7.1   The Research Process

The model in figure 7.1 assumes that the production of generally valid conclusions is based on the ability of researchers to control their own subjectivity through the rigour of their research method. Objective, or at least generalizable, knowledge is assumed to be separable from subjectivity. Feminists have challenged this dualism extensively and effectively.[17] The simple claim that the personal is political undermines the validity of knowledge that excludes women's experiences. Feminists have shown the power that can be exercised over women, and their 'subjugated knowledges', through defining objective knowledge as superior to personal experience. It is the assertion of women's experience as valid that has powerfully demonstrated the subordination of women to men in every area of social life. Women's accounts of what their lives are like have forced reconceptualizations of social relationships and the nature of power; experience challenges the validity of 'objective' masculinist knowledge.

This challenge, however, does not make all feminist knowledge necessarily equally valid. The validity of experience is in constant tension with the limitations of experience which social sciences try to transcend. Women's accounts of other women's power over them (through, for example, racism, class, sexual orientation and physical ability) have shown clear, painful and

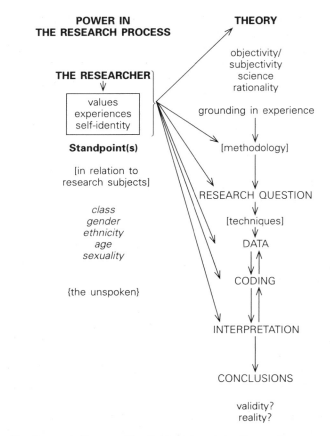

Figure 7.2   The Research Process: The Subjectivity of the Researchers

persistent social divisions between them, and so problems in how to validate feminist knowledge of what the social world is like. It is an uncomfortable conclusion for feminism that women can put considerable effort into achieving their own subordination to men, or into subordinating other women.

Feminism is then faced with a dilemma. Feminists want to make political and moral judgments about the illegitimacy of men's power over women, or of women's power over each other. But such judgments rest on general statements about the nature of social life – about, for example, the extent of male control of women's bodies. We cannot develop strategies for changing power relations if we do not understand power. Like other researchers, we need ways of knowing social life that give us more or less valid knowledge. Feminist innovation in methodology has been through trying to grasp the parts that experience, emotion and subjectivity play in the research process, rather than seeing these as weaknesses to be controlled. Figure 7.2 suggests additional factors that impinge on what can be known through the research process.

If we locate the researcher as an actor in the research process, we open the way to recognition of the power relations within which the researcher is located. Each researcher brings particular values and particular self-identities to the research and has lived through particular experiences. While these values, identities and experiences do not rigidly determine particular points of view, they do give researchers variable standpoints in relation to subjects of research.[18] Since differences may be more apparent to the subjects of research than to the researcher, they constrain what it is possible to know about, and affect our emotional sensitivities.

The point here is not that we know the ways in which particular stances may systematically affect research, but that we do *not* know. The masculinist methodologies and rules of validation that have been developed to control subjectivity do not fully recognize the unpredictability, variability and complexity of the human interactions in ways which take account of power in the research process. We can never be sure that we know what is unspoken or unthought.[19]

Postmodern or post-structuralist methodologies that attempt to deconstruct texts, discover subjugated knowledges and analyze discourses tend to be even less explicit than modern methodologies about the place of the researcher in the research. Feminist researchers have been very successful in, for example, recovering women's history, and giving voice to women's experiences which have previously been silenced. But this does not necessarily entail sensitivity to where the 'knower' is situated. While the work of Michel Foucault, for example, has been particularly influential in allowing women to see power relations in the social construction of sexuality and the body, his own gender-blindness allowed him to ignore the ways women experience men's power over them.[20]

The conception of the research process shown in figure 7.2 is fairly far removed from an orderly and logical progression of rules of validation. In drawing on theory the researcher has to make a series of decisions about epistemology – about what theory of knowledge they subscribe to. In particular researchers have to decide how far their theory is grounded in experience, and in whose experience, and how they understand the nature of 'reality'. It is the *different decisions* taken at this stage that account for the considerable variations within feminist methodology and between feminist researchers.

The process of interpretation can now be seen as a site of struggle at a critical point of the research, and one on which the presence of the researcher in the research process has a profound effect. Research based on interviews, however, also brings in the subjects of research, which makes interviews social events and research more clearly a social process.[21] In figure 7.3, the place of interviews and of those who are researched is suggested.

By taking interviews to be social events, we can envisage interview research as a learning process both for researchers and for those who are researched.[22] A number of feminists have written on the problems of how to take account of social relationships in the research process. Figure 7.3 serves to indicate relevant relationships:

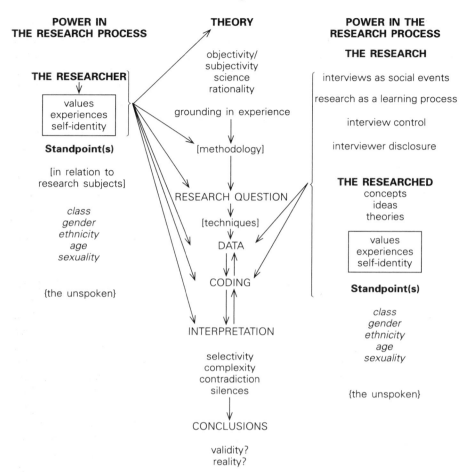

Figure 7.3 The Research Process: A Learning Process

1 inside the research team where conventionally in the UK, and elsewhere, relationships are hierarchical and very generally male-dominated, even though most contract researchers are women;[23]

2 between the researcher and the researched as they interact in the stylized social events that constitute interviews;[24]

3 between researchers, the researched and wider social connections. The standpoints of both researchers and the researched situate them socially in ways which may or may not be apparent or salient to them in the same ways. Power relations in the research process can be recognized and made overt, but differences such as age, class, gender, ethnicity and religion impinge on the possibilities of interaction and interpretation, and so on how the social world is known.[25]

Feminists have had to accept that there is no technique of analysis or methodological logic that can neutralize the social nature of interpretation. We cannot read meaning *in* interview texts, allowing them to propose their own meanings, without also reading meaning *into* them, as we make sense of their meanings. Feminist researchers can only try to explain the grounds on which selective interpretations have been made by making explicit the process of decision-making which produces the interpretation, and the logic of method on which these decisions are based. This entails acknowledging complexity and contradiction which may be beyond the interpreter's experience, and recognizing the possibility of silences and absences in their data.

Feminists can aim at reflexivity, in the sense of continuous critical reflection on the research processes we use to produce knowledge. These aims, however, are not necessarily (or ever?) realized as we might wish. As systematic self-knowledge is not easily available, we cannot break out of the social constraints on our ways of knowing simply by wanting to. A continuous critique of research conclusions is required from those whose standpoints differ from our own.

In figure 7.4, we show that by taking the place of the researched into account, we can also raise questions about what the research is for. Introducing policy implications into our conclusions opens up new problems about claims to valid knowledge. The differing conclusions to which researchers come are based on the interaction of their various standpoints with their interpretations of their data. The same interview transcripts are then open to different interpretations, and so to different conclusions on policy. This is not to say that all interpretations are equally valid. Adopting a relativist position on policy offers freedom to masculinist researchers or those on the 'new right' to suggest further constraints on women's lives. Distinguishing between policies is always a matter both of values and of the power of the theory used.

By asking 'for whom' policies are intended, we recognize variability in the research process. The initial conclusions of the WRAP team value the autonomy of young women, so our policy recommendations are aimed at empowering young women to take more control of their sexual safety. Forming our conclusions then demands that we make explicit what concepts and values we draw on in thinking about such issues as agency and empowerment, and reflecting on what affects constraints on sexual safety. This process of reflection reveals the extent to which young women can collude in their own subordination, and the tremendous efforts they make to produce themselves as successfully feminine. Our values do not simply inform our conclusions in any determinist way, but interact with the knowledge we have produced: our conclusions favour feminist policies that empower young women, over masculinist policies that reaffirm sexuality as an area to be controlled and policed. While our policy recommendations are consistent with our value position, we also claim that we have valid grounds for coming to these conclusions.

The process of interpretation that is so central to this claim of validity

Janet Holland and Caroline Ramazanoglu

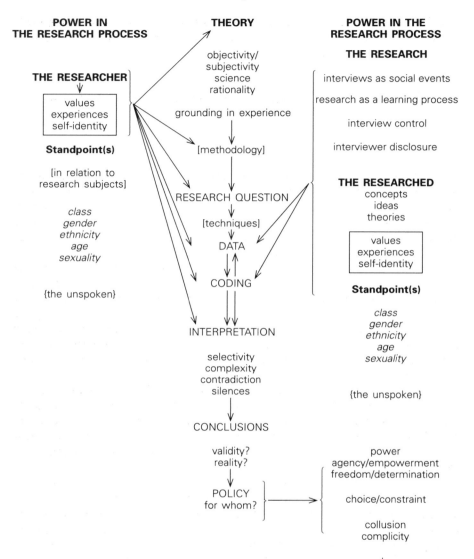

POWER IN THE RESEARCH PROCESS

THEORY

POWER IN THE RESEARCH PROCESS

THE RESEARCHER

values
experiences
self-identity

Standpoint(s)

[in relation to
research subjects]

*class
gender
ethnicity
age
sexuality*

{the unspoken}

objectivity/
subjectivity
science
rationality

grounding in experience

[methodology]

RESEARCH QUESTION

[techniques]

DATA

CODING

INTERPRETATION

selectivity
complexity
contradiction
silences

CONCLUSIONS

validity?
reality?

POLICY
for whom?

THE RESEARCH

interviews as social events

research as a learning process

interview control

interviewer disclosure

THE RESEARCHED
concepts
ideas
theories

values
experiences
self-identity

Standpoint(s)

*class
gender
ethnicity
age
sexuality*

{the unspoken}

power
agency/empowerment
freedom/determination

choice/constraint

collusion
complicity

values

Figure 7.4 The Research Process: Interpretation in its Place

134

remains problematic and contested. But this does not mean that feminists should lack confidence in their conclusions. In the next section we consider some implications of this claim.

Locating Researcher and Researched in the Research Process

The Interview as a Social Event: An Interactive Learning Process

The unstructured interview has been variously described as naturalistic, auto-biographical, in-depth, narrative or non-directive. Whatever the label used, the informal interview is modelled on the conversation and, like the conversation, is a social event with, in this instance, two participants. As a social event it has its own set of interactional rules which may be more or less explicit, more or less recognized by the participants.

In addition to its generally social character, there are several ways in which the interview constitutes a learning process. At the level of this process, participants can discover, uncover or generate the rules by which they are playing this particular game. The interviewer can become more adept at interviewing, in general, in terms of the strategies which are appropriate for eliciting responses, and in particular, in our case, in enabling people to talk about the sensitive topic of sexuality, and thus to disclose more about themselves.

Often neither young women nor men in our studies had had the opportunity to talk about the issues in the terms in which they were raised, or to think about sexuality and sexual experience in relation to themselves in the ways invited by the interview. The interviewees, then, could learn more about themselves in both the process and content of the interview, as indeed could the interviewer.

In this context issues of control and power in the research and interview context become crucial in shaping the production of data for interpretation. We can imagine an ideal of research as a collaborative interactional process in which the 'work' consists of the construction of meanings, with reciprocal inputs from researcher and researched, arriving at agreed conclusions on interpretation of the content, or data of the research. This is an ideal to which some feminists aspire. They seek reciprocity in the research relationship and are sensitive to intrusion into women's lives; they want to 'realize the meanings', the lifeworld of the women they research, in a way that makes sense for the women themselves.[26] To this end some attempt to involve the researched in the entire research process, starting with setting the agenda for research, undertaking it in a reciprocal relation, through to interpretation and writing-up (or producing some statement) of the results.[27] There is a conflict between the requirements made of a researcher through their membership of an academic or disciplinary community, and the needs and interests of the women they research. Measor identifies the problem precisely in the context of the interview. The interview, she says, 'involves entering another person's social world and their perspective, but remaining alert to its configurations at the same time. . . . There is a contradiction in aiming for ultimate rapport and yet treating the person's account both critically and sociologically'.[28]

The researcher has the power to define the research situation and to reconstitute the content of the interview, the statements of the researched, in her own terms. Her 'standpoint' in relation to the researched in terms of a number of social categories may vary in ways which enhance the possibilities for control. An aware, feminist researcher may be older, more educated, from a different social class and ethnic background than the woman she interviews, who may in turn defer to her, or feel relatively powerless on one or other of those grounds. It is true too that those same 'standpoint' factors which mark differences between women may give the researched the power to control what information they are prepared to disclose to the researcher, and possibly (probably?) inhibit disclosure.

Feminists have identified some of the problems of exploitation of women as subjects of research, and of women interviewing women. The 'naturalistic' interview, conducted with empathy by a woman, might lead women into considerable revelation. Despite different standpoint factors, identification could operate, particularly if the researcher uses shared experience (for example as mother, wife or worker) to facilitate rapport. The interviewee may have a perception of a similar, shared, subordinated power position. Women can be easy targets for women interviewers, as Finch points out: 'I have also emerged from interviews with the feeling that my interviewees need to know how to protect themselves from people like me'.[29] In the broader context of research, we could imagine an example where women, themselves exploited in the research process, might exploit the women they research. A young woman research assistant, without power in the research context, may conduct empathetic, revelatory interviews with women, to have the data she collects removed entirely from her control by the person who runs the research project of which it is a part.

Interpretation is always structured at least in part by how the researched enter into the research process set up by the researchers. The difficulty of managing interviews so as to allow the experience of the researched to come through can be illustrated by considering what an interview can do to an interviewer.

Effects of the Research on Interviewers

It is sometimes difficult for researchers to envisage the effects on them of interviews on sensitive topics. Julia Brannen, referring to a study of marital breakdown, speaks of her respondents using the interview as catharsis, and likens the situation to a psychoanalytic or psycho-therapeutic interview.[30] Liz

Kelly, conducting interviews with women who had been sexually abused as children, reports having to stop interviews because 'women were visibly distressed'.[31] She often spent as much time talking informally with the women as in the extremely long interviews which she undertook. She reports that 'Interviewing and transcribing the tapes was much more time-consuming and emotionally draining than I had anticipated'.[32]

Many of the interviews in the WRAP study were emotionally draining and demanding. One member of the WRAP team interviewed a young woman who had been extremely violently raped by a number of men, narrowly escaping with her life. The interview made extreme demands on the interviewer, although the young woman involved, a rape survivor, not victim, as she put it, had done a massive amount of work on herself and the experience. Just reading the transcript is emotionally shocking. In another case a young man clearly wanted to discuss the death of his mother some years earlier, but the interviewer was reluctant to respond to this need for two reasons. First, responding as a researcher, it was likely that it would be difficult to pursue the objectives of the research, a discussion of sexual behaviour and sexuality, if the young man's need to talk about his mother was accepted. Second, the researcher had very recently suffered a bereavement with the unexpected death of a close member of her family, and felt that the discussion would be emotionally unbearable. In the event, since his need was clearly strong, the researcher invited the young man to talk about his mother and his bereavement, and doing so in fact offered a basis for discussing intensely personal, but relevant issues in the rest of the interview. But the personal emotional cost to the interviewer was quite high.

In the WRAP team we were fortunate in having colleagues with whom to discuss emotionally disturbing and demanding interviews (although they were not always available at the precise moment at which they were needed). But the impact of interviews on sensitive topics on interviewers should not be underestimated, and a support structure is advisable.

When interviews are emotional or distressing, there are clear problems in deciding what sense to make of them, but these problems occur generally in interviews and raise questions about what we can take interviews to mean. We consider this point in the next section.

Language and Meaning

The essence of the naturalistic interview is flexibility and responsiveness, although it is clear that the researcher, and indeed the researched, come to the situation with an agenda. In the WRAP studies we had a series of topics which we wished to explore, but there was no set way in which they were to be covered. The intention was to be very responsive to the concerns of the respondent, if necessary letting them talk their way into what was important for them in an interview lasting on average one and a half hours. We also had to stay open to the meanings which the accounts of sexuality had for the young people themselves, and to possible different meanings in the way we understood and responded to what they were saying. Julia Brannen highlights the problem for the researcher:

> At the outset of the interview the interviewer is faced with the problem of whether and how to name the topic under investigation. Sensitive researchers tread warily at the beginning of interviews and don't reveal all their hand at the outset. It is important not to prejudge the research problem by labelling it or defining its boundaries too closely; respondents may thereby define the problem in their own terms.[33]

It can be very difficult for respondents to talk about sensitive issues with an interviewer. In our case, quite often young people did not have an appropriate language with which to discuss sexual matters. What was available was either the clinical/scientific, which is somewhat removed from their own vocabularies, or the obscene/crude, which they were often uncomfortable with in an interview. But beyond the limitations of the descriptive vocabulary for bodily parts and sexual acts lies the absence of a language to describe the ambiguities and uncertainties about sexuality and sexual behaviour which many of them felt, and particularly to describe female sexuality and desire in positive terms. There is no language to describe a woman's desire to both have and not to have sex, or indeed the pressures on her to do both.

Insofar as there is a possible way of talking about the sensitive topics involved, the researcher needs to be able to pick up and use the language of the respondents as it is offered, which is what we attempted to do in the WRAP studies. Some interviewees are reluctant to use slang or colloquial terms without the approval of the interviewer, but there are many terms for the body parts and activities involved, so it is difficult for the interviewer to introduce such terms without some knowledge of the social setting and environment of the interviewees. As time went on, the WRAP interviewers became more conversant with local terminologies, but given variations by class, age and ethnicity in the sample, it was somewhat difficult to be conversant with all potential variants, and the research provided a learning process for the researchers. Wight, studying the sexuality of 14-to-16-year-old working-class boys in Glasgow, consulted with his respondents and as a result deliberately used their own slang in his interviews, to make them feel more at ease and to avoid confusion.[34]

Silverman and Perakyla touch on some of these issues in their conversation analysis of transcripts of HIV and AIDS counselling sessions.[35] They found that patients paused or hesitated before first mentioning terms relating to sexual intercourse or contraceptives, and similarly in relation to 'dreaded issues' (in this context the possibility of getting ill and dying of AIDS). They suggest that this could be the result of general cultural norms about delicate topics, but they also found that these hesitations were what they called 'locally managed', that they took on a particular character in the specific setting and exchange, and that patients and counsellors 'mirrored' each other in subsequent exchanges. They saw the pattern of conversation as indicating an acceptance of the issue as delicate and a willingness to deal with it as such. They also argue that this constitutes 'elegant interactional work' by both parties, not difficulties in communication.

We suggest that in the WRAP studies, the difficulties which the young women in particular have in talking about issues related to sexuality, and the hesitations, silences and contradictions which abound in their responses, themselves reflect the contradictory nature of the social construction of feminine sexuality, rather than any local problem of communication between interviewee and interviewer. We argue this by connecting the experience of the interviews to feminist theories and accounts of experiences. There were instances where the interviewer spoke the silence, voiced the unvoiced. In the following example a young woman is describing a situation where she has asked a man to use a condom because she was worried about HIV and AIDS, but could not tell him so. She has difficulty in the interview in saying what it was that she said, just as she had difficulty in saying what she wanted in the sexual situation:

Q: What counts in that situation is how it feels.
A: Yes. You don't, you don't. I wouldn't swear he was safe. He hadn't got anything. But you just don't know. But I said, listen, don't, don't . . .
Q: Don't come inside you . . .
A: Don't come inside me. I've never talked like this . . .
Q: These things are important to talk to people about.
A: That's what I said, yeah.

In two other examples, the interviewer felt strongly that some crucial meaning, or explanatory factor, lay behind the entire narrative provided in the interview, but did not voice it since she also felt that it was the interviewee's to reveal, or perhaps to own.

In each case the interviewee did eventually make this meaning explicit. One young man revealed at the end of a very long interview that it was his religious conviction which kept him a virgin at 21, prefacing his explanation with the statement, 'Don't you want to know why'? The interviewer interpreted this comment as a criticism of the fact that she had not asked the question, nor made the suggestion.

This failure to voice the unvoiced was made explicit in the second instance, where again a 21-year-old virgin, this time a woman, after the long interview was over and the tape turned off, revealed that it was 'race' and the way that it situated her which made it impossible for her to become sexually active. She spent a further hour describing her experience of 'race' and racism, and the ways in which it intersected with her gender to construct her sexuality. When the interviewer revealed that she had sensed that something like this was the case but had had felt inhibited from expressing it, the interviewee responded: 'Why didn't you just say!?' A problem for any interpretation of transcripts is that the unvoiced can never be fully grasped in an interview, and we can only negotiate recognition of what may be hinted at.[36]

In the young women's accounts of their sexual experiences in the WRAP study, a considerable degree of violence emerged.[37] But it proved extremely difficult for the interviewers to raise the issue of violence with the young men we interviewed later. While some young men did talk about experiencing certain kinds of violence, usually fighting other men, or being attacked themselves, none admitted to 'hitting a woman'. Other researchers have found that women's reports of male aggression or force do not coincide with men's reports.

While interviewees may give interviewers information on their actions, they can present other meanings too. One young woman, who was not sexually active at the time of the interview, gave an analysis of the meanings of condom use through her reflections on the experiences of others. She asserted that she would use a condom in a sexual relationship, and tried to describe why some people would not. In doing so she seems to cover most of the problems and issues involved in condom use – opening an interpretation to the interviewer:

> Most of them [her friends] do say if they were to have sex they would use a condom, and they say they wouldn't – I mean they say we'd probably feel embarrassed, you know, saying 'do you mind using a condom?' and stuff, but most of them say that – like if I was to have sex it would probably be because we like foreplay, you know, sort of getting into it, and then afterwards it would kind of ruin it if you was to say, excuse me, could you go and get a condom please. I don't know, it just seems an offputting idea. That's the only bit I'm sort of – that's why I'd say that the sort of carried-away situation where you wouldn't use a condom and like that, that's the only way we wouldn't use one. Other than that we would. But most of us would feel embarrassed at asking a boy, I don't know why.

In interpreting this passage we want to go beyond the text to 'see' embarrassment as a 'real experience'. We validate this conclusion through our theory of the social construction of femininity, and our own experience as women. We can also 'find' in the text a notion of the essential spontaneity of the sexual event, and the desire to protect herself against infection. These meanings struggle for ascendancy here; a struggle complicated by the slippage between what she sees as her own position on the issue and what she is trying to describe as that of her friends.[38]

In another interview, a young woman returned to the topic of pleasure, raised earlier by the researcher, which she did not pursue at the time, revealing the pressure on her to engage in sexual activities in which she was not particularly interested, in order to meet male needs:

> Actually, seeing as you asked me earlier, 'did you find it enjoyable or pleasurable?' – I find everything enjoyable and pleasurable except for the actual penetration, so I mean, why bother? I think really if you're with a guy and you are going to do everything but, it's obviously a big tease.

In this extract the researcher can 'find' a clear reference to experience – a preference for non-penetrative sex – which can be compared with accounts given by other interviewees. We have here one statement which 'fits' with other sources of information about the 'realities' of sexual encounters. But the next statement does not inform us about 'teasing' behaviour. Rather it shows how this young women conceives non-penetrative sex as problematic in view of her assumptions about men's needs.

Obviously the text of a transcript does not reveal all that went on in the interview: language was not the only thing exchanged. Body language, non-verbal exchanges, distress and laughter are all part of that interchange, and all need to be taken into account in understanding and interpreting what the young women and young men were trying to communicate about their sexuality and sexual experience. The WRAP interviewers keep detailed descriptive field notes of the interviewee and interview to supplement the script.

In coding and analyzing the complexities of different levels of information, hints, images and meanings in these interview transcripts, we draw not only on our reading of them as texts, but on the interaction of three levels of conceptualization: the terms and meanings offered by the young women and explicit in the data, such as those in the extract above; the interviewer's field notes made after the interview, which entail some reflection on meanings in the interview; and team members' discussion, interpretation and coding of these data in the light of feminist and sociological theory, as well as our own sexual experiences.

The sense we make of interviews, in the light of the numerous complications suggested above, interacts with our sense of appropriate policy strategies. We turn briefly now to the some ethical considerations raised by the application of feminist conclusions.

Ethical Issues in Policy Recommendations

The issue of whose knowledge is produced from interviews, and to what ends it should be put, is particularly salient in the case of feminist research. Feminist methods, and the interaction between the feminist researcher and the researched, may facilitate or encourage exposure which could lead to potentially damaging revelation. The researched may incriminate themselves by revealing illegal activities – in our studies under-age sex and drinking, drug use and dealing, and other illegal activities emerged. What the researched say might reflect badly on them and damage their reputation or that of others if reported – this is clearly an issue when sexual behaviour is the topic for discussion.

What the researched say, or might have to say if they could talk about it, could be psychologically, emotionally, personally or socially problematic or damaging for them. Brannen, Dodd and Oakley report responses of this type in a study of marital difficulty and breakdown;[39] Kelly has talked about it in the context of long interviews on child sexual abuse.[40] Physical abuse and violence raise similar issues. In some instances, feminists have been unable to publish the results of their research on women for fear that it might be damaging to those women. In the WRAP studies some young women (and one young man) were able to talk about their experience of being sexually abused as a child. Research situations in which interviewees reveal such difficult and potentially harmful material also raise questions of the appropriate interviewer response and whether it is within the role of the researcher to counsel and offer comfort.

Punch has discussed some of the ethical dilemmas which confront the qualitative researcher, particularly ethnographers and those who have extremely sensitive material disclosed to them in the course of research.[41] He argues that to protect the researched, ethical codes which call for informed consent have been developed in the social sciences. Research subjects have the right to be informed both that they are being researched and about the nature of the research. He suggests, however, that these ethical codes can be no more than guidelines, since the situation in ethnographic research is often such that the activity cannot be interrupted in order to give detailed information about the fact of the research and gain consent from all participants. But he goes further to suggest that deception may be appropriate in some situations, although the responsible ethnographer should always bear in mind and respect 'privacy, harm, identification and confidentiality'. His conclusion is that 'Some measure of deception is acceptable in some areas where the benefits of knowledge outweigh the harms and where the harms have been minimized by following convention on confidentiality and identity'.[42]

Punch's pragmatism seems to place him on slippery moral ground, and many feminist researchers would blanch at this approach. Judith Stacey argues that ethnography is potentially the most exploitative method, creating a particular contradiction between feminist ethics and methods: 'I find myself wondering whether the appearance of greater respect for and equality with research subjects in the ethnographic approach masks a deeper, more dangerous form of exploitation'.[43] At the extreme she sees the problem in terms of betrayal; the researcher is freer than the researched to leave the system of relationships within which the ethnography has been conducted, and constructs her own version of the experiences of the researched. Stacey draws parallels between the ways that feminists concerned with methodology have grappled with these issues and the ways that 'postmodern' ethnographers have done so. The similarities lie partly in reflexivity, and partly in a recognition which lays bare the limitations of the research process.

Drawing policies from confused and contested meanings can never be an orderly or value-free process. Feminism plays methodological, moral and political roles in struggling to ensure that as much of women's experience as possible can be grasped, and that appropriate policy recommendations can be drawn from this experience.

Through a Glass, Darkly?

In discussing something of the difficulties of interviewing on sensitive subjects we have tried to problematize the central place of interpretation in the research process. As researchers we need to be continuously aware of how problematic interpretation is and will remain. But this does not mean that we are condemned to a feeble, disempowering relativism, which considers a view that produces the backlash to be as valid as a view from under the lash. Experience remains one essential and informative source of validity which is open to reflexive interpretation.[44]

If we cut through the complexities of epistemological differences, we can show, rather crudely, three possible positions that feminists can take in producing more or less valid conclusions from interviews. (There are roughly three positions current in social research, but these are overlaid by multiple variations and qualifications which we do not consider here).

1   The data produced by researchers can be regarded as in some way directly reflecting an unproblematic reality. Truth is then connected to reality through set procedures of interpretation. Interpretation can be seen as a process which can be contaminated by failure to control the subjective, political, personal. Opinion pollsters tell us what people 'really' think about selected issues. The overt problem in this view is not how to interpret the text, but how to avoid contaminating the connection between truth and reality. This methodology is then very concerned with the minutiae of interview techniques, control of bias, sampling accuracy, and generally with the mechanisms of reliability and validity. It assumes that reality can be accessed through correct technique. Human subjectivity is acknowledged as a problem but is controlled through the sophistication of sampling and the research instruments.

While some feminists may operate with these as implicit assumptions, feminism has made this approach problematic because the 'truths' produced are overwhelmingly the 'truths' of patriarchal societies which render women's experience marginal, deviant or trivial. Feminism then seems to rule out the possibility of a direct relation between the texts we produce in research and an agreed, shared social reality. Transcripts cannot mirror social life.

2 At the other extreme, the assumption that there is a reality which is knowable through interviews is rejected. In this view, interview transcripts and comparable texts cannot reflect reality since we have no way of knowing the relationships between truth and the interview text. An interview is a specific account given to a particular interviewer at a particular moment. An interview with the same person would have produced a different text in any other circumstances. We cannot then take these singular texts as in any way accessing reality, or recording past actions. They are accounts in which people present themselves to specific audiences. We can only allow diverse accounts to speak for themselves through multiple possible readings of transcripts as texts.

This approach, and the influence of ethnomethodology, has had an appeal to some feminists in privileging the validity of women's accounts of their experience, and in allowing the experience of the silenced to be heard and shared. The growing influence of post-structuralism and postmodernism on feminism has given a new respectability to the view that women's lives are contradictory and so feminism itself should be fragmented, plural, multiplex. We can only analyze unstable, fragile, shifting social constructions.

What is problematic here is that this relativist view of women's lives producing many truths does not fully acknowledge the factors influencing researchers' interpretations of women's lives and women's diversity. Feminist researchers who interview others to produce feminist knowledge can never simply allow the experience of the other to speak for itself (this would be publication rather than research – which is important but different). To treat what people say to interviewers simply as textual leaves us unable to show how we have come to any conclusions. It does not expose interpretation as a social process, or the relevant 'relations of ruling', in deciding between possible notions of what is there.

3 The middle way between these extremes is the one adopted by the WRAP team, along with most feminists. The great attention paid to method and methodology in recent years by feminists indicates both the central importance of clarifying how we come to conclusions, and the very considerable difficulty of doing so. These difficulties have provoked considerable methodological variation within feminism.[45]

If we assume that there is some material reality in people's lives – such as the reality of gendered relationships between women and men – this does not ensure a means of accessing it. Any understanding of the nature of 'real' relationships involves a degree of conceptualization, and so some process of interpretation of our 'evidence' for the existence of these relationships.

The middle way is then first to claim that there is some level of reality which can be accessed through people's accounts, but also to accept that there is no precise solution as to exactly *how* this can be done. Ultimately we do not know whether or not we have done it.

Interpretation then becomes revealed as the key methodological step in this process of attempting to link data and social relationships. A number of factors interact in unpredictable ways in any process of interpretation: feminist theory and political values, the standpoint and subjectivity of the researcher, the social event of the interview, the ways in which interviewees formulate their accounts on that occasion, and their own standpoints and values.

Over the years, feminists have made a convincing case that women 'really' are dominated by men in many respects and many situations. This is a claim that has rested heavily on women's own accounts of their experiences, but these accounts have forced a reconceptualization of violence, sexuality, marriage, domestic labour and so on. Women's accounts have not then simply spoken for themselves; they have been actively interpreted and conceptualized by feminists.

This process of interpretation, as we have tried to show here, is both positive and creative, but also flawed in the sense that we can never be sure that we have got it right. There are no general rules of validation that can impose an abstract order on the confusion and complexity of daily life. This flaw does not lie specifically in feminism, but in the tension between the vulnerability and the power of any social researcher who tries to read through their data to some version of social reality behind it.

Sociologists, like other social scientists, have responded to this problem by diversifying into schools of thought each with their own methodological *solution* to the problem of knowing (or not knowing) what is 'really' the case. Research methods courses generally teach students these solutions. (The unreflexive solutions which operate in the middle ground between certainty and relativism are often hard for students to grasp, if not positively obfuscated, which is perhaps not surprising given the uncertainties of the task.)

Feminists are continually showing that this problem is not solved, but rather is with us at the start of every research project and must be resolved at the point of interpretation in that project. Some form of openly reflexive interpretation then seems essential if we are to claim any validity for our conclusions.

Sheila Rowbotham has said: 'It is now possible to look back at ourselves through our own cultural creations, our actions, our ideas, our pamphlets, our organizations, our history, our theory'.[46] In this view it is possible to see through the 'glass' of interview accounts, but sometimes the glass, or our own reflection in it, is all we can see. In any research project the quest for valid knowledge is at odds with a desire for order, stability and certainty in our methodology.

We 'know', however, that feminism is not just chasing shadows, because experience tells us so. We recognize domestic violence, male power, gender socialization, when these are identified as public political issues (although all women do not necessarily recognize or experience them in the same ways). But this is not to privilege experience, subjectivity or emotion as general means of validation – there are always limits to experience, as painful struggles around difference show. New 'cultural creations' give us new ways of knowing sexuality, but no stable rules of validation which can ensure that feminists always know best. Feminist struggles to assert the centrality of gender relationships in women's lives are also struggles to rework the unstable politics of daily life.[47] In these struggles, the validity of our interpretations depends on the integrity of the interaction of our personal experiences with the power of feminist theory and the power, or lack of power, of the researched. Our conclusions should always be open to criticism.

Notes

1   A version of this chapter was given as a paper, 'Accounting for sexuality, living sexual politics: can feminist research be valid?' at the British Sociological Association annual conference, April 1993.
2   C. Ramazanoglu (1989b).
3   D. Smith (1989), pp. 35–6.
4   *Ibid.*, p. 35.
5   *Ibid.*, p. 36.
6   *Ibid.*
7   P.H. Collins (1990), pp. 202–3.
8   Smith (1989), p. 57.
9   These divisions can be seen, for example, in the differences between S. Hekman (1990), Stanley and Wise (1990) and contributors to Harding and Hintikka (1983).
10 This chapter draws on our experiences of working in a team and discussing interpretations with colleagues. We are grateful to Janet Ransom for comments on some points. The views expressed here are our own.
11 More detailed results of this research are available as WRAP Papers from Tufnell Press, 47 Dalmeny Rd, London N7 ODY. Prices on request.
12 This point, which we discuss further below, is informed by an unpublished paper by Rachel Thomson (1989) 'Interviewing as a process: dilemmas and delights', written as part of her MA degree, in which she analyzes her experience of interviewing young women.
13 The Women, Risk and AIDS Project study of young women was staffed by the authors and Sue Scott, now at the University of Stirling, Sue Sharpe, a freelance author and researcher, and Rachel Thomson, now at the Sex Education Forum of the National Children's Bureau, working collectively. The Project was funded by a two-year grant from the ESRC and supplementary support from the Department of Health, Goldsmiths' College, and the Institute of Education. The WRAP team interviewed 150 young women in depth between 1988 and 1990. A pre-selection questionnaire (completed by 500 young women) provided a statistical profile of a large (non-random) sample from which we generated two purposive

samples (one in London, one in Manchester). The defining variables were age (16–21), social class, power (based on level of educational attainment and/or type of work experience), ethnic origin and type of sexual experience.

The Men, Risk and AIDS Project (MRAP) was a comparative study of 46 young men in London between 1991 and 1992. A pre-selection questionnaire was also used in this project giving additional statistical data on 250 young men. Tim Rhodes, now at the Centre for Research on Drugs and Health Behaviour, was a team member on this project. This project was funded by a one-year grant from the Leverhulme Trust and supplementary support from the Department of Health and Goldsmiths' College.

In both studies the main technique used was an unstructured interview, which was tape-recorded, transcribed and computerized. The interviews were informal and intensive, covering sensitive areas about sexual experience. The interview transcripts constitute our main source of data, but are supplemented by the interviewers' field notes and a sub-sample of second interviews with 20 young women.

14 C. Ramazanoglu (1990).
15 There are some notable exceptions such as contributions to Bell and Newby (1977) and to Bell and Roberts (1984).
16 Figure 7.1 may appear to represent a hypothetico-deductive model of research, in which a hypothesis or research question is derived from theory and tested against data produced by the researcher, as opposed to an analytical inductive model in which the researcher collects data and generalizes from it. Our purpose is to show that feminist methodology disrupts both these positions, since they do not take account of research as a social process.
17 See, for example, Harding (1987); D. Smith (1988a); Cain and Finch (1981).
18 E.g. Hartsock (1983); Cain (1990).
19 Cain (1993).
20 Ramazanoglu and Holland (1993).
21 Thomson (1989).
22 *Ibid.*
23 Kay (1990); Bell (1977).
24 Brannen (1988).
25 See, for example, Cain and Finch (1981), and Hartsock (1983).
26 Acker *et al.* (1983); Mies (1983).
27 Graham (1984).
28 Measor (1985), p. 63.
29 Finch (1984), p. 80.
30 Brannen (1988).
31 Kelly (1988).
32 *Ibid.*, p. 10.
33 Brannen (1988), p. 553.
34 Wight (in prep.).
35 Silverman and Perakyla (1990).
36 See also Opie (1992).
37 Holland *et al.* (1992).
38 Holland (1993).
39 Brannen *et al.* (1991).
40 Kelly (1988).
41 Punch (1986).

42   *Ibid.*, p. 41.
43   Stacey (1988), p. 22.
44   See also Fuss (1989).
45   Harding (1992).
46   Sheila Rowbotham (1973b, p. 28), cited in T. de Lauretis (1986), p. 4.
47   T. de Lauretis (1986).

Chapter 8

The Work of Knowledge and the Knowledge of Women's Work

Miriam Glucksmann

Feminist research could be argued to offer a distinctive approach along a number of different dimensions: its substantive concerns which determine the subject matter of enquiry and the kinds of questions that are asked; its approach towards what it is studying, which is premised on certain broad epistemological and philosophical positions that set limits on the types and range of research methods and techniques it adopts; its overt political commitment which aims for an active relation between feminist research and feminist political practice, such that the output of the research, the knowledge that is produced, contributes in some way to transforming the relations of inequality and domination that are its central topics of investigation.

Over the last decade and a half reams of books and articles have been written about the first two of these dimensions and a large body of work has developed in the last few years in particular around the debates in feminist epistemology.[1] Historically this mushrooming of published work has accompanied the other feature of the period, namely the expansion of Women's Studies and Gender Studies as academic courses and the (qualified) acceptance of feminism within certain sectors of the academy.

Yet the same positive comments cannot be made about the third aspect of feminist research. On the contrary, the relation between feminist theoretical work and political practice has become more problematic as time has passed; less has been written about it; the earlier hopes for a fairly direct political input have a starry-eyed and naive ring to our ears today and have given way to more general notions such as 'empowerment'. Feminist research became more academic while feminist politics as we knew it went into decline. However this development must be seen in the context of the political sea-change that has occurred in Britain since the late 1970s. The many and various groupings that went to make up the Women's Liberation Movement have all but disappeared. Earlier certainties about the aims of feminism and how to achieve them gave way to defensiveness in the face of charges of essentialism and to fragmentation in response to the emphasis on differences between women. Writing about gender inequality obviously has a different quality and impact when it is orientated towards an active political movement rather than towards a primarily academic audience. It is not that the relation between theory and practice could ever have been simple or unproblematic but at least it was possible to think about there being one. Clearly both the kinds of questions that are asked and the kinds of answers that are given depend on and are shaped by the context in which they are raised and the audience they address. For example, where divisions between women had previously been viewed as a political problem to be overcome, in many quarters, the very fact of difference came to be reified into an abstract principle and taken to justify the impossibility of any generalizable theory or practice.

For those engaged in action research of various kinds or where their project is directly linked with a particular campaign or commissioned by feminist organizations the problem does not arise, or certainly not so acutely. Much of the work currently being done (including that of other contributors to this book) in the areas of, for example, domestic violence, women and AIDS, community health care, or the gender impact of different strategies of economic development, can be seen to have some effect. But for many of us there is an ongoing struggle to avoid being submerged either by political defeatism or by postmodern paralysis. However I believe that in a period of relative political quiescence, when a large body of feminist research is in danger of losing its radical edge or of becoming a purely academic exercise, the challenge is to recognize the constraints and parameters that now exist for what they are and as externally imposed, and to take on board their inevitable implications for the relation between feminist research and its reception, who it is for and what happens to the knowledge it produces. Part of the reflexivity of the feminist researcher must be to include an appreciation of the limits of what could possibly be achieved in the particular political context of the time.

In this chapter the central issue that I want to address is the different and unequal relation to knowledge of the researcher and researched. However 'feminist' in terms of aims, perspective or methods adopted, I want to suggest that it is impossible to overcome within the research context the inequalities of knowledge between researcher and researched. Rooted as these are in the real social divisions of knowledge that are created between people in contemporary society they represent a central contradiction that inevitably characterizes academic feminist research. No amount of sensitivity or reciprocality, for example in the interview situation, can alter the fact that while the task of the researcher is to produce knowledge, those being researched have a quite different interest in and relation to their situation.

Yet there has been a tendency in much of the writing on feminist research to focus on the research process itself, in particular on the relationship between the researcher and researched, as if it were a form of political practice. The amount of angst suffered and enormous efforts expended in the attempt to create an egalitarian and reciprocal relation within the research process would seem to imply that there is some perfect model of researcher/researched relation to be achieved and that if we succeed, then this counts as *being* or *acting* feminist. While no one actually argues explicitly that feminist research *is* feminist politics I do detect an undercurrent, an unwitting implication perhaps, in many of the best known writings on the subject.[2] Of course one should expect continuity of behaviour, approaches and attitudes on the part of feminists within the research situation and towards politics more generally but this need not amount to conflating the two.

Such a slippage, whether implicit or explicit, would, in my view, rest on a confusion of levels and be in danger of attempting to establish an egalitarianism in the research situation as a substitute for establishing it in the 'real world'. Nobody imagines that we could transform the various forms of *gender* subordination either through or within the research process. Equally, the same must also hold true for unequal relations between women: we do not and could not overcome the structured inequalities between women within the research process. Yet the creation of a transparent and equal relation between researcher and researched where each is equally involved and each gains something from the process does sometimes appear to become the main objective of the research.

The search for 'feminism within the research situation', if one can call it that, could well be interpreted as a response to the problems of lack of external political context that I have already alluded to. We find a quasi-solution for frustration in the current political climate by focusing down onto the research process, perhaps the one situation in which we can have an active role and over which we do have some control. But failing to recognize the limitations that are necessarily built into social research can lead to a misguided voluntarism which implies that we could, if we tried hard enough, equalize the relation between, say, a woman researcher and the women she is interviewing. It can also lead to a concern with the internal dynamics of the research situation taking precedence over what the research is ostensibly about.

In making this point I want to emphasize that I am not taking issue with any of the injunctions about how to behave as a researcher, how to conduct qualitative research, how to act towards the people that one is interviewing, and how to avoid using them as 'research objects'.[3] Rather the point I am making is that the researcher's self-awareness and reflection on her research should include a realistic appraisal of the limits of research as a locus for authentic political activity.

Researching Women's Work

Before discussing the significance of inequalities of knowledge in the research situation I want to summarize my own work since the reflections that follow flow to a large extent from it. My research trajectory mirrors the changes of the last fifteen years. During that period I have undertaken three projects on working-class women's work. The first, based on working on the assembly line in a motor components factory for nine months, grew directly out of my involvement in the Women's Liberation Movement in Britain and was undertaken in the spirit of exploring one of the major political problems perceived by socialist feminists in the mid 1970s – that of understanding why feminism appeared not to be relevant to, or not to involve, working-class women. I left my academic job and went to work in the factory in order to experience that kind of life and work for myself, in the hope of gaining some insight into what it was like to be an unskilled, badly paid manual worker, and at the same time to learn about gender domination and subordination in employment, about class differences between women and men, and about ethnic divisions between women in a specific sector of work.

My motives were not academic and I did not see what I was doing as research, but more as learning than producing knowledge, let alone as partici-pant observation. When I set out I had no intention of writing a book. At the time 'research' such as this was in any case definitely not on the academic agenda. *Women on the Line* was eventually published in 1982 (after a long delay because of legal problems[4]) and was soon being described as a piece of 'ethnographic research' and used on research methods courses as an example of participant observation. This was a forceful indication of how much times had changed! Although when asked to give talks about it, I was quite capable of justifying the approach I had adopted on legitimate methodological grounds and to discuss the ethics of covert versus overt modes of participant obser-vation, this was certainly not the outcome I had in mind at the outset.

The next two pieces of research were more historical and based princi-pally on interviews with older women who had worked during the inter-war period either as assemblers in the London area or as textile or other manual workers in the north-west. These later projects were stimulated by the earlier experience of assembly line work since I wanted to discover the origins of the very rigid sexual division of labour that characterized mass production indus-try. My use of historical material was premised on the belief that long-term comparisons help to develop understanding of large-scale transformations in social inequalities or in subordination in the domestic economy, and hence of the possibility of political change, rather than researching into history for history's sake.

However, by the mid 1980s, when I began working on what was to become *Women Assemble*,[5] I was under no illusions about the possibilities of research feeding directly into the feminist movement or being directly 'for' the people it was 'about'. Rather I was aiming at a recuperative history, which gave voice to women who had worked on assembly lines in the new mass production industries such as electrical engineering and food process-ing. Traditionally industrial sociology had defined men working in car fact-ories in the 1950s as the quintessential assembly line workers; I wanted to redress the balance and then look at some of the theoretical implications of recognizing that hundreds of thousands of women had worked as assemblers in other industries, and at an earlier period, for received arguments about

Fordism and the labour process. A further aim was to develop a means of analyzing the class relations of different groups of workers, so suggesting a way of distinguishing in class terms between different groups of women (as well as between men, and between women and men). My overall political aim was, necessarily under the changed circumstances, longer-term and more theoretical: to contribute by means of this case study to our developing theory of the relation between gender and class as intertwined structural inequalities.

Subsequently my interest in whether the women had bought the products that they had made and in the links between their domestic labour and paid employment led to a more recent project broadly concerned with the relation between production and consumption in the domestic and market economies, and the structural transformation in the relation between these two spheres that occurred in Britain between 1920 and 1960. My aim was again to use history not as an end in itself but rather as a means of throwing light on the formation of present-day gender inequalities and to distinguish between different forms and patterns of gender inequality in each sphere, the mechanisms that generate, perpetuate or undermine them, and how the forms change over time. This research was also by means of a case study and largely based on oral history: I interviewed two generations of women in the Greater Manchester area who had been employed in the 1930s and in the 1950s in an attempt to ascertain the impact of the full-time employment of married women on their domestic division of labour, consumption and use of domestic technology.[6]

All of these projects relied on the cooperation of working-class women whose life histories and circumstances were very different from my own. Even though the research might, and this is the most I could hope for, have some relevance to the understanding of structured inequalities of gender affecting these and other women which would be a necessary precondition for undermining and abolishing gender domination in the hopefully not-too-distant future, I could not kid myself that it has any practical significance for those women in the here-and-now. This difference between me and the people I was researching, and the fact that they could not realistically constitute an audience or outlet for the research, has forced me to think about the relation between researcher and researched in a particular way.[7]

Whose Research and for Whom?

I turn now to what I have called the central contradiction of academic feminist research, at least of the qualitative oral history variety, namely the inequalities of knowledge in the research situation. I use this as an umbrella term to include two broad dimensions of unequal relations which shape the relation between researcher and researched. One concerns the different relation to the production of knowledge and thereby to the research situation or interview as the means of producing knowledge. The other concerns differences in the kinds and range of knowledge possessed by researcher and researched and the role of the researcher in handling and responding to these.

To say that researcher and researched have a different relation to the research situation is only to restate the obvious, but this difference has extremely profound implications. However, since such effects sometimes become obscured or forgotten in the temptation to create a reciprocal relation, it is important to keep well aware of them. For example, in my own case I took an assembly line job in order to learn something, whereas the other women were there in order to earn a living. My survival strategy in response to the pace and tedium of the job was to try to understand the occupational structure, the labour process and so on, whereas my co-workers had quite other strategies. I was there to know, and I learned from them, but they had no interest in producing anything written or for external consumption from what they knew of the set-up. And why should they when it was me who was concerned with analyzing women's work? Although we sat and talked about our lives all day this was not a form of consciousness-raising; even though the topics covered might have been similar, the purpose of the discussion was largely for social interaction and to pass the time. It was not a collective enterprise in producing knowledge. The eventual output in the form of the book was accessible to and of interest to only a narrow range of people, and not to those it was about.

In the oral history interview situation similar considerations also apply.[8] The researcher defines the subjects to be covered and poses the questions in a particular way. She is not entering the lives of her interviewees in the long term and again there can be little question of developing collective knowledge. She initiates the interview and runs it on her terms and for her purposes; she determines what goes on in it and what she does with the material she acquires. The researcher selects from it in order to answer *her* questions. They are not the questions of the interviewees, and the interviewees are not writing it up. They are likely to have quite other interests in their life stories than what the researcher treats as significant and they are not in a position to appreciate why certain points are more significant to the researcher than others. Nor in most instances would they probably care. What is in it for them is never what is in it for you. Even if they were interested it is usually not for the *knowledge* of it.

To illustrate, one problem that I encountered when doing interviews for my project on mass production in the inter-war period in the London area was to keep the people I was interviewing off the subject of the Second World War. Once they started talking about this it was disastrous because I could rarely get them back to describing their working life before the war. Clearly their experiences of the blitz and evacuation were far more significant, or at least memorable, than boring assembly line work. But my project was not about the war, nor a life-history project, and although interesting in themselves and for another project their accounts of what happened to them during the war were of little relevance for me at the time.

This very different relation to the research process is an inevitable feature of research. But while conventional value-neutral observers of the traditional variety had no problem with it, feminist researchers have found it much more difficult to accept. Hence the temptation to mistake good rapport or a friendly woman-to-woman interview or lively discussion about some of the topics for reciprocality or equal involvement in the research process, rather than coming to terms with the fact that a 'good' interview is no more or no less than that. The researcher might come away with a good feeling but does the interviewee?[9]

These considerations apply even when those being interviewed are interested in the process for their own reasons and do take an active role in determining what subjects are covered. In fact several of the people I interviewed in the Greater Manchester research were writing up their own autobiographies or were involved in local oral history projects. I was really struck when a group of women I turned up to interview in Salford greeted me saying that they had seen me before – in the local history library. They had been looking up newspapers from the 1930s on microfilm to find out what films had been showing at the local cinemas as material for a play they were writing about life in Salford before the war to be performed in old people's homes! They talked enthusiastically about the value of preserving the past and made many helpful suggestions about other things I should find out about the area and gave names of other people to contact. They were quite at home with the interview situation and more or less ran it themselves after I had explained what I was interested in, asking each other questions and prompting each other on particular subjects.

It was in many ways an ideal interview with active participation by the interviewees, yet despite all of this what came out of it was not a collective production of knowledge. What I found most significant from their testimony was not what was most significant to them. I reinterpreted what they said, for instance about married women's employment, in the light of other documentary evidence and in comparison with the accounts of what women in Bolton had said about the same subject. This group of Salford women were adamant that there had been very little work for married women before the war; they all defined themselves primarily as mothers and wives (in that order) and talked at length about their work in the home. Yet all turned out to have engaged in full-time paid work for virtually the whole of their married lives, though mostly in casual and multiple part-time jobs. But they hardly spoke about this. The women in Bolton, on the other hand, were mostly retired weavers who had carried on the established tradition of married women working, farming out their children to relatives or neighbours while they were at work. This group spoke in detail about all the mills they had worked in and about changes in the industry. But they were not at all forthcoming about their domestic labour or about problems in organizing their domestic lives. From the point of view of my project, which was looking at the effects of employment on the domestic division of labour, it was the contrast between these two groups which highlighted what was specific about each and their very different relation to domesticity and to paid employment. *My* problem was to analyze and explain this difference. On the other hand, in order for this to have become a collective enterprise in producing knowledge and mutual understanding, the women of Bolton would have had to talk to the women of Salford. By the time I wrote up my conclusions I had filtered their experience through a number of different sieves and interpreted it in the light of material culled from a variety of other sources. Even when the women took an active interest in the research process or asked, as several did, whether others had recounted experiences similar to theirs and what differences I found between south-east and north-west England, there was no getting away from the fact that it was my project, and not theirs, and I was 'using' their experience as raw material for my analysis. How much can be drawn from 'experience' and the problems of interpreting it represent another problematic issue for oral history to which I shall return.

To summarize, whatever interest those being researched have in the content or procedure of the research process their relation to it is quite other than that of the researcher whose prime object, unlike theirs, is to produce knowledge, even if she intends to 'give it back' in some form. However much the researcher aims to avoid treating the people she is researching as 'objects', and however 'good' the rapport appears to be, there can be no getting away from the fact that those being researched are the 'subjects' of the research. The line between being a subject and an object in this context is a pretty fine one, and exists, more likely than not, only in the researcher's head.

Divisions of Knowledge

The second dimension of the inequality of knowledge in the research situation derives from socially determined structural divisions in knowledge between people formed in society at large. These divisions in knowledge (amount of formal education, qualifications and credentials; skills possessed; type of vocational or professional training etc.) are integral to the division of labour of industrial societies. Some people have much greater access than others to knowledge and the economic and social power that accompanies it. Some people specialize in producing knowledge, others in disseminating and reproducing it, others in consuming it, while many do not engage in any of these activities.

Divisions in knowledge exist alongside the other social divisions of class, gender and race, overlaying and crisscrossing them. Constituting as they do a distinct form of inequality, they must also be recognized as one (amongst others) of the sources of division between women. As such they necessarily affect the research process. To put it bluntly the feminist researcher is usually a highly formally educated intellectual whose work is to read, think, write and ultimately produce knowledge. But the same is not usually the case for the many working-class people who are studied by academic oral historians.[10] Inequalities in knowledge of this kind are bound to enter into the interpretation of oral testimony as well as into the interview situation itself, though they will vary considerably in significance depending on the degree of social distance between researcher and researched.

Again this is a rather self-evident point but it does affect how researchers use and interpret their interviewees' testimony. This was brought forcefully home to me for example in attempting to analyze the dynamics of gender subordination in mass production work. I could not rely for my explanation entirely on the women assemblers' own understanding of their situation, precisely because a central aspect of their subordination was that they acquired only a fragmented and partial knowledge of the assembly line process as a whole. One reason for this was that a defining characteristic of the labour process was to put into practice Taylorist principles of dividing conception from execution, and subdividing functions into separate tasks in a minutely detailed division of labour. Assemblers usually operated only one or two machines and were only given enough information to operate these. They had little knowledge of the process as a whole or of the functions of other grades of workers, especially of those higher than themselves in the hierarchy. Thus one clear instance of gender inequality on the shop floor was that of knowledge: men controlled the machinery, which included knowing more about the production process, while women operated it. This lack of formal knowledge was further compounded by the fact of being tied to a particular place in the line all day and not moving around the different parts of the factory: the assembly line also subdivided women's experiences.

But in addition – and this is a different sense of inequality of knowledge – their knowledge and understanding of their situation was from their standpoint. The knowledge of the male supervisors who controlled the line, though broader than that of the women, was also from their own standpoint, that of an overseer. And similar points could be made about the accounts that labourers or engineers or managers would have given of the production process and work force; it was all from a particular position or standpoint.[11] In the conflict-ridden situation of the factory, where different groups of workers did have quite objectively distinct interests deriving from their place in the division of labour (for example the supervisors had an interest in assemblers working as fast as possible since the size of their wage was linked to output), the 'standpoint' nature of knowledge was particularly pronounced.[12]

So how was I to document and analyze the subordination of women assemblers? Clearly the women were not in a position to give an overall picture of the labour process, nor, by implication, of exactly how they were dominated by it. On the other hand it was me, rather than them, who was primarily interested in constructing a knowledge of women's subordination at work. Even though my aim was to privilege their situation, my analysis could not be based on their account alone. 'Telling it like it was' as they recounted it could only have reproduced the women's own fragmented experience. It had to be complemented by material from a number of other sources, sources which – and this is significant in view of the inequalities of knowledge – I, unlike the assemblers, was in a position to acquire and to which I had relatively easy access because of my particular training and status.

These included interviews with supervisors and managers, company archive material, surveys and other documentary data from the inter-war period, trades union journals, census data and other official statistics, a whole range of secondary data and so on. So in writing about the domination of women assemblers I deployed many different sources and kinds of data, and synthesized them into an analysis which attempted to explain the assemblers' position and indicated why they experienced it in the way that they described. Their accounts were thus the primary, but by no means the only, material relevant to generating an understanding of the dynamics by which they were subordinated. In this way the arguments that I developed were 'multi-sourced' and welded from different elements. Although my approach was from a committed standpoint I would argue that the resulting analysis referred to socio-structural divisions (as opposed to divisions only of interpretation, experience or standpoint) by attempting to explain its subject matter from the outside with the aid of substantiating data rather than just accepting at face value what the women said. To have done the latter would not have done the women any favours.

Epistemological Debates and Historical Method

The foregoing discussion has hinted that the use of people's accounts of their past 'experience' has definite limitations and involves specific epistemological problems relating both to the use of 'accounts' and of 'experience' as the basis for constructing theory. It may be worth addressing some of these directly before turning to more practical issues since I have already argued implicitly for a particular epistemological position.

Oral testimony could never, by its very nature, provide an unmediated account of anything. The experience is mediated by memory, and the memory by the circumstances in which it is elicited. Until recently oral historians accepted this limitation as part and parcel of building up popular memory as a means of recovering 'lost' voices from the past. But the impact of postmodern philosophy and deconstructionism has resulted in fundamental questioning of procedures hitherto considered unproblematic.

This is not the place to embark on an extended discussion of these philosophical positions and I want only, and very briefly, to situate the method of multi-sourcing outlined earlier among other approaches to oral history which vary considerably in the weight given to experience as a basis for knowledge. Presenting it schematically they could be said to range on a continuum from, at one end, frameworks which accept people's memories of experience at face value and as the basis for an account of the past, to, at the other end, the position that such data represents only what it is, people's memories of experience, and cannot provide a route to knowledge of 'the' past. In the former case researchers would attempt to let the oral evidence 'speak for itself' while in the latter no claims for meaning would be made for it other than as a text. At this end of the continuum there are also important differences: so for those who believe that there is no way of moving from representation to what is being represented the problems are of one kind. However, for those who believe that there is no referent either, but only statements and sentences (in this case, no such thing as society but only myriad discourses) the problems are quite other. But for both there would be no possibility of critical assessment, by reference to material external to the discourse, of the relation between discursive and extra-discursive events.

An alternative position, at a tangent to this continuum, is the hermeneutic approach, which concentrates on the meaning that the action or experience, or the memory of it, holds for the actor. The aim is to arrive at an understanding of the consciousness of reality/the world/the past and the meaning people ascribe to these rather than of the reality itself. This method, with its long and respectable tradition in mainstream sociology, is enjoying a new vogue in perhaps unexpected quarters. However feminists adopting this framework[13] insist on the role of the researcher and the nature of the research process being conceptualized as an integral part of the outcome of the research. (Here feminist reflexivity is at odds with the traditional approach which maintains the desirability of detached value-neutrality on the part of the researcher and the possibility of producing objective findings unaffected by the interests or role of the researcher.) The feminist injunction is the principled response to the belief that researchers together with their research subjects construct a negotiated reality, on the premise that there is no one reality, that it is always mediated by the meaning it holds for the actor, that it is always constructed, that there are multiple constructions and all may be equally valid. Close attention is paid to the dynamics of the research process and to the participation of the researcher in the construction of reality. The researcher's own responses and understandings, and the meanings it has for her, thus become integral components of the final product.

But, for those caught up more closely with contemporary philosophical concerns, the quest for subjective meaning may be abandoned altogether in favour of approaching testimony in quite other ways. One alternative is for historians to treat it as a form of myth-making about the past. In this case they would deal with memories qua myths, and attempt to study people's mythical construction of the past.[14] A different alternative, especially for those who have rejected (along with the referent) 'the grand narrative' in favour of the 'little story', is to treat oral testimony purely as discourse. In this case the transcript becomes a text, to be analyzed as such, in linguistic or other terms.[15] It stands alongside other cultural products, as a text amenable to methods akin to those of literary criticism or discourse analysis.

But – rephrasing here arguments made above about the limits on what can be gleaned from accounts of experience and their value as one source amongst many – since my research interests lie principally in the realm of the extra-discursive, I attempt to construct an external referent by which to assess the testimony as discourse. So in terms of these debates my position is more 'realist' and retains aspects of 'grand narrative'. I attempt to create an overall structure of discursive and extra-discursive reality, into which I slot testimony along with other evidence. Moreover my frame of reference is external to that of the subjects of my research while permitting interpretation of their frame of reference. So, for example, while an assembly line structures and subdivides discourses, I find it more reasonable to theorize it predominantly as existing for the production of material objects under particular economic relations, and to situate the discursive interpretations, including my own, within an overall extra-discursive reality. Developing an alternative reference to the same referent would seem to be an essential requirement for a critical appreciation of what people say. Otherwise, the only alternatives would be to accept it at face value or to treat it as a text, and both of these would imply abandonment of analysis at the level of social structure altogether.

Practicalities and Ethics

Although these fundamental questions were at the back of my mind while actually doing the interviews my immediate concerns were in fact much more mundane. The sort of practical problems that I encountered probably confront everyone doing similar research, but precisely those problems that demanded the most attention never seemed to be dealt with in methods textbooks. Perhaps this is because they sound so obvious, if not silly, when written down. So at the risk of restating the obvious I shall turn now to some of these practicalities under three broad headings: finding people to interview, handling the interview situation, and the ethics of the data-processing stage.

Finding People to Interview

My most time-consuming problem was undoubtedly finding the women that I wanted to interview. In the first oral history project these were women in the south-east who had worked on assembly lines before the war. So the youngest were now going to be in their mid seventies and most in their eighties. The pattern of employment had been for women to leave factory work on marriage or at the birth of their first child. So many would have stopped being assemblers before 1939. Even if, as in a sizeable minority of cases, they had continued in employment until retirement age, they would still have retired at least fifteen years before the time of interview. The most difficult problem was therefore to locate such women. In a more self-contained industrial town or smaller community with which you, as researcher, are familiar, finding such women might not pose much problem but I had no knowledge whatsoever of the southern suburbs of London which turned out, after much searching, to be the most suitable for my purposes. In the end my contacts were made through a variety of means: community and company-based pensioners' organizations, sheltered accommodation, local firms, relatives of friends.[16] But to say this belies the hundreds of telephone calls, the numerous letters written (many unanswered), the newspaper advertisements placed, the enquiries to trades unions and voluntary organizations and the many other leads that led nowhere. This stage took months and I often despaired of ever finding anyone. Even after I had got on the right track many was the occasion when the person I turned up to interview had worked before the war but not in a factory or if in a factory then in the office or canteen rather than on the shop floor!

In the later project on the north-west I also had to start from scratch since I had hardly ever been to Bolton, Oldham or Salford before. Naively I imagined that it would be easier to locate people there than in London and I started off with great expectations of interviewing pairs of mothers and daughters who had engaged in factory work in the 1930s and 1950s. Again, the first three or four months of a one-year project were consumed in familiarizing myself with the subject and area and trying to set up interviews. Eventually I had to give up the search for 'the' definitive labour history of women's work in the Manchester area which would provide all the essential background information and just accept that it did not exist. I also found it very wearing to have to make phone calls to so many different kinds of people and explain my project in terms that made sense to them. You have to be in the right mood and feeling self-confident which I often was not after not getting anywhere by the tenth call of the day. In the end my expectations had to alter: although I did interview one mother and daughter pair of 96 and 72, and included questions about mothers and daughters in all of the other interviews, the women I found to interview had engaged in a wider variety of jobs than I had really wanted and many more in textiles. I am also now convinced that if I had stood in Salford precinct or Bolton market wearing a sandwich board saying who I wanted to contact I would have found as many, or more, suitable interviewees as through the more conventional and laborious methods.

Linked to finding the women to interview was the problem of how to introduce myself to them, and here I probably contravened all the rules. I found that formality in describing the project, or sending the customary letter explaining myself and guaranteeing them confidentiality definitely put some people off, somehow suggesting to them that there might be something to hide, and making them reluctant to take part. Similarly, while several of those who lived on council estates were worried about admitting any stranger into their flat for fear of burglary or attack and wanted identification, others became nervous at anything official-sounding or on headed paper. So flexibility in presenting myself – appearing non-threatening while at the same time being above board – was all-important. Although some did want to remain anonymous I was surprised that many in fact actively wanted their actual names to appear. They seemed genuinely pleased to see themselves in print and quite a number voiced the opinion that people like them, or the sorts of work that they did, were vary rarely written about and they wanted the real details to be included.

Handling the Interview Situation

The interview itself also presented a challenge, of gaining as much information as possible in the short time available. I found that an hour was around the maximum optimal time, and since it took some time getting into it (and usually having a cup of tea), there was probably not much more than half to three-quarters of an hour of 'prime' time. The presence of the husband was an occasional obstacle: sometimes the woman kept deferring to him and let him answer questions put to her or he just took over. I discovered that the best policy if he would not keep quiet was to interview him too and do them in turn. The worst occasion was when the husband sat in the room throughout the session with his head hidden behind a newspaper, having a silent but definite impact on interviewer and interviewee!

I alluded earlier to the problem of going off the subject: it is tricky when people start talking about things that are more significant to them than the content of your questions to get back on the track without being rude. However it was easier if the subject was the blitz or something external than if it was personal or emotional, bereavement in many cases, and rape in a few. Often then I gave up on what I had actually come for. On the other hand many of the women were lonely and wanted company and then it could be awkward to leave, even after staying to chat for some time, and this often induced guilt feelings about 'using' them. Some people said the best things after the tape recorder had been switched off, and some would only answer 'yes' or 'no' to questions and required constant prompting.

My own experience of factory work undoubtedly helped me to speak in words that were understandable to the retired women I was interviewing. I felt more manipulative, and that I was playing a part, when adapting my language to ask retired managers or engineers about their 'female operatives'. I remember feeling particularly ill-at-ease (internally) when interviewing the managing director of a company in a local Conservative club under a large portrait of Margaret Thatcher. To him I was the brisk professional concerned with industrial efficiency. But I suspect that being a credible actor must be a part of all qualitative interviewing.

The Ethics of the Data-Processing Stage

The final point that I want to make is that ethical considerations enter equally, if not more, into the stage of processing the data as into the interview situation. Usually the researcher has sole access to and total control over the tapes or transcripts. No one else oversees which parts she selects as of significance. For instance, in making excerpts it is only too easy to place together quotations from different sections of the interview so giving much stronger emphasis to a point than if each quotation stood alone. While there is some external constraint on ethical standards in the actual collection of data, there is very little over what is done with the material. Each researcher is left on trust to draw the difficult line between interpreting the data in terms of its relevance to her research questions as opposed to twisting it in a way that amounts to a misrepresentation of what was said. Showing the end result, as opposed to the unedited transcript, to the people whom it was based on is one way of guarding against this. But basically the problem remains, inherent in the structure of the research process as discussed above, and the fact that it is the researcher's project rather than a collective one. But I feel there should be just as much of an ethical question mark over the use made of interview material as over how it was elicited.

In the course of my two projects many people with whom I would not normally have come into contact welcomed me into their homes and lives. What I learned from them often led me to change my ideas and pursue new questions (housing conditions and contraception) or some areas in much greater depth (the technology and economics of clothes washing). What I eventually wrote up was undoubtedly better for their suggestions about the project as well as for their personal testimony. It remains a supreme irony to me that in contemporary political circumstances, and in spite of my wish to contribute to a politics of abolishing gender subordination affecting these and other women, the research is probably of greater benefit to me than to them, in the short term at least. I have to believe that things might change in the long run.

Conclusion

In conclusion, given that the structural inequalities of gender remain as persistent as ever (if not more entrenched) in a politically quiescent period such as we have experienced in Britain in recent years, the importance of developing a thorough historical understanding of their dynamics remains central for the consolidation of a politics of transforming them. Even, or especially, during a period of social fragmentation and political dissipation, I feel that it is necessary to resist the tendency of such processes to invade or overwhelm attempts to achieve a broad and long-term historical perspective. It is this belief that has underpinned the research that I have been describing, my use of diverse methods and sources, and my focus on the changing conditions and experience of working-class women's labour.

But the relationship between knowledge and politics will necessarily differ in circumstances when there is an active and widespread women's movement and when there is not. In the former case the possibility may exist for developing knowledge in a more collective way and less academically and individually, and also for there to be a positive connection between 'theory and practice'. In the latter case the onus falls on feminist researchers neither, on the one hand, to succumb to defeatism, nor, on the other, to confuse research practice for feminist politics, but to recognize the more attenuated relation between the theoretical work we do and any social transformation for what it is.

Notes

1 For a critical overview of debates on feminist epistemology see Mary Maynard's discussion in chapter 1 above; Stanley (1990a); and Harding (1991).
2 This comment applies to several of the contributions in Roberts (1981) and in Bell and Roberts (1984). See also Stanley and Wise (1983).
3 Sociological research methods and ethics generally appear to have learned much from feminism here, despite the frequently rehearsed argument (expressed, for example, by Hammersley (1992)), that there is nothing distinctive about feminist methods since all 'good' research is in fact characterized by similar practices. Whilst this may well be so, it is nevertheless significant that the argument is so often made as a defensive stance against feminist sociology.
4 The book appeared under a pseudonym: R. Cavendish (1982). The legal problems are instructive in themselves. When writing up my experiences I deliberately used the real name of the factory, the area, and the product and I included a discussion both of the industry and the local employment structure. All this had, eventually, to be removed, and the products, labour process, workers, firm, location and myself disguised so as to be unrecognizable. British libel law places the onus of proof on the author, and the original publisher was not prepared to take the risk of libel action. If charged the only admissible evidence I could have used in defence would have been already published material, which was non-existent. Alternatively the workers could have been called as witnesses. Obviously I did not even consider this – it would have guaranteed them the sack. Although my intention had not been to single out the particular company for special criticism (indeed it was typical of many others) an account of a factory located in its actual geographical and industrial context could have been of some practical use to local feminists and trades unionists. Ironically, and in spite of all the measures taken to ensure anonymity, an excerpt was quoted in one of the tabloid newspapers soon after publication which immediately identified the factory at least to those working there!
5 Glucksmann (1990).
6 This project was made possible by the award of a Hallsworth Senior Research Fellowship at the University of Manchester Department of Sociology in 1990–1.

7 This differs considerably from that described by Ann Oakley, to take one very well known example. She emphasized the shared nature of her own and her interviewees' experiences of childbirth which enabled her to be a source of information and support for them and to make the research process into more of an interactive endeavour. See Oakley (1981).

8 These remarks refer specifically to academic oral history. More generally understood oral history comprises a broad variety of activities, including community projects, people's autobiography, or reminiscence therapy, all of which take different forms and are conducted on a different basis from academic research. I should like to thank Mike Roper for helpful comments on current debates in oral history.

9 I certainly did not come away feeling good on the occasion when I was on the other side of the microphone being interviewed about my involvement in the student movement of the late 1960s. In fact I felt awful afterwards. I had dredged my memory for what the interviewer wanted to know: what I had thought *then* about various political arguments and strategies and why. All sorts of memories were churned up and then left up in the air without being resolved. Also I found it very hard to refrain from saying what I *now* thought in hindsight about what had happened then and only talk as if it were still in the present. And of course I did not know whether the researcher thought it was a good interview.

10 The situation would of course be different if the research was about people similar to the researcher in education and profession. But very few research those in a superior position to their own. It is much easier to 'equalize' downwards than upwards!

11 While working in the motor components factory I nearly fell off my stool one day to see an erstwhile academic colleague who was an industrial sociologist being taken on a guided tour of the shop floor. On comparing notes later we could have been in different factories. Even the firm's official account of its employment policies and wages structure was completely at odds with what I knew.

12 Clearly, no suggestion could seriously be made here that adding up the accounts from all the different standpoints would somehow lead to the 'truth'. Put like this it is obvious that there is none. But I would also reject the relativism that would result from recognizing all standpoints as equally valid.

13 For examples of this approach see the accounts in Stanley (1990a); Smith (1988a); and for the same argument as applied to auto/biography, Stanley (1990c).

14 See especially Samuel and Thompson (1990), Introduction and Part I; also Popular Memory Group (1982).

15 Many examples of this approach can be found in issues of the journals *Oral History* and *History Workshop* from the mid 1980s onwards. For feminist discussion of this and related matters see Gluck and Patai (1991), and, for an anthropological approach, Tonkin (1992).

16 See Glucksmann (1990), pp. 24–5 for a more detailed account of finding interviewees.

Chapter 9

Doing Feminist Women's History: Researching the Lives of Women in the Suffragette Movement in Edwardian England

June Purvis

Introduction

My aim in this chapter is to discuss some of the problems I have encountered when undertaking research into the suffragette movement in Edwardian England, especially the Women's Social and Political Union (WSPU), founded on 10 October 1903 by Mrs Emmeline Pankhurst and her eldest daughter, Christabel, with the expressed aim of obtaining votes for women on equal terms with men.[1] In particular, for illustrative purposes, I shall focus upon the experience of prison life for those WSPU members who were jailed as a result of activities they engaged in when fighting for the right of women to enfranchisement. My account of this process is inevitably influenced by contemporary debates about what is 'feminist' women's history and so some discussion, albeit brief, of this concept is necessary.

Feminist Women's History in England

The growth of recent interest in feminist women's history may be traced to the somewhat inaccurately called 'second wave' of the organized women's movement in Western Europe and the USA from the late 1960s. As feminists at that time analyzed the oppression, subordination and inequalities that women experienced in society, many turned to the past to explore the lives of our foremothers. In particular, in England, some feminists within socialist/ marxist circles wrote influential texts that explored how history had been largely written by men and focused upon male agency, male activities and male experiences. Of particular importance was Sheila Rowbotham's book *Hidden From History: 300 Years of Women's Oppression and the Fight Against It*, first published in 1973 and generally regarded as being the catalyst for the growth of research into women's lives in the past.[2] Since that time there has been an outpouring of publications making visible women's lives in the past, some of these accounts being more explicitly feminist than others.

In England, then, the growth of feminist women's history in the 1970s and 1980s was especially intertwined with socialist politics, the views of radical feminist historians, such as Dale Spender, Elizabeth Sarah and Sheila Jeffreys, being very much a 'minority voice'.[3] While some argued for a separate *her*story others hoped for a grander rewriting of the historical record. During the 1980s, however, as the Women's Movement became much more fragmented, an awareness grew of how the division into the usual 'Big Three' perspectives – socialist, radical and liberal feminism – excluded other feminisms.[4] In particular, black and lesbian feminists raised key questions about racism and heterosexuality, pointing out how their experiences as women had been marginalized in both feminist theory and practice.[5] As the differences between women began to be voiced, feminist women's history (and Women's Studies) became much more separate from political struggles than had been the case earlier when the commonalities that all women shared were emphasized.

Such debates were not impervious to developments in the United States where feminist women's history had a much stronger foothold in the academy than in this country. However, by the 1990s, the situation had changed there too as the discipline became less feminist and more descriptive, shifting to what we may more accurately term 'women's history', that is, a history that takes women as its subject matter but is not necessarily informed by the ideas and theories that would constitute a feminist analysis. The reasons for this are many, not least being the 'turn to culture', to post-structuralism, postmodernism and deconstruction within the broad interdisciplinary field of Women's Studies and the erosion, generally, of historical influence.[6]

Debates in the USA about 'transforming' feminist women's history through focusing on gender rather than women, through studying language and discourses rather than material reality and experience, and through deconstructing the term 'women' and concentrating upon the differences between women rather than their commonalities, have profound implications for the future development of the field.[7] Although I do not have the space within the confines of this chapter to explore in depth such complex issues, I wish to argue firstly that we must bring women 'back' into feminist women's history and study them as women, and secondly, that we must study the material forces that have shaped their lives and experiences, even though these experiences may be mediated through the 'lenses' of the individuals' own histories, ideologies and cultures.[8] Finding out about women's daily experiences and, therefore, where possible, finding women's own words in the past is a critical aspect of 'feminist' research.[9]

These ideas, then, some of which I shall refer to later in this chapter and in the conclusion, are the thoughts that inform this account of researching the prison experiences of suffragettes in Edwardian England from a 'feminist' perspective.

Consultation of Sources

I began my task by consulting relevant secondary sources and then moving into a careful perusal of the primary texts. Although the dividing line between a 'primary' and a 'secondary' source is somewhat arbitrary, the former is usually regarded as a text that came into being during the period of the past that is being researched while the latter is usually seen as a text that is produced much later than the events being studied, offering an interpretation and conversion of the primary data into an account that may be consulted by others. Secondary sources are especially useful for giving an overview of themes related to the proposed research, and for also providing many references to primary sources that might be followed. Such references are especially helpful since historical work is generally esteemed to be 'serious and scholarly' to the extent that it is based on original primary sources.[10]

Consultation of Secondary Sources

The first WSPU act that ended in imprisonment is well documented in the secondary sources. On the evening of 13 October 1905, Christabel Pankhurst and Annie Kenney, a young working-class factory worker, attended a Liberal Party meeting held in the Free Trade Hall, Manchester. One of the speakers, Sir Edward Grey, had already been sent a request to receive a deputation from the WSPU in support of women's enfranchisement, but no reply, as expected, had been received. At the meeting, Annie and then Christabel asked the question 'Will the Liberal government give women the vote?'[11] The women were told to put the question in writing since it could then be dealt with during question time – which did not happen. Undaunted, Annie then unfurled a white calico banner on which was written 'Votes for Women' and asked again, 'Will the Liberal government give women the vote?' The women were forcibly removed from the hall. Outside the auditorium, Christabel spat at a policeman, an act that she knew would constitute a technical assault and thus bring the issue of women's enfranchisement 'into Court, into prison'.[12] For their offences, Christabel was sentenced to a fine of 10s 6d or seven days' imprisonment and Annie to 5s or three days; both chose prison.

This assertive questioning of leading members of the Liberal Party who were expected to form the next government in the 1906 general election was one of the early and innovative strategies adopted by the WSPU in its demands for votes for women on equal terms with men. Other activities used at this time also broke the taboo on female modesty and could result in arrest and imprisonment. These included demonstrations, mass marches, deputations to the House of Commons, public meetings and street-corner speaking. However, it was especially from 1912, when more extreme forms of militancy, such as attacks on public buildings and art treasures, arson, vandalizing pillar-boxes, and widespread window-breaking took place that arrest and imprisonment became most common and newsworthy.[13] Although property was attacked, the aim was never to endanger human life.

These so-called 'militant' activities are often contrasted in the secondary sources with the law-abiding, 'constitutional' means adopted by the much larger National Union of Women's Suffrage Societies (NUWSS), formed in 1897 and led by Millicent Garrett Fawcett.[14] From 1905 until the outbreak of the First World War in 1914 about 1,000 women and about 40 men were sent to prison because of their suffrage activities, although not all of these prisoners were WSPU members.[15] On 2 July 1909, Marion Wallace Dunlop, an artist, authoress and WSPU member, was sentenced to one month's imprisonment in the Second Division (where suffragettes were commonly placed) for defacing the wall of St Stephen's Hall. She asked to be treated as a political offender and thus to be placed in the First Division, the common location for all political prisoners. When her request was refused, she began, on her own initiative, a hunger strike. After striking for ninety-one hours, she was released. The action she had taken, however, was soon adopted by others; indeed, by August, hunger striking was the normal practice of imprisoned suffragettes.[16]

In October of that year, a new policy of forcible feeding of suffrage prisoners who refused food was initiated in Winson Green Gaol, Birmingham. That too became common practice over the next four and a half years until, with the outbreak of war in August 1914, the WSPU ceased all militant action. Forcible feeding was justified by the government as a means of 'saving' the life of those who refused nourishment, of 'preserving' a prisoner's health, and of 'preventing', in the case of death through starvation, a charge of manslaughter.[17] Under the Prisoners' Temporary Discharge for Ill-Health Act, rushed through parliament in April 1913, forcible feeding became even more of an ordeal for those subjected to it since the new Act allowed prisoners who had damaged their own health through their own conduct to be released into the community and then, once fit, to be re-arrested to continue their sentence. Under the 'Cat and Mouse Act', as it became known, a 'mouse' weakened by hunger striking and forcible feeding could be released, often for a period of five to seven days, in order to regain sufficient strength to be re-arrested and then freed again, until the full sentence was served.

The descriptions of these prison experiences in the secondary sources tend to follow a particular pattern. One of the earliest and most influential accounts of the suffrage movement was written by a participant and observer who, as a member of the constitutional NUWSS, was critical of the militant politics of the WSPU. Ray Strachey's *'The Cause': A Short History of the Women's Movement in Great Britain*, first published in hardback in 1928 and then reprinted in a widely accessible and much cited paperback by Virago in 1978, presents the WSPU as engaging in 'propaganda', its deliberate policy being to seek 'sensational achievement rather than anything else'.[18] Its leaders 'did not care' whom they shocked and antagonized and 'deliberately put themselves in the position of outlaws dogged by the police'.[19]

Not surprisingly, Strachey blames the WSPU women themselves for their treatment in prison with what Dodd has termed an 'illiberal callousness'.[20] Unwilling to acknowledge the hunger strike as a political strategy, she sees the torture and agonies of forcible feeding as the victims' fault. The prisoners 'struggled so violently against it', she suggests, that the process became 'dangerous' and the prison officials were 'obliged' to let them starve till they came to the edge of physical collapse, and then to let them go.[21] Although Strachey's account was not the 'first' history of the suffrage movement, it was one of the most widely read.[22] Consequently its narrative with the 'naming of heroines and villains' was repeated at regular intervals in other suffrage accounts.[23] Even Rosen, in what has been called a 'definitive study'[24] of the WSPU, speaks in a matter-of-fact way of how forcible feeding involved mouths being prised open, lacerations, phlegm, vomiting, pain in various organs, loss of weight 'and so on'.[25]

The few secondary sources that deviate from this dominant, although not exclusive,[26] narrative present a very different picture of prison life since they attempt to present the case from the viewpoint of the militants themselves. Thus in 1973, Raeburn concluded that the suffragettes 'were cruelly persecuted and misrepresented for their efforts to achieve basic equality'[27] while, some twelve and fifteen years later respectively, the well-known feminist historians, Martha Vicinus and Liz Stanley, also present sympathetic accounts. Vicinus offers a compelling analysis of the way the suffragettes believed that only by giving their bodies for the women's cause through such public activities as going on delegations, speaking on soapboxes, selling literature – and ultimately, for many, the bodily sacrifice of prison and hunger striking – would they win the necessary spiritual victory that would enable them to enter the male political world.[28] Stanley, in a life of Emily Wilding Davison, the WSPU militant who died on 8 June 1913 as a result of injuries sustained four days earlier when, at the Derby races, she ran onto the course and fell under the hooves of the King's horse, explores the way the WSPU operated as a feminist organization through women's friendship networks.[29]

The work of these three authors in particular convinced me that there was a fuller story to tell about the prison experiences of the suffragettes. Thus I went back to the primary sources and read personal texts of the women themselves – such as unpublished and published letters, unpublished and published testimonies, and published autobiographies.

Consultation of Primary Personal Sources

Although prison conditions might vary, depending on the year in which the sentence was served and upon local variations and personnel, common admission procedures stripped the individual of self-identification. On entry to Holloway in 1908, for example, the women were immediately called to silence by the wardresses, locked in reception cells, and then sent to the doctor before they were ordered to undress. Once they had been searched to make sure they concealed nothing, their own clothes were stored by the authorities and details requested about name, address, age, religion and profession and whether she could read, write and sew. A bath was then taken. Although each bather was separated from the next by a partition, low doors enabled wardresses to overlook such a private bodily funtion. Once dried, the prisoner was told to dress herself from clothes lying in piles on the floor. Second-class prisoners wore green serge dresses, third-class brown. All had white caps, blue and white check aprons, and one big blue and white handkerchief a week. Every garment was branded in several places, black on light things, white on dark, with a broad arrow. Underclothing was coarse and ill-fitting; shoes were heavy and clumsy and rarely in pairs while the thick and shapeless stockings, black with red stripes going round the legs, had no garters or suspenders to keep them up. On the way to her cell, the prisoner was given sheets for the bed, a toothbrush (if she asked for it), a Bible, prayer book and hymn book, a small book on 'Fresh Air and Cleanliness' and a tract entitled 'The Narrow Way'. Once in the cell, which might be about 9 feet high and either about 13 feet by 7 feet or 10 feet by 6 feet, she was given a yellow badge bearing the number of her cell and the letter and number of its block in the prison. From now until her release, the inmate would be known only by her cell's number.[30]

Prison regulations imposed a certain routine on daily life.[31] At this period in Holloway, for example, a waking-up bell rang about 5.30 a.m., an hour and three quarters before a breakfast consisting of a pint of sweet tea, a small brown loaf and two ounces of butter (which had to last all day) was handed to the prisoner in her cell. Before the daily half-hour of chapel the prisoner had to empty her slops, scrub the floor and the three planks that formed her bedstead, fold up the bedclothes into a roll and stow them away with the mattress and pillow, and polish with soap and bath-brick the tin utensils of her cell. 'Inspection' each day ensured that the task was done in the required manner. In chapel and at the daily hour of exercise in a gravelled yard, talking was not permitted. Lunch was at noon and a supper consisting of a pint of cocoa with thick grease on top plus a small brown loaf was taken at 5 p.m. The electric light in the cell was controlled from outside and turned off at 8 in the evening.

During the first four weeks of imprisonment, the rest of the prisoner's time was spent in her cell which was often airless, especially in summer; a certain amount of 'associated labour' had to be undertaken, which might involve making nightgowns or knitting men's socks. Once a week a bath was taken and twice a week books could be borrowed from the poorly stocked prison library. After four weeks, prisoners were allowed to take their needlework or knitting to the hall downstairs, which was more airy, and sit side by side, although talking was still forbidden. Those serving one month or less in the Second Division were not entitled to receive any visits from friends nor to have any correspondence with them. Special permission to visit might sometimes be obtained by making special application to the Home Office or through an MP. Those whose sentences exceeded a month were entitled to a visit at the end of a month, and on that occasion not more than three friends were allowed to see the prisoner. The prisoner was also entitled to write a letter at the end of a month's imprisonment, for which writing materials in addition to the slates and slate pencils given on admission were permitted.[32] A reply to that letter might be sent to the prison and then given to the prisoner.

While all suffragette prisoners shared with other women inmates this structuring of their daily lives (even though the formal rules were frequently subverted), their differential status was also apparent. Since it was commonly recognized that the militants did not belong to the so-called 'criminal classes'[33] they were usually segregated from the other women by being placed in separate cell blocks and being kept separate in communal activities, such as chapel and exercise. Often they were placed in the newer, lighter cells, as Maud Joachim found when she entered Holloway Gaol in 1908.[34] But above all else, the recognition of the suffragettes as 'not ordinary' inmates was marked by their collective belief in 'the cause'. As Corbett notes, it was a common identity as suffragettes that the movement forged and from which it drew its strength.[35]

Such a theme was frequently articulated by WSPU leaders and rank and file members alike. Emmeline Pankhurst, the much loved leader of the WSPU, implored in 1909 'Women! Comrades! Dear Fellow-workers! I charge you, love this Movement, work for it, live for it', in one of her powerful addresses. 'Let no thought of your own comfort and happiness hinder you from rendering it your whole service', she continued. 'Give it your thought, your time, your all.'[36] For Emmeline Pethick-Lawrence, treasurer of the WSPU and one of its leaders until ousted by Mrs Pankhurst and Christabel in 1912, women of the upper, middle and working classes found a 'new comradeship with each other' in the suffrage cause. 'Neither class, nor wealth, nor education counted any more', she claimed, 'only devotion to the common ideal'.[37] Although by 1912, when the more extreme forms of militancy were common, there was a marked decline in the rate of new members joining the WSPU,[38] time and time again suffragette prisoners testified that they endured the hardships of prison life because they believed in the movement, the feeling of collectivity that was fostered, the common bond that united all women and the dignity of women to stand up and fight for what they believed in.

Patricia Woodlock, honorary secretary of the Liverpool branch of the WSPU and imprisoned many times, did not hesitate 'to put the welfare of her sex before her own freedom'.[39] Emily Wilding Davison, imprisoned eight times, stressed that the perfect militant warrior 'will sacrifice all . . . to win the Pearl of Freedom for her sex'.[40] Mary Nesbitt, coming out of jail in 1912, emphasized, 'I was deeply impressed by the *wonderful* spirit of loyalty and love for the cause and for our leaders – all, irrespective of class, creed or age, were unwavering'.[41] Ethel Smyth, also in prison in 1912, remembered the women 'forgetful of everything save the idea for which they had faced imprisonment'.[42] For women such as these, and many more, the fight for women's enfranchisement was like a religion, the women themselves being a 'spiritual army' that sought a new way of life.[43]

Despite the sense of unity and comradeship the suffragettes felt as they faced the common external reality of prison life, however, their shared experiences were not experienced equally but fractured on a number of differences. This is not surprising given the complexity of women's lives within a radical women's political movement that was both in opposition to, and yet a part of, an Edwardian culture that expected women to be ideally located within the private sphere of the home rather than the male world of politics. Differences would also be accentuated by the fact that hunger striking and force-feeding were acts committed by, and on, individuals in their own cells. Whether force-fed by a cup, tube through the nostril (the most common method) or tube down the throat into the stomach (the most painful), the individual suffragette struggled on her own. The forcible feeding of the disabled May Billinghurst in Holloway in January 1913 brought a particular wave of revulsion since she was 'small, frail, and ha[d] been a cripple all her life'.[44] She told how the three doctors and five wardresses who held her down:

> forced a tube up my nostril; it was frightful agony, as my nostril is small. I coughed it up so that it didn't go down my throat. They then were going to try the other nostril, which, I believe, is a little deformed. They forced my mouth open with an iron instrument, and poured some food into my mouth. They pinched my nose and throat to make me swallow.[45]

After ten days of 'almost incredible suffering', when she was fed three times every twenty-four hours, she was released 'a physical wreck'.[46] For the disabled such as May, paralysed as a child and confined to a tricyle for mobility, forcible feeding was a particular act of courage.[47]

Age, too, would be another possible line of difference. The three grandmothers, Mrs Heward, Mrs Boyd and Mrs Aldham, in Holloway in 1912, as well as the 78-year-old Mrs Brackenbury, may have found prison life especially tiring.[48] And the younger women, still menstruating, may have found the supply of sanitary towels inadequate. Phyllis Keller found none available during her time of imprisonment and had to write to her mother to ask for a box of 'the old fashioned, washable sort'.[49] Yet despite the importance of such factors as age and disability in fracturing prison experiences, the personal accounts of suffragette prisoners reveal that the most commonly recorded differences related to marital status, social class background and rank within the WSPU.

Most of the suffragette prisoners appear to have been spinsters rather than married women. Of the 108 women arrested for stone-throwing after a demonstration to the House of Commons on 29 June 1909, for example, 80 were termed 'Miss' and 26 'Mrs'.[50] Yet whether married or not, the women were not separated from their lives outside the prison: the sexual politics of home, work and politics could intermesh with prison life in complex yet different ways.[51]

Single women may have worried about employers, parents, friends and lovers, and some might have had dependents. The 80 single women arrested and imprisoned for stone-throwing on 29 June 1909 included a number engaged in paid work – Miss Ivy Beach and Nellie Godfrey were both businesswomen; Sarah Carwin, Helen Grace Lenanton, Rachel Graham and Ellen Pitman were nurses; Millicent L. Brown, Alice E. Burton, Emily Wilding Davison, Florence T. Down, Elizabeth Roberts, Irene Spong and Alice M. Walters were teachers; Kitty Marion an actress; Kathleen Streatfield an artist; Jessica Walker a portrait and landscape painter; and Harriet Rozier 'a typical working women, having had to earn her bread since she was nine years old'.[52] Employers may not have looked kindly upon such behaviour, especially when it involved the inconvenience of 'absenteeism'. Florence T. Down, for example, was an elementary school teacher, and therefore particularly vulnerable to hostility since her salary was paid out of public funds.[53] Kitty Marion, the actress, could find that even one night in a cell, resulting in one missed performance, 'was sufficient to damage [the] chances of future employment'.[54]

Worries about dependents and parents must also have been common for single women. Dora Montefiore, a widow, found the visit of her daughter, who was pregnant with her first child and far from strong, a bittersweet experience. 'I could not bear that she should see me, her mother, in prison dress', wrote Dora in her autobiography.[55] She worried too about how she could send money to her son who was entirely dependent upon her financially for his engineering studies:

> The end of the month was approaching, and I had had one or two sleepless nights in prison wondering how I should send him his allowance which was due at the end of the month, and wishing at the same time I might be able to send him a message of love and of sorrow for the trouble I knew I was causing him by the publicity of my actions.[56]

When Miss Charlotte Marsh was serving a three-month prison sentence in Winson Green Prison in 1909, during which she was tube-fed 139 times, her father became dangerously ill. Although the prison authorities knew of his illness, they did not release Charlotte until 9 December, one day after they received the news that he was dying. Travelling straight to Newcastle by train, she found her father unconscious. He died without recognizing her.[57]

Married women, especially those with small children, were likely to be anxious about how their families coped in their absence. A typical example is that of Sadd Brown writing to her husband from Holloway on 16 March 1912. She had discovered in her bag a photo of her children and now kissed them every night and was glad that they were always looking at her. 'Let them know a little where I am so that they can send their loving thoughts to me', she pleaded, 'they need not think because I am shut up I have done wrong'. When she got into her narrow bed at night, her thoughts however flew to her husband '& your strong loving arms'.[58] Her undated letter to her children and Mademoiselle, written on dark brown lavatory paper, probably six days later, is especially poignant:

> My three little Darlings & Mlle
>   Mummy thanks you ever so much & also Mlle for the letters – they were such a joy & I wanted to kiss them all over – but I am going to kiss all the writers when I see them & I don't think there will be much left when I have finished. I have got such a funny little bed, which I can turn right up to the wall when I don't use it. I am learning French & German so you must work well or Mummy will know lots more than you. Next time you see Granny I want you to give her a big kiss and hug from me with lots of love – Now 1. 2. & 3 it is Mummy's bed time – so goodnight ... Lots of love & kisses
>   Mummy
> Mrs. Pankhurst thinks there is enough evidence against her to give her 7 years.
> Don't forget Matilda's bedstead.[59]

As all these accounts by single and married women reveal, prison life could be interwoven with a range of duties as wage or salary earners, daughters, friends, wives and mothers.

It is commonly assumed that suffragettes were middle-class women, 'the educated and well-to-do'.[60] Obviously working-class women, especially in comparison with leisured middle-class and upper-class women, would have less time and money to give to the cause. Nevertheless, there were a number of working-class militants. Indeed, even by 1912, nine years after the WSPU was founded, Ethel Smyth found in Holloway more than a hundred women, 'rich and poor ... young professional women ... countless poor women of the working class, nurses, typists, shop girls, and the like'.[61] These working-class women would have to rub shoulders with their more elevated sisters, such as Miss Janie Allan, a millionairess of the Allan Line, Lord Kitchener's niece Miss Parker, several cousins of Lord Haig's, Mrs Barbara Ayrton Gould (daughter of Hertha Ayrton, the scientist who invented the safety lamp for miners) and Alice Morgan Wright, an American sculptress.[62]

The official line of the prison authorities was that all prisoners were treated alike, irrespective of their class background, a claim of which some in the WSPU became very suspicious. Lady Constance Lytton, an upper-middle-class spinster, believed she had received preferential treatment in Newcastle Prison when, on hunger strike in October 1909, she was not forcibly fed and was released after only two days, officially because of her heart condition. Although Constance did indeed have a weak heart and had been, in her own words, 'more or less of a chronic invalid'[63] throughout the great part of her youth, she felt that her family background and political connections (her brother was the Earl of Lytton and a member of the House of Lords) had influenced the prison authorities; lesser known women and women in poorer health than she was had been imprisoned longer and forcibly fed. An incident later in the year confirmed her doubts. On 21 December, Selina Martin, a working-class woman of 'high character',[64] was arrested and remanded for a week in Walton Gaol, Liverpool, bail being turned down. Refusing to eat prison food, she and another working-class woman, Leslie Hall, were forcibly fed – despite the fact that it was contrary to the law for remand prisoners to be treated in this way. After being kept in chains at night, Selina was frog-marched up the steps to a cell where she was forcibly fed again. Since frog-marching involved seizing her arms and legs and carrying her head downwards, her head bumped on each step. The brutality of the incident was reported in many of the major newspapers and on the front page of the 7 January 1910 issue of *Votes for Women*.

Constance, in Manchester at the time, shared her concerns with a distressed Mary Gawthorpe, another WSPU worker, who confided that the women were 'quite unknown – nobody knows or cares about them except their own friends. They go to prison again and again to be treated like this, until it kills them!'[65] Constance determined to try out whether the prison authorities would recognize her need 'for exceptional favours' if they did not know her name.[66] Thus, after some elaborate planning, including removing her own initials from her underwear, she assumed the guise of 'Jane Warton', a working woman, and re-joined the WSPU under her new name. 'Jane Warton' protested against forcible feeding outside Walton Gaol – and was arrested. Sentenced to a fortnight in the Third Division, she went on a hunger strike.

Before the first forcible feeding, neither her heart was examined nor her pulse felt. After a struggle, the doctor managed to insert a steel gag which fastened her jaws wide apart, far more than they could go naturally, and caused intense pain. Then:

> he put down my throat a tube which seemed to me much too wide and was something like four feet in length. The irritation of the tube was excessive. I choked the moment it touched my throat until it had got down. Then the food was poured in quickly; it made me sick a few seconds after it was down and the action of the sickness made my body and legs double up, but the wardresses instantly pressed back my head and the doctor leant on my knees. The horror of it was more than I can describe. I was sick over the doctor and wardresses, and it seemed a long time before they took the tube out. As the doctor left me he gave me a slap on the cheek, not violently, but, as it were, to express his contemptuous disapproval.[67]

This scene was repeated another seven times before Constance's true identity was discovered and she was released. Although she had proved her point about the differential prison treatment of women from differing social backgrounds, she never fully recovered from her ordeal, but suffered a stroke in 1912 and died in 1923.

Class differences between women prisoners may have been more accentuated after 15 March 1910 when Rule 243a was added to the regulations governing prison life. The new rule, framed with the suffragettes in mind, permitted the Secretary of State to approve 'ameliorations . . . in respect of the wearing of prison clothing, bathing, hair-cutting, cleaning of cells, employment, exercise, books, and otherwise'.[68] Under the new rule, for example, friends and relatives outside could send in food parcels. In Holloway on 8 June 1912, Margaret Thompson went around distributing the 'much praised' shortbread she had been sent while Miss Allan put cake, strawberries and cherries on her plate.[69]

It was at this time too that the suffragette prisoners had another lesson in the ways the prison authorities could offer 'preferential' treatment to certain of their members, on this occasion according to their rank within the WSPU. When Mrs Pankhurst and Emmeline and Frederick Pethick-Lawrence were sentenced on 22 May 1912 to nine months in the Second Division, they had all proclaimed their intention of hunger striking unless they were accorded the normal rights of political offenders and transferred to the First Division. Five days after their removal there, on 15 June, the WSPU held a meeting at the Albert Hall where Mabel Tuke announced that if the government did not transfer all seventy-five WSPU members currently in prison also to the First Division, all, including the leaders, would hunger strike. The audience cheered when she told them that messages from the prisoners in Holloway, Winson Green Gaol, Birmingham, and Aylesbury Prison, would now be read out. The prisoners in Holloway were typical in expressing their sense of community and 'oneness' with each individual WSPU member:

> We, the prisoners of liberty in Holloway Gaol, send to you, the soldiers of liberty in our great campaign, our greetings and our love. We are with you in spirit, and it is our daily and hourly joy to know that the battle is being carried on without ceasing against oppression and repression. We are assured that every woman in our ranks will do her duty. We and you have put fear behind us, and those who fight against the fearless wage a losing war.[70]

When the government refused to transfer all suffragette prisoners to the First Division, the threatened hunger strike began on 19 June. Frederick Pethick-Lawrence was force-fed five times, his wife once. Mrs Pankhurst, lying in bed, very weak from starvation, was in the cell next to Emmeline Pethick-Lawrence when she heard a sudden scream come from her friend and then the sound of a prolonged and very violent struggle. 'I sprang out of bed', Mrs Pankhurst recalled in her autobiography, 'and, shaking with weakness and with anger, I set my back against the wall and waited for what might come'.[71] When the doctors and wardresses appeared at her door, she grabbed a heavy earthenware water jug from a nearby table and cried, 'If any of you dares so much as to take one step inside this cell I shall defend myself'.[72] The group retreated.

By 6 July, all the hunger strikers had been released, including forty-five women who were freed before their sentences had expired.[73] This was the last attempt made by the prison authorities to forcibly feed Emmeline Pankhurst. The government was too worried about her possible death, on their hands, and thus instant martyr status, to dare attempt such an assault again.[74]

For many of the rank and file members, the worst feature of their prison experiences was the 'public' violation of their bodies when being forcibly fed. Helen Liddle Gordon hated the lack of privacy when enduring the pain of forced feeding.[75] Nell Hall spoke of the 'frightful indignity' of it all.[76] For Sylvia Pankhurst, the sense of degradation endured was worse than the pain of sore and bleeding gums, with bits of loose jagged flesh, the agony of coughing up the tube three or four times before it was successfully inserted, the bruising of her shoulders and the aching of her back.[77] Sometimes, when the struggle was over, or even in the heat of it, she felt as though she was broken up into many different selves, of which one, aloof and calm, surveyed all the misery, and one, ruthless and unswerving, forced the weak, shrinking body to its ordeal.[78] Although the word 'rape' is not used in the personal accounts of force-fed victims, the instrumental invasion of the body, accompanied by overpowering physical force, great suffering and humiliation, was akin to it.[79] The knowledge that new tubes were not always available and that used tubes may have been previously inflicted on diseased persons and the mentally ill or be dirty inside the tube, issues that had been openly discussed in *Votes for Women*,[80] undoubtedly added to the feelings of abuse, dirtiness and indecency that the women felt. WSPU members must have greeted the news of the cessation of militancy on 13 August 1914 with great relief, although sad at the thought that the vote had not been won and at the prospect of the killing and slaughter that war would bring.[81]

Problems when Consulting and Interpreting Personal Texts

Personal texts are one of three main groupings of texts that the researcher might consult and, as I have argued elsewhere, such texts will contain an inevitable bias in the selection and presentation of content since they are written from the subjective perspective of the author(s).[82] Although I knew this, what I was not prepared for was the way the consultation and interpretation of these primary documents became very much a 'personal' involvement for me. As my research progressed I felt (and still do feel) that I had a duty to read, and make public, the words of women whose pain in the name of the feminist movement is so vividly related and whose experiences have been so misrepresented in most secondary sources. In trying to understand their lives, I reflect on my own and those of other feminists I know today. Our views too are often misrepresented, our demands for a more equal society not listened to, our full rights as citizens on equal terms with men still not achieved. In particular, as mentioned earlier, black women and lesbian women today have made us all aware of how their voices have been silenced and marginalized in feminist theory and practice. When reflecting on the present and trying to interpret the past, I have to ask whether I, as a researcher, am also 'silencing' the voices of such women.

So far in my research I have found few references to black women. Several Indian women, for example, marched in 'The Women's Coronation Procession' held on 17 June 1911 as a complement to the coronation of King George V. Although the WSPU organized the day, most of the major suffrage societies, including the NUWSS, participated, and it is highly likely that Mrs Roy, wife of an Indian barrister, Mrs Bhola Nauth, Honorary Secretary of the Indian Women's Educational Fund, and Mrs Mukerjea, President of the Indian National Union,[83] were non-militant, constitutional suffragists rather than militant suffragettes. I could not, therefore, use 'race' as a line of differentiation when analyzing women's prison experiences, although Edwardian feminist discourse often reinforced rather than challenged 'racist' assumptions.[84] Whether heterosexuality/lesbianism should be used as another line of differentiation has been more troublesome. 'Celibacy', for example, was openly discussed within the militant movement. Indeed, Cecily Hamilton, for a few months a member of the WSPU and then, for somewhat longer, of the also militant Women's Freedom League and the less political Women Writers' Suffrage League, of which she was one of the founders, advocated celibacy in her book *Marriage as a Trade*.[85] Christabel Pankhurst too, in *The Great Scourge and How to End It*, in warning of the dangers of marriage for women through husbands infected with VD advocated 'Votes for Women, which will give to women more self-reliance and a stronger economic position, and chastity for men'.[86] The call for celibacy may indicate that, as in the case of many of the other women quoted here, such women prioritized other women in their lives and may, perhaps, be called 'lesbians'. However, the difficulty of defining what is 'lesbianism' has made it problematic for me to interpret any one voice quoted in this chapter as a 'lesbian' voice – since no one woman I have quoted has identified herself as such.[87] I have, therefore, not used sexual orientation as a major fracturing point in the prison experiences of the suffragettes – although it may have been so. Instead, I have concentrated upon those social factors that are most clearly evident in the sources I have read.

In conducting my research, therefore, I become increasingly aware of the continuity and change between past and present, of the struggles and gains of women living in Edwardian society and of women living today, and of the way feminist 'politics' is not confined to an analysis of the formal structures of any one political organization. This reflexive process whereby one's own consciousness may provide insights into the lives of women in the past, and vice versa, is indeed an integral part of the 'feminist' research process.

Finding women's voices in the past, as I have done here, is critical for challenging the dominant narrative about prison life presented in the majority of secondary sources. And when using this material, the researcher usually adopts one or both of two main types of analysis.[88] If we see the creators of these personal texts as witnesses, and use their descriptions of people, places and events to provide us with information, we may call this *descriptive analysis*. If, on the other hand, we treat the creators of these personal documents as representative of particular social groupings, the label might be *perspective analysis*. The distinction between the two is important to bear in mind since the checks that need to be made about the documents will vary according to the kind of analysis involved. With descriptive analysis, the accuracy of the account is the central concern, and in order to assess this, comparisons will be made with other accounts describing the same phenomenon. With perspective analysis, on the other hand, the accuracy of the account does not necessarily matter. What is important is whether the document is representative of the perspectives of the social categories to which one is assigning the author(s): for example, constitutional feminists or militant feminists. Once again, the document will be compared with others, but this time with those produced by other members of that social category. As we shall see in the following discussion, one may use both descriptive and perspective analysis when interpreting the range of documents considered in this chapter. However, before we do this, there are some questions we must ask of the personal texts themselves, as of all sources generally.

Not every WSPU prisoner recorded her experiences; neither has every recorded account survived. Consequently I have to rely upon those unpublished accounts carefully preserved in such places as the Museum of London and the Fawcett Library[89] and upon the more common published testimonies, such as autobiographies. Some unpublished accounts, written perhaps on scraps of paper or in a diary, may have been thrown away or may be stored in a desk or drawer, still waiting to be discovered; others may be kept in private hands, unknown and unavailable to the researcher.[90] Published accounts are more likely to have been written by middle-class rather than working-class women since they were more likely to have had the time and education to engage in such an undertaking, as well as knowledge of and access to the largely male world of publishing. Issues such as these raise the question of how representative any one personal document, unpublished or published, may be of prison life generally or of any particular social grouping of women. What the researcher tries to do is immerse herself in the sources, get a 'feel' for the time and place, and then engage in descriptive analysis, comparing the descriptions of prison life offered in one account with others. From this mass of information, one or more accounts will be selected as 'typical'.

My approach here has been to follow this method, selecting certain quotations from women's writing as a way of 'getting at' typical experience. Although the text itself is not that experience but a representation of it, we cannot dismiss it as 'mere abstraction'. Even though 'experience' may be mediated through the discourses of the day, we must recognize that this is how the woman herself wanted to be represented.[91] Generally, too, it is important for us to find out as much as possible about how the personal documents were produced, who wrote and created them and why, and what sources of information were drawn upon.

Personal testimonies about prison life, written while in prison, are the source closest in time and place to the event in question and, therefore, the source most favoured by historians.[92] However, the personal letters we have considered here were produced under certain social conditions that framed the women's writing. Prison regulations stipulated that permission to write and receive letters was given to prisoners for the purpose of enabling them to keep up a connection with their 'respectable friends and not that they may be kept informed of public events'. Furthermore, all letters had to be legibly written and would be read by the prison authorities. Any of 'an objectionable tendency, either to or from prisoners, or containing slang, or improper expressions' would be 'suppressed'.[93] Letters intended for a private audience, such as friends, lovers, relations and family, were likely, therefore, to cover 'selected' matters, even though they were probably written in an intimate and private style. Some information might not be communicated because of censorship or through fear of upsetting the intended receiver.

Ada Wright, in Aylesbury Prison in 1912, in an unpublished letter dated 6 June to Mrs Arncliffe Sennett, pointed out: 'I try to write almost as I would if not supervised – It is the only way if letters are to be letters (I have had to revise this letter to you, however)'.[94] Myra Sadd Brown's unpublished letter to her husband of 16 March 1912 expressed, as we saw earlier, affectimate thoughts for him and their children during her absence in prison; however, she also felt it necessary to reassure him that all was well – 'On the whole we are not having a bad time, but the difficulty is to kill time. . . . We are all of us happy & get up to larks whenever the occasion serves'.[95] Letters such as these, produced under prison regulations, are therefore likely to contain many 'silences' and 'gaps' and the researcher is unsure how much 'to read between the lines'.

Personal letters written under prison regulations to 'respectable friends' knowing that they might be published in a public form were likely to be shaped by different concerns. It is highly probable that both Emmeline and Christabel Pankhurst were aware that their letters dated 21 November 1908, to Emmeline Pethick-Lawrence, might be given a more public exposure since Mrs Pethick-Lawrence and her husband were joint editors of *Votes for Women*. Sections of the letters contain statements of praise, warmth and encouragement for all WSPU members, rather like some of the public addresses these leaders gave. Christabel, for example, a brilliant politician, states at some length:

> From the visitors we have gained quite a lot of information as to how things are going on, and, as you may suppose, I am simply delighted by the progress the movement is making. I think you are all doing splendidly . . .
>
> Please tell the members of the Union how happy we feel and how contented to be here, because of what they are doing outside.[96]

Letters composed surreptitiously, in contravention of prison rules, to be smuggled out to friends for their personal perusal or for publication in a daily newspaper, might contain normally censured material. Katherine Gatty, in Holloway in June 1912, was denied the right to write and receive letters since, along with four other women, she had refused to undertake any prison work. Anxious to enlist outside publicity that might help the five to be given political status and thus placed in the First Division, she had no choice but to write in secret on dark brown lavatory paper:

> I want this to get into the *Standard* or *Daily News* or *Manchester G* on Wed. next if possible. God grant it reaches you safely. I had the utmost difficulty in getting it written & incredible difficulty in obtaining the paper & the envelope . . .
>
> As a signal that you have safely received this message through the Enemy's lines – send me a small (sample size only) quantity *again* of what I asked you to send me from Hospital. It will hearten us Five to know you know about us & are helping us. You see, as most of the Suffragist prisoners are at work (including the Two Leaders) it is not to be expected that Clements Inn should bother to fight for our little grievances. . . .
>
> Will you do all you can on & after Wed. to get answers from the Doctor, Matron, Governor, & Chaplain about our Removal to the 1st Div. . . . Will you also try to get MPs & the Home Sec. etc., written to about us all & the Five & me.[97]

The existence of the document itself shows how militants could circumvent the official rules. And the content of the letter reveals not only a deep commitment to the fight for political status but also the fact that individual WSPU members would act on their own initiative, taking a line independent of the leadership. As Stanley notes, the WSPU was never a single static entity but 'a shifting alliance of different interests, motivations and philosophies'.[98] Yet invaluable as such texts are, I frequently encountered innumerable problems (and incredible sadness) when using them. Often the writing tool for such secret correspondence would be whatever could be smuggled into a cell, such as 'a small bit of pencil',[99] which, against the dark brown of the lavatory paper, is often difficult to read – especially if the handwriting is also unclear.

Some personal testimonies of prison life, as we have seen, were published in newspapers such as *Votes for Women* or in leaflet form.[100] Such texts were likely to be read by other WSPU members and thus to influence the form and shape of any future story that might be told. Indeed, the emphasis, from 1909, upon forcible feeding in these accounts tends to repeat very similar details, with a depressing regularity. However, it is virtually impossible to find out how any one published account was produced and whether it was edited or altered in some way. Issues such as these pose, as mentioned earlier, the difficulty of how lived experience may be presented in a published form – a problem that is also central to autobiographies.

An autobiography may be defined as the written story of one's life. The idea that the key feature of a woman's autobiography is the search for a gendered 'self' may imply, of course, that the author is presented in a favourable light and others less so. Yet even if this is not the case, as subjective accounts of events, autobiographies, like all personal texts, contain an inevitable bias in the selection and presentation of content.[101]

In particular, most of the published autobiographies by militants were written long after the events described, when the participants were middleaged or elderly. One would, therefore, expect memory not to be entirely accurate – although Mary Richardson claimed in 1953 that, as she grew older, her memory leant further and further backward into the past so that she vividly recalled those times.[102] Often, of course, an autobiographer would draw upon a range of sources other than memory – but not all state what these sources might be! We are fortunate in that the 92-year-old Margaret Thompson tells us that her account is based on notes written about her experiences 'soon after they had been gone through'. In particular, some pages in the account of her third imprisonment were 'copied from a diary scribbled by me, on the back of a calendar, in prison in 1912'.[103] One would expect an autobiography based on such sources, close in time to the events, to be more reliable in its descriptions of such events that autobiographies written later. Nevertheless, even when a diary is kept, with no expected audience, we must not forget that, as with autobiographies, the events described have been selected and shaped in ways the author desired. And in the particular case referred to here, obviously the size of the calendar would be a key factor determining how much was written.

Many suffrage autobiographers looked back to their campaigning days with nostalgia. This seems to have been especially so in the inter-war years. But as Hilda Kean argues, it was more than nostalgia that the suffragettes wanted to record.[104] During the inter-war years it became increasingly apparent that the promises of the suffrage struggle had not been realized; women had not advanced as much as it was hoped. Cicely Hamilton lamented in 1935 that 'the battle we thought won is going badly against us'; women were 'back at the secondary existence, counting only as "normal" women, as wives and mothers of sons'.[105] In particular, it seems that 'old', militant feminists were seen as politically anachronistic, part of a political era that no longer existed. As Vera Brittain noted, many young women regarded their mothers' struggles for equality as a closed chapter of history – ' "Why go on with that old stuff? ... It's simply flogging a dead horse!" '[106]

Many of the militants were, understandably, very critical of Strachey's history of the suffrage movement, published in 1928, and also of Sylvia Pankhurst's *The Suffragette Movement*, published three years later. Indeed, although Christabel was the Pankhurst daughter with the university degree and a leader of the WSPU, it is Sylvia's history, not Christabel's,[107] that is vividly written and the most frequently cited. As Jane Marcus notes, *The Suffragette Movement* has become the standard reading of first wave feminism, stubbornly held and hardly challenged.[108] Yet Sylvia's biography intrudes on the narrative in subtle and less subtle ways, making it a 'personal' document, an autobiography as well as a history. Her account is strongly influenced by her deep resentment of her mother's preference for Christabel, always 'the apple of her eye'[109] and by her socialist feminist perspective which was often at odds with the more radical feminist views of Mrs Pankhurst and Christabel and of the politics they advocated. In 1913, for example, Sylvia broke from the WSPU, mainly because she had appeared on a public platform with the socialist George Lansbury and thus broken Christabel's 'golden rule' forbidding WSPU members from appearing in public with men.[110] For many of the militants writing an autobiography after the publication of *The Suffragette Movement*, therefore, the aim may have been not only to explore one's own identity and part in the suffrage struggle, but also an attempt to write an alternative history to that already on offer.

The liberal feminist, Ray Strachey, with her own axe to grind, concludes in a review of Sylvia's book that as a contribution to history 'it is worthless. Its omissions are as noticeable as its injustices, and its onesidedness of view is as apparent as the progressive turbulence of the movement itself'.[111] Such a judgment is too harsh. Although the 'onesidedness' may weaken the usefulness of the autobiography for descriptive analysis, it does not affect its usefulness for perspective analysis. Indeed, it is precisely this 'onesidedness' of view that makes an autobiography of interest to the feminist researcher since it reveals information about the perspective of the author, in this case that of a socialist feminist. And despite its bias, Sylvia's own voice rings clearly through her 'history'. Her descriptions of her prison experiences compare favourably with other accounts we have considered here.[112]

Conclusion

I have tried in this chapter to convey something of the process of what doing 'feminist' women's history means to me through concentrating upon the prison experiences of suffragettes in Edwardian England. No account is final, but some key themes keep recurring in my thoughts. First, by using a range of personal documents I have explored how central the sense of collectivity and of comradeship was for the suffragettes who were sent to prison – although the shared experience of prison life was not experienced equally but differentiated on a number of grounds, such as marital status, social class, rank within the WSPU, age and disability. I have, therefore, attempted to respect the mass of evidence that supports the sense of a feminist community amongst the militants in Edwardian England while also taking on board the notion of the 'differences' between women, so prevalent in feminist thinking today. I must ask therefore – am I in danger of trying to 'fit' empirical data from the past 'into' a conceptual framework derived from where I stand in the present?

I take some comfort in the knowledge that all historians, of whatever persuasion, cannot but be selective in the choice of the so-called 'facts' and in the use and construction of theory and interpretative frameworks.[113] Value-neutrality is not possible and which facts are selected depends, to a large extent, upon the questions the researcher is asking. Feminist historians openly discuss these issues; immersed in feminist debates today, they are only too aware of the danger of projecting ideals and values back in the past 'as an anachronism'.[114] By using the notion of 'difference', we can write a more sophisticated history of the militants while also recognizing their emphasis upon the common bonds between all women.

Secondly, as I have revealed, it is critical to find the voices of the suffragettes themselves, in their own personal accounts, since their words challenge those interpretations about prison life offered in the dominant discourse that has been constructed by both female and male historians alike. Examining the material conditions of women's lives and their experiences of those conditions seems to be the most legitimate way to construct a feminist women's history that has women centre stage.

Notes

1 This research is not yet completed and is being financially supported by the University of Portsmouth to which I express grateful thanks. Since members of the WSPU engaged in 'militant' acts (see note 14) they are usually referred to as 'suffragettes' whereas the non-militant suffrage workers are usually termed 'suffragists'.

2 Rowbotham (1973a).

3 J. Rendall (1991), p. 48.

4 Hinds *et al.* (1992), p. 7.

5 For black feminism see, for example, Carby (1982); Amos and Parmar (1984); and Bryan *et al.* (1985). Influential American publications at this time included Moraga and Anzaldua (1981); hooks (1982); Hull *et al.* (1982). For lesbian critiques see especially M. Wittig 'The straight mind', first read in New York at the Modern Language Association Convention in 1978 and reprinted in M. Wittig (1992); Rich (1980); Freedman *et al.* (1985).

6 Bennett (1989), p. 256.

7 See especially Scott (1988) and Riley (1988). For useful critiques of Scott and Riley see Stanley (1990d); Jackson (1992). For useful overviews of the development of feminist history in the UK see Hall (1992) and Hannam (1993).

8 Bennett (1993), p. 175. For discussion of the term 'experience' in regard to women's lives see especially Pierson (1991) and Scott (1992).

9 For a useful overview of the problems that may arise when oral history is utilized as a tool of feminist scholarship see Gluck and Patai (1991).

10 Marwick (1989), p. 199.

11 Rosen (1974), p. 50. Other secondary sources on the suffrage movement include Strachey (1928); E.S. Pankhurst (1931); Fulford (1957); C. Pankhurst (1959); Rover (1967); D. Mitchell (1967); Raeburn (1973); Liddington and Norris (1978); Hume (1982); Harrison (1982); Garner (1984); Holton (1986); Kent (1987); Tickner (1987); Leneman (1991).

12 C. Pankhurst (1959), p. 51.

13 Holton (1986), p. 4.

14 According to Garner (1984), p. 11, by 1914 the NUWSS had 480 affiliated societies with 53,000 members. The analytical imprecision of the terms 'militant' and 'constitutional' is explored in Holton (1986), p. 4, where she points out that if 'militancy' involved a preparedness to resort to extreme forms of violence, few 'militants' were 'militant' and then only from 1912 onwards. If, as Holton argues, militancy connoted amongst suffragists a willingness to take the issue onto the streets, or if it sometimes indicated labour and socialist affiliations, then many 'constitutionalists' were also 'militant'.

15 I have calculated these figures from *Roll of Honour, Suffragette Prisoners 1905–1914* (n.d.) Keighley, Rydal Press. It is extremely difficult to be accurate here. I have assumed those with Christian names I identify as female to be women, and vice versa for the male sex. There are also 49 persons listed with a surname and no Christian name or initial, e.g. Vertue.

16 Rosen (1974), p. 121.

17 *Ibid.*, pp. 127–8.

18 Strachey (1928), p. 309.

19 *Ibid.*, p. 310.

20 Dodd (1990), p. 135.

21 Strachey (1928), p. 314.

22 For earlier histories see especially A.E. Metcalfe (1917).

23 J. Marcus (1987), p. 3.

24 Review by F.M. Leventhal of Rosen's *Rise Up Women!* and Morgan's *Suffragists and Liberals* in *The Times Literary Supplement*, 19 September 1975.

25 Rosen (1974), p. 124.

26 The other key narrative of the fight for the vote comes from E.S. Pankhurst (1931). As we shall see later, Sylvia herself was imprisoned and force-fed, and presents a picture of prison life similar to that discussed in the rest of this chapter. However, overall her account is written from a socialist feminist perspective and therefore she is very critical of WSPU politics – see note 110.

27 Raeburn (1973), p. 241.

28 M. Vicinus (1985), p. 263 and p. 268.

29 L. Stanley with Ann Morley (1988).

30 Mrs Pankhurst 'Suffragists in Prison', *The Daily Telegraph*, 18 February 1908.

31 The following information is taken from M. Joachim 'My life in Holloway Gaol' *Votes for Women*, 1 October 1908, pp. 4–5 and Daisy Dorothea Solomon, *My Prison Experiences*, leaflet, n.d. (1909?), reprinted from the *Christian Commonwealth*, 25 August 1909.

32 'House of Commons, Tuesday, No. 17', speech of Mr Gladstone, *The Times*, 18 November 1908.

33   Tickner (1987), p. 107.
34   Joachim 'My life in Holloway Gaol', p. 5.
35   Corbett (1992), p. 162.
36   E. Pankhurst 'March, breast forward!', *Votes for Women*, 2 July 1909, p. 880.
37   E. Pethick-Lawrence (1938), p. 188.
38   Rosen (1974), p. 211.
39   'Patricia Woodlock – Procession and Meeting', *Votes for Women*, 25 June 1909, p. 843.
40   E. Wilding Davison, 'The Price of Liberty', reprinted in *Daily Sketch*, 28 May 1914.
41   Mary Nesbitt, unpublished letter to Miss Sinclair dated 1 May 1912, Suffragette Fellowship Collection, Museum of London.
42   E. Smyth (1934), p. 211.
43   Vicinus (1985), p. 260.
44   *Votes for Women*, 24 January 1913, p. 238.
45   'Treatment of militant women', *Votes for Women*, 24 January 1913, p. 244.
46   *Ibid.*; *Votes for Women*, 24 January 1913, p. 238.
47   Dove (1988), p. 7.
48   M.E. Thompson and M.D. Thompson (1957), p. 50.
49   Interview undertaken by the author with Phyllis Keller's daughter, Pam Henderson of Bucks Green, Sussex, on 29 July 1992. Phyllis Keller was imprisoned in Holloway in March 1912.
50   *Votes for Women*, 2 July 1909, pp. 876–9.
51   See Holton (1992).
52   *Votes for Women*, 2 July 1909, pp. 876–9.
53   *Ibid.*, p. 877; Liddington and Norris (1978), p. 220.
54   Julie Holledge (1981), p. 56.
55   D.B. Montefiore (1927), p. 105.
56   *Ibid.*, pp. 105–6.
57   'Releases of prisoners', *Votes of Women*, 17 December 1909, p. 181.
58   Unpublished letter dated 16 March 1912 from Myra Sadd Brown in Holloway, Fawcett Library Autograph Letter Collection, Vol. XX.
59   Unpublished, undated letter (*c.* 22 March 1912) from Myra Sadd Brown written from Holloway on dark brown lavatory paper, Fawcett Library Autograph Letter Collection.
60   Rosen (1974), p. 76. Rosen believes that from the autumn of 1906 support for the WSPU came from 'the educated and well-to-do, rather than from the rank and file of the Labour movement'. I am less sure about this.
61   Smyth (1934), p. 211.
62   Z. Procter (1960), p. 109.
63   C. Lytton and J. Warton, Spinster (1914), p. 1.
64   *Votes for Women*, 14 January 1910, p. 242.
65   Lytton and Warton (1914), p. 235.
66   *Ibid.*, p. 235.
67   *Ibid.*, pp. 269–70.
68   Rosen (1974), p. 134.
69   Thompson and Thompson (1957), p. 49.
70   'Mass meeting in the Albert Hall', *Votes for Women*, 21 June 1912, p. 614.
71   E. Pankhurst (1914), p. 254.

72 *Ibid.*, p. 255.
73 Rosen (1974), pp. 166–7.
74 Mrs Pankhurst was, however, arrested, released and re-arrested many more times under the Cat and Mouse Act. Fears about her death were frequently expressed by the press in 1913 and 1914. In her autobiography, *My Own Story* (1914), p. 298, she notes how she was released from prison in May 1913 'because, had I remained there much longer, I should have been a dead woman'.
75 Helen Liddle Gordon (1911), p. 58.
76 Nell Hall-Humpherson, *Suffragette*, leaflet, n.d.
77 E.S. Pankhurst (1931), p. 444.
78 *Ibid.*
79 Tickner (1987), p. 107.
80 See, for example, 'The dangers of forcible feeding', *Votes for Women*, 8 October 1909, p. 19.
81 Rosen (1974), p. 248 – the news was conveyed in a circular from E. Pankhurst to all WSPU members addressed as 'Dear Friend'.
82 J. Purvis (1992), p. 275. The other main categories I identify are *official texts* which includes state, bureaucratic, institutional and legal texts, such as census data, government reports, official reports of societies and organizations, and *published commentary and reporting* which includes such texts as novels, writings of literary, social and political figures, newspapers, films and paintings. Subjective experiences will, of course, also shape many of the texts in these two other main categories. Furthermore, Michel Foucault and other influential twentieth-century post-structuralists such as Roland Barthes have questioned the authority of a person as the autonomous author of a text and argue that the text itself has a life of its own, independent of the authorial meanings inscribed in it. We are all, authors and non-authors alike, shaped by culture, but this is not to say that human agency is an illusion. As Gabrielle Spiegel (1990) argues we must explain cultural expressions in terms of historically situated authorial consciousness. For a recent feminist history that draws upon post-structuralist insights into the ways in which meanings are constructed and cultural practices organized see Walkowitz (1992).
83 A. Burton (1991), p. 66.
84 *Ibid.* See also A.M. Burton (1992) and Valverde (1992).
85 C. Hamilton (1909).
86 C. Pankhurst (1930), p. 37.
87 For a discussion of such problems when researching lesbians in the past see Lesbian History Group (1989) especially the chapter by S. Jeffreys, 'Does It Matter If They Did It?'
88 Purvis (1992), p. 276.
89 I would like to thank Nicola Johnson and Diane Atkinson at the Museum of London, London Wall, London EC2Y 5HN, and David Doughan at the Fawcett Library, Old Castle Street, London Guildhall University, London E1 7NT for their many kindnesses to me during the course of my researches.
90 D. Doughan (1992), p. 134.
91 Corbett (1992), pp. 8–9.
92 See Tosh (1991), p. 33.
93 These regulations are stated on the back of a letter written by Myra Sadd Brown to her husband on 16 March 1912 on official notepaper from 'H.M. Prison

Holloway'. The letter states she is in good health and that she encloses a parcel of soiled linen for washing. Fawcett Library Autograph Letter Collection, Vol. XX.

94 Unpublished letter dated 6 June 1912 from Ada Cecile Wright in Aylesbury Prison to Mrs Arncliffe Sennett, Maud Arncliffe Sennett Collection, British Library C121g1 Vol. 18.

95 Unpublished letter dated 16 March 1912 from Myra Sadd Brown in Holloway to her husband, Fawcett Library Autograph Letter Collection, Vol. XX.

96 *Votes for Women*, 26 November 1908, p. 148.

97 Unpublished letter from Katherine Gatty, dated 17 June [1912], written on dark brown lavatory paper, Maud Arncliffe Sennett Collection BL C121g1 Vol. 18.

98 Stanley with Morley (1988), p. 175.

99 Unpublished letter by Ada Wright in Aylesbury Prison dated 11 June 1912, Maud Arncliffe Sennett Collection, BL C121g1 Vol. 18.

100 In addition to those sources cited see the leaflet *Fed by Force, How the Government Treats Political Opponents in Prison, Statement of Mrs. Mary Leigh (who is still in Birmingham Gaol)*, leaflet published by The National Women's Social and Political Union, n.d. (1909 ?).

101 The literature on women's autobiography as a genre is now extensive – but see Jelinek (1980); Benstock (1988); Stanton (1987); Brodzki and Schenck (1988); Newman (1991); Stanley (1992). Of particular relevance for this chapter is Davis *et al.* (1982).

102 Richardson (1953), p. x.

103 Thompson and Thompson (1957), 'Introduction'.

104 H. Kean (in prep.). I am grateful to Hilda for allowing me to see her stimulating paper and to refer to it.

105 C. Hamilton (1935), p. 251.

106 V. Brittain 'Women still wait for equality', *Daily Herald*, 26 March 1938, reprinted in Brittain and Holtby (1985), pp. 144–5.

107 C. Pankhurst (1959).

108 J. Marcus (1987), p. 5.

109 E.S. Pankhurst (1931), p. 267.

110 Romero (1987), p. 68.

111 *The Woman's Leader*, 20 February 1931, p. 19.

112 E.S. Pankhurst (1931). See, for example, pp. 230–8.

113 For an early influential book dealing with this theme see Carr (1961).

114 Bock (1989), p. 8.

Bibliography

ACKER, J., BARRY, K. and ESSEVELD, J. (1983) 'Objectivity and Truth: Problems in Doing Feminist Research', *Women's Studies International Forum*, vol. 6, no. 4, pp. 423–35.

ALTHUSSER, L. (1971) 'Ideology and State Apparatuses: Notes Towards an Investigation', in ALTHUSSER, L. *Lenin and Philosophy and Other Essays*, London, New Left Books.

AMOS, V. and PARMAR, P. (1984) 'Challenging Imperial Feminism', *Feminist Review*, 17 (Autumn).

APPLE, M. (Ed.) (1982) *Cultural and Economic Reproduction in Education*, London, Routledge and Kegan Paul.

ATHENS, L. (1980) *Violent Criminal Acts and Actors*, London, Routledge and Kegan Paul.

ATKINSON, P. (1990) *The Ethnographic Imagination: Textual Constructions of Reality*, London, Routledge.

BELL, C. (1977) 'Reflections on the Banbury Restudy', in BELL, C. and NEWBY, H. (Eds) *Doing Sociological Research*, London, Allen and Unwin.

BELL, C. and ENCEL, S. (1978) *Inside the Whale*, Sydney, Pergamon.

BELL, C. and NEWBY, H. (Eds) (1977) *Doing Sociological Research*, London, Allen and Unwin.

BELL, C. and ROBERTS, H. (Eds) (1984) *Social Researching: Politics, Problems, Practice*, London, Routledge and Kegan Paul.

BENEKE, T. (1982) *Men on Rape*, New York, St Martin's Press.

BENNETT, J.M. (1989) 'Feminism and History', *Gender and History*, vol. 1, no. 3 (Autumn).

BENNETT, J.M. (1993) 'Women's History: A Study in Continuity and Change', *Women's History Review*, vol. 2, no. 2.

BENSTOCK, S. (Ed.) (1988) *The Private Self: Theory and Practice of Women's Autobiographical Writings*, London, Routledge.

BERGER, J. and LUCKMANN, T. (1971) *The Social Construction of Reality*, Harmondsworth, Penguin.

BHAVNANI, K-K. (1990) 'What's Power Got to Do with It? Empowerment and Social Research', in PARKER, I. and SHOTTER, J. (Eds) *Deconstructing Social Psychology*, London, Routledge.

BHAVNANI, K-K. (in prep.) 'Tracing the Contours: Feminist Research and Feminist Objectivity', in AFSHAR, H. (Ed.) *Feminist Understandings of Race and Gender*, London, Macmillan.

BILLIG, M. (1982) *Ideology and Social Psychology*, Oxford, Basil Blackwell.

BLAIR, I. (1982) *Investigating Rape*, London, Heinemann.

BLAND, L. (1985) 'In the Name of Protection: The Policing of Women in the First World War', in SMART, C. and BROPHY, J. (Eds) *Women in Law*, London, Routledge.

BOCK, G. (1989) 'Women's History and Gender History: Aspects of an International Debate', *Gender and History*, vol. 1, no. 1.

BOURDIEU, P. (1977) *Outline of a Theory of Practice*, Cambridge, Cambridge University Press.

BOWLES, G. and DUELLI KLEIN, R. (Eds) (1983) *Theories of Women's Studies*, London, Routledge and Kegan Paul.

BRAH, A. (1992) 'Difference, Diversity, Differentiation', in DONALD, J. and RATTANSI, A. (Eds) *'Race', Culture, Difference*, London, Routledge.

BRANNEN, J. (1988) 'Research Note: The Study of Sensitive Subjects: Notes on Interviewing', *Sociological Review*, vol. 36, no. 3, pp. 552–63.

BRANNEN, J. (Ed.) (1992) *Mixing Methods: Qualitative and Quantitative Research*, Aldershot, Avebury.

BRANNEN, J. (1993) 'Research Note: The Effects of Research on Participants: Findings from a Study of Mothers and Employment', *Sociological Review*, vol. 41, no. 2, pp. 328–46.

BRANNEN, J., DODD, K. and OAKLEY, A. (1991) 'Getting Involved: The Effects of Research on Participants', paper for the BSA Annual Conference *Health and Society*.

BRITTAIN, V. and HOLTBY, W. (1985) *Testament of a Generation: The Journalism of Vera Brittain and Winifred Holtby*, ed. P. BERRY and A. BISHOP, London, Virago.

BRODZKI, B. and SCHENK, C. (Eds) (1988) *Life/Lines: Theorizing Women's Autobiography*, Ithaca, Cornell University Press.

BROWNMILLER, S. (1975) *Against Our Will*, New York, Bantam.

BRYAN, B., DADZIE, S. and SCAFE, S. (1985) *The Heart of the Race: Black Women's Lives in Britain*, London, Virago.

BRYMAN, A. (1988) *Quantity and Quality in Social Research*, London, Unwin Hyman.

BUNCH, C. (1987) *Passionate Politics: Feminist Theory in Action, Essays 1968–1986*, New York, St Martin's Press.

BURAWOY, M. *et al.* (1991) *Ethnography Unbound: Power and Resistance in the Modern Metropolis*, Berkeley, University of California Press.

BURGOS, M. (1989) 'Life Stories, Narrativity, and the Search for Self', *Life Stories/Recits de Vie*, 5, pp. 29–37.

BURTON, A. (1991) 'The Feminist Quest for Identity: British Imperial Suffragism and "Global Sisterhood", 1900–1915', *Journal of Women's History*, vol. 3, no. 2 (Fall).

BURTON, A.M. (1992) 'The White Woman's Burden: British Feminists and "The Indian Woman", 1865–1915', in CHAUDURI, N. and STROBEL, M. (Eds) *Western Women and Imperialism: Complicity and Resistance*, Bloomington and Indianapolis, Indiana University Press.

CAIN, M. (1986) 'Realism, Feminism, Methodology and the Law', *International Journal of the Sociology of Law*, vol. 14.

CAIN, M. (1990) 'Realist Philosophy and Standpoint Epistemologies *or* Feminist Criminology as a Successor Science', in GELSTHORPE, L. and MORRIS, A. (Eds) *Feminist Perspectives in Criminology*, Milton Keynes, Open University Press.

CAIN, M. (1993) 'Foucault, Feminism and Feeling: What Foucault Can and Cannot Contribute to Feminist Epistemology', in RAMAZANOGLU, C. (Ed.) *Up Against Foucault: Explorations of Some Tensions Between Foucault and Feminism*, London, Routledge.

CAIN, M. and FINCH, J. (1981) 'Towards a Rehabilitation of Data', in ABRAMS, P., DEEM, R., FINCH, J. and ROCK, P. (Eds) *Practice and Progress: British Sociology 1950–1980*, London, Allen and Unwin.

CAMERON, D. and FRAZER, E. (1987) *The Lust to Kill: A Feminist Investigation of Sexual Murder*, New York, New York University Press.

CAPUTI, J. (1987) *The Age of Sex Crime*, Bowling Green, OH, Bowling Green State University Press.

CAPUTI, J. (1993) 'The Sexual Politics of Murder', in BART, P. and MORAN, E.G. (Eds) *Violence Against Women*, London, Sage.

CARBY, H.V. (1982) 'White Woman Listen! Black Feminism and the Boundaries of Sisterhood', in CENTRE FOR CONTEMPORARY CULTURAL STUDIES *The Empire Strikes Back: Race and Racism in 70s Britain*, London, Hutchinson.

CARLEN, P. (1992) 'Criminal Women and Criminal Justice: The Limits to, and Potential of, Feminist and Left Realist Perspectives', in MATTHEWS, R. and YOUNG, J. (Eds) *Issues in Realist Criminology*, London, Sage.

CARR, E.H. (1961) *What is History?*, London, Macmillan (reprinted by Penguin, Harmondsworth, 1964).

CARR-HILL, R. and MAYNARD, M. (1989) *Working in the Tourist Sector in York*, York, IRISS, University of York.

CAVENDISH, R. [GLUCKSMANN, M.] (1982) *Women on the Line*, London, Routledge and Kegan Paul.

CENTRE FOR STAFF DEVELOPMENT IN HIGHER EDUCATION (1985) *Through a Hundred Pairs of Eyes*, anti-racist video and accompanying guide, London, CSDHE.

CHAMBERS, G. and MILLER, A. (1982) *Investigating Sexual Assault*, Edinburgh, HMSO.

CHESNEY-LIND, M. and SHELDEN, R.G. (1992) *Girls, Delinquency and Juvenile Justice*, Pacific Grove, CA, Brooks/Cole Publishers.

CICOUREL, A.V. (1974) *Method and Measurement in Sociology*, London, Collier-Macmillan.

CLIFFORD, J. (1981) 'On Ethnographic Surrealism', *Comparative Studies in Society and History*, 23, pp. 539–64.

CLIFFORD, J. (1983) 'On Ethnographic Authority', *Representations*, vol. 1, no. 2, pp. 118–46.

CLIFFORD, J. (1986) 'Introduction: Partial Truths', in CLIFFORD, J. and MARCUS, G. (Eds) *Writing Culture: The Poetics and Politics of Ethnography*, Berkeley, University of California Press.

CLIFFORD, J. and MARCUS, G. (Eds) (1986) *Writing Culture: The Poetics and Politics of Ethnography*, Berkeley, University of California Press.

COCKBURN, C. (1991) *In the Way of Women: Men's Resistance to Sex Equality in Organizations*, London, Macmillan.

COHEN, S. (1989) *Against Criminology*, London, Routledge.

COLE, E.B. and COULTRAP-MCQUIN, S. (1992) *Explorations in Feminist Ethics: Theory and Practice*, Bloomington and Indianapolis, Indiana University Press.

COLES, B. and MAYNARD, M. (1990) 'Moving Towards a Fair Start: Equal Gender Opportunities and the Careers Service', *Gender and Education*, vol. 2, no. 3, pp. 297–308.

COLES, B., MAYNARD, M. and RIDING, J. (1988) *Fair Start: Equal Gender Opportunities and the Work of the Careers Service*, York, IRISS, University of York.

COLLINS, J. (1983) 'The Meaning of Lies: Accounts of Action and Participatory Research', in GILBERT, N.G. and ABELL, P. (Eds) *Accounts and Action*, Aldershot, Gower.

COLLINS, P.H. (1986) 'Learning from the Outsider Within: The Sociological Significance of Black Feminist Thought', *Social Problems*, vol. 33, no. 6.

COLLINS, P.H. (1990) *Black Feminist Thought: Knowledge, Consciousness and the Politics of Empowerment*, Boston and London, Unwin Hyman.

CONNELL, R.W. (1987) *Gender and Power*, Stanford, CA, Stanford University Press.

COOK, J. and FONOW, M. (1986) 'Knowledge and Women's Interests: Issues of Epistemology and Methodology in Feminist Sociological Research', *Sociological Inquiry*, no. 56, pp. 2–29 (reprinted in NIELSEN, J. McCARL (Ed.) *Feminist Research Methods: Exemplary Readings in the Social Sciences*, London, Westview Press, 1990).

CORBETT, M.J. (1992) *Representing Femininity: Middle-Class Subjectivity in Victorian and Edwardian Women's Autobiographies*, Oxford, Oxford University Press.

DALY, K. and CHESNEY-LIND, M. (1989) 'Feminism and Criminology', *Justice Quarterly*, vol. 5, no. 4.

DAVIS, T., DURHAM, M., HALL, C., LANGAN, M. and SUTTON, D. (1982) ' "The Public Face of Feminism": Early Twentieth-Century Writings on Women's Suffrage', in CENTRE FOR CONTEMPORARY CULTURAL STUDIES (Ed.) *Making Histories: Studies in History-Writing and Politics*, London, Hutchinson.

DE CERTEAU, M. (1988) *The Practice of Everyday Life*, London, University of California Press.

DE LAURETIS, T. (1986) 'Feminist Studies/Critical Studies: Issues, Terms and Contexts', in DE LAURETIS, T. (Ed.) *Feminist Studies/Critical Studies*, Bloomington, Indiana University Press.

DEEM, R. and BREHONY, K. (1992) 'Why Didn't You Use a Survey so You Could Generalise Your Findings? Methodological Issues in a Multiple-Site Case Study of School Governing Bodies after the Education Reform Act', paper presented to ESRC seminar on Methodological and Ethical Issues Associated with Research into the 1988 Education Reform Act, University of Warwick, 2 July 1992.

DEVAULT, M. (1990) 'Talking and Listening from Women's Standpoint: Feminist Strategies for Interviewing and Analysis', *Social Problems*, vol. 37, no. 1.

DOBASH, R.E. and DOBASH, R.P. (1992) *Women, Violence and Social Change*, London, Routledge.

DODD, K. (1990) 'Cultural Politics and Women's Historical Writing: The Case of Ray Strachey's *The Cause*', *Women's Studies International Forum*, vol. 13, nos. 1/2, Special Issue *British Feminist Histories*, ed. by L. Stanley.

DONALD, J. (1985) 'Beacons of the Future: Schooling, Subjection and Subjectification', in BEECHEY, V. and DONALD, J. (Eds) *Subjectivity and Social Relations*, Milton Keynes, Open University Press, pp. 214–50.

DONALD, J. and RATTANSI, A. (Eds) *'Race', Culture, Difference*, London, Routledge.

DOUGHAN, D. (1992) 'The End of Women's History? A View from the Fawcett Library', *Women's History Review*, vol. 1, no. 1.

DOVE, I. (1988) *Yours in the Cause: Suffragettes in Lewisham, Greenwich and Woolwich*, Lewisham Library Service and Greenwich Libraries.

DUELLI KLEIN, R. (1983) 'How to Do What We Want to Do: Thoughts about Feminist Methodology', in BOWLES, G. and DUELLI KLEIN, R. (Eds) *Theories of Women's Studies*, London, Routledge and Kegan Paul.

EATON, M. (1986) *Justice for Women*, Milton Keynes, Open University Press.

EDWARDS, R. (1990) 'Connecting Method and Epistemology: A White Woman Interviewing Black Women', *Women's Studies International Forum*, vol. 13, no. 5, pp. 477–90.

FERNANDO, S. (1992) 'Blackened Images', *Ten. 8: Critical Decade: Black British Photographs in the 80s*, vol. 2, no. 2, pp. 140–6.

FILMER, P., PHILLIPSON, M., SILVERMAN, D. and WALSH, D. (1972) *New Directions in Sociological Theory*, London, Collier-Macmillan.

FINCH, J. (1984) ' "It's Great to Have Someone to Talk To": The Ethics and Politics of Interviewing Women', in BELL, C. and ROBERTS, H. (Eds) *Social Researching: Politics, Problems, Practice*, London, Routledge and Kegan Paul.

FLAX, J. (1987) 'Postmodernism and Gender Relations in Feminist Theory', *Signs*, vol. 12, no. 4, pp. 621–43 (reprinted in NICHOLSON, L.J. (Ed.) *Feminism/Postmodernism*, London, Routledge, 1991, pp. 39–63).

FONOW, M.M. and COOK, J. (Eds) (1991a) *Beyond Methodology: Feminist Scholarship as Lived Research*, Bloomington, Indiana University Press.

FONOW, M.M. and COOK, J. (1991b) 'Back to the Future: A Look at the Second Wave Feminist Epistemology', in FONOW, M.M. and COOK, J. (Eds) *Beyond Methodology: Feminist Scholarship as Lived Research*, Bloomington, Indiana University Press.

FOUCAULT, M. (1981) *The History of Sexuality, Vol. 1*, Harmondsworth, Penguin.

FOUCAULT, M. (1986) *The History of Sexuality, Vol. 2*, Harmondsworth, Viking.

FRAZER, E., HORNSBY, J. and LOVIBOND, S. (1992) *Ethics: A Feminist Reader*, Oxford, Blackwell.

FREEDMAN, E.B., GELPI, B.C., JOHNSON, S.L. and WESTON, K.M. (Eds) (1985) *The Lesbian Issue: Essays from SIGNS*, Chicago and London, University of Chicago Press.

FULFORD, R. (1957) *Votes for Women: The Story of a Struggle*, London, Faber and Faber.

FUSS, D. (1989) *Essentially Speaking: Feminism, Nature and Difference*, London, Routledge.

GAME, A. (1991) *Undoing the Social: Towards a Deconstructive Sociology*, Milton Keynes, Open University Press.

GARDNER, C.B. (1980) 'Passing By: Street Remarks, Address Rights and the Urban Female', *Social Forces*, 56.

GARDNER, C.B. (1988) 'Access Information: Private Lines and Public Peril', *Social Problems*, 35.

GARDNER, C.B. (1990) 'Safe Conduct: Women, Crime and Self in Public Places', *Social Problems*, vol. 37, no. 4.

GARNER, L. (1984) *Stepping Stones to Women's Liberty: Feminist Ideas in the Women's Suffrage Movement 1900–1918*, London, Hutchinson.

GEERTZ, C. (1973) *The Interpretation of Cultures*, New York, Basic Books.

GELLNER, E. (1970) 'Concepts and Society', in WILSON, B. (Ed.) *Rationality*, Oxford, Blackwell.

GELSTHORPE, L. (1990) 'Feminist Methodologies in Criminology', in GELSTHORPE, L. and MORRIS, A. (Eds) *Feminist Perspectives in Criminology*, Buckingham, Open University Press.

GELSTHORPE, L. (1992) 'Response to Martyn Hammersley's Paper on "Feminist Methodology" ', *Sociology*, vol. 26, no. 2.

GELSTHORPE, L. and MORRIS, A. (1988) 'Feminism and Criminology in Britain', *British Journal of Criminology*, vol. 28, no. 2.

GLASER, B. and STRAUSS, A. (1967) *The Discovery of Grounded Theory*, Chicago, Aldine.

GLEESON, D. (Ed.) (1983) *Youth Training and the Search for Work*, London, Routledge and Kegan Paul.

GLUCK, S.B. and PATAI, D. (Eds) (1991) *Women's Words: The Feminist Practice of Oral History*, London, Routledge.

GLUCKSMANN, M. (1982) *see* CAVENDISH, R. (1982).

GLUCKSMANN, M. (1990) *Women Assemble: Women Workers and the New Industries in Inter-War Britain*, London, Routledge.

GOLDE, P. (1970/1986) *Women in the Field: Anthropological Experiences*, Berkeley, University of California Press.

GORDON, H.L. (1911) *The Prisoner: A Sketch*, Letchworth, Garden City Press.

GRAHAM, H. (1983) 'Do Her Answers Fit His Questions?', in GAMARNIKOW, E., MORGAN, D., PURVIS, J. and TAYLORSON, D. (Eds) *The Public and the Private*, London, Heinemann.

GRAHAM, H. (1984) 'Surveying through Stories', in BELL, C. and ROBERTS, H. (Eds) *Social Researching: Politics, Problems, Practice*, London, Routledge and Kegan Paul.

GRAMSCI, A. (1971) *Selections from the Prison Notebooks*, ed. Q. Hoare and G. Nowell-Smith, London, Lawrence and Wishart.

GREEN, P. (1993) Review of *Feminist Perspectives in Criminology* (Gelsthorpe and Morris), *British Journal of Criminology*, vol. 33, no. 1, pp. 112–13.

GRIFFIN, C. (1985) *Typical Girls: Young Women from School to the Job Market*, London, Routledge and Kegan Paul.

GRUBIN, D. and GUNN, J. (1991) *A Study of Convicted Rapists*, London, Home Office.

GUBA, E.G. (1990) 'Subjectivity and Objectivity', in EISNER, E.W. and PESHKIN, A. (Eds) *Qualitative Inquiry in Education: The Continuing Debate*, Columbia University, New York, Teachers College Press, pp. 74–92.

HALL, C. (1992) 'Feminism and Feminist History', in HALL, C. *White, Male and Middle-Class: Explorations in Feminism and History*, Cambridge, Polity Press.

HALL, S. and JEFFERSON, T. (1976) *Resistance through Rituals: Youth Sub-cultures in Post-War Britain*, London, Hutchinson.

HALL-HUMPHERSON, N. (n.d.) *Suffragette*, leaflet.

HAMILTON, C. (1909) *Marriage as a Trade*, London, Chapman and Hall (reprinted by The Women's Press, London, 1981).

HAMILTON, C. (1935) *Life Errant*, London, J.M. Dent.

HAMMERSLEY, M. (1992) 'On Feminist Methodology', *Sociology*, vol. 26, no. 2 (May), pp. 187–206.

HANMER, J. and SAUNDERS, S. (1984) *Well Founded Fear*, London, Hutchinson.

HANNAM, J. (1993) 'Women, History and Protest', in RICHARDSON, D. and ROBINSON, V. (Eds) *Introducing Women's Studies*, Basingstoke, Macmillan.

HARAWAY, D. (1988) 'Situated Knowledges: The Science Question in Feminism and the Privilege of the Partial Perspective', *Feminist Studies*, vol. 14, no. 3 (Fall), pp. 573–99.

HARDING, S. (1986) *The Science Question in Feminism*, Milton Keynes, Open University Press.

HARDING, S. (Ed.) (1987) *Feminism and Methodology*, Milton Keynes, Open University Press.

HARDING, S. (1990) 'Feminism, Science and the Anti-Enlightenment Critiques', in NICHOLSON, L.J. (Ed.) *Feminism/Postmodernism*, London, Routledge, pp. 83–107.

HARDING, S. (1991) *Whose Science? Whose Knowledge? Thinking from Women's Lives*, Milton Keynes, Open University Press.

HARDING, S. (1992) 'The Instability of the Analytic Categories of Feminist Theory', in CROWLEY, H. and HIMMELWEIT, S. (Eds) *Knowing Women: Feminism and Knowledge*, Cambridge, Open University Press in association with Polity Press.

HARDING, S. and HINTIKKA, M.B. (Eds) (1983) *Discovering Reality: Feminist Perspectives on Epistemology, Metaphysics, Methodology and Philosophy of Science*, Dordrecht, Reidel.

HARGREAVES, A. (1982) 'Resistance and Relative Autonomy Theories', *British Journal of Sociology of Education*, vol. 3, no. 2, pp. 107–26.

HARGREAVES, D.H. (1967) *Social Relations in a Secondary School*, London, Routledge and Kegan Paul.

HARRISON, B. (1982) 'The Act of Militancy: Violence and the Suffragettes, 1904–1914', in HARRISON, B. *Peaceable Kingdom: Stability and Change in Modern Britain*, Oxford, Clarendon Press.

HARTSOCK, N.E.M. (1983) 'The Feminist Standpoint: Developing the Ground for a Specifically Feminist Historical Materialism', in HARDING, S. and HINTIKKA, M. (Eds) *Discovering Reality: Feminist Perspectives on Epistemology, Metaphysics, Methodology and Philosophy of Science*, Dordrecht, Reidel, pp. 283–311.

HEIDENSOHN, F. (1968) 'The Deviance of Women: A Critique and Enquiry', *British Journal of Sociology*, vol. 19, no. 2.

HEIDENSOHN, F. (1985) *Women and Crime*, London, Macmillan.

HEIDENSOHN, F. (1992) *Women in Control? The Role of Women in Law Enforcement*, Oxford, Oxford University Press.

HEKMAN, S. (1990) *Gender and Knowledge*, Cambridge, Polity Press.

HESTER, M., KELLY, L. and RADFORD, J. (Eds) (in prep.) *Violence Against Women: Research of the British Sociological Association's Violence Against Women Group*.

HIGGINBOTHAM, E. (1982) 'Two Representative Issues in Contemporary Sociological Work on Black Women', in HULL, G.T., SCOTT, P.B. and SMITH, B. (Eds), *All the Women Are White, All the Blacks Are Men, But Some of Us Are Brave: Black Women's Studies*, New York, Feminist Press.

HILLIARD, B. and CASEY, C. (1993) 'Sex Pests in Uniform', *Police Review*, 19 February.

HINDS, H., PHOENIX, A. and STACEY, J. (Eds) (1992) *Working Out: New Directions for Women's Studies*, London, Falmer Press.

HOFF, L. (1990) *Battered Women as Survivors*, London, Routledge.

HOLDER, R., KELLY, L. and TARA-CHAND, A. (1992) *Challenging Domestic Violence: A Resource for Training and Change*, Hammersmith and Fulham Community Safety Unit.

HOLLAND, J. (1993) *Sexuality and Ethnicity: Variations in Young Women's*

Sexual Knowledge and Practice, WRAP Paper 8, London, The Tufnell Press.

HOLLAND, J., RAMAZANOGLU, C., SHARPE, S. and THOMSON, R. (1992) 'Pleasure, Pressure and Power: Some Contradictions of Gendered Sexuality', *Sociological Review*, vol. 40, no. 4, pp. 645–74.

HOLLEDGE, J. (1981) *Innocent Flowers: Women in the Edwardian Theatre*, London, Virago.

HOLTON, S.S. (1986) *Feminism and Democracy: Women's Suffrage and Reform Politics in Britain 1900–1918*, Cambridge, Cambridge University Press.

HOLTON, S.S. (1992) 'The Suffragist and the "Average Women"', *Women's History Review*, vol. 1, no. 1.

HOOKS, B. (1982) *Ain't I A Woman: Black Women and Feminism*, Boston, South End Press.

HOOKS, B. (1984) *Feminist Theory: From Margin to Center*, Boston, South End Press.

HOOKS, B. (1991) *Yearning: Race, Gender, and Cultural Politics*, London, Turnaround.

HUDSON, A. (1990) ' "Elusive Subjects": Researching Young Women in Trouble', in GELSTHORPE, L. and MORRIS, A. (Eds) *Feminist Perspectives in Criminology*, Milton Keynes, Open University Press.

HULL, G.T., SCOTT, P.B. and SMITH, B. (Eds) (1982) *All the Women Are White, All the Blacks Are Men, But Some of Us Are Brave: Black Women's Studies*, New York, Feminist Press.

HUME, L.P. (1982) *The National Union of Women's Suffrage Societies 1897–1914*, New York and London, Garland Publishing.

JACKSON, S. (1992) 'The Amazing Deconstructing Woman', *Trouble and Strife*, 25 (Winter).

JAGGAR, A. (1983) *Feminist Politics and Human Nature*, Totowa, NJ, Rowman and Allanheld.

JAYARATNE, T.E. and STEWART, A. (1991) 'Quantitative and Qualitative Methods in the Social Sciences: Current Feminist Issues and Practical Strategies', in FONOW, M.M. and COOK, J. (Eds) *Beyond Methodology: Feminist Scholarship as Lived Research*, Bloomington, Indiana University Press.

JEFFERSON, T. (1992) 'Wheelin' and Stealin'', *Achilles' Heel*, Summer, pp. 10–12.

JEFFREYS, S. (1989) 'Does It Matter If They Did It?', in LESBIAN HISTORY GROUP *Not a Passing Phase: Reclaiming Lesbians in History 1840–1985*, London, The Women's Press.

JELINEK, E. (Ed.) (1980) *Women's Autobiography: Essays in Criticism*, Bloomington, Indiana University Press.

JOACHIM, M. (1908) 'My Life in Holloway Gaol', *Votes for Women*, 1 October, pp. 4–5.

JONES, D.S. and NELSON-LE GALL, S. (1986) 'Defining Black Families: Past and Present', in SEIDMAN, E. and RAPPAPORT, J. (Eds) *Redefining Social Problems*, New York, Plenum Press.

KAY, J. (1990) 'Research Note: Constructing the Epistemological Gap: Gender Divisions in Sociological Research', *Sociological Review*, vol. 38, no. 2, pp. 344–51.

KEAN, H. (in prep.) 'Searching for the Past in Present Defeat: Mid-War British Feminism and Historical Identity', *Women's History Review*.

KELLY, L. (1988) *Surviving Sexual Violence*, Cambridge, Polity Press.

KELLY, L. (1990) 'Journeying in Reverse: Possibilities and Problems in Feminist Research on Sexual Violence', in GELSTHORPE, L. and MORRIS, A. (Eds) *Feminist Perspectives in Criminology*, Buckingham, Open University Press.

KELLY, L. (1992) 'The Connections Between Disability and Child Abuse: A Review of the Research Evidence', *Child Abuse Review*, vol. 1, no. 3, pp. 157–68.

KELLY, L. and RADFORD, J. (1988) 'On the Problem of Men', in SCRATON, P. (Ed.) *Law, Order and the Authoritarian State*, Milton Keynes, Open University Press.

KELLY, L. and REGAN, L. (1990) 'Flawed Protection', *Social Work Today*, 17 April.

KELLY, L., REGAN, L. and BURTON, S. (1991) *An Exploratory Study of the Prevalence of Sexual Abuse in a Sample of 16–21 Year Olds*, Final Report to the ESRC.

KELLY, L., REGAN, L. and BURTON, S. (1992a) 'Defending the Indefensible? Quantitative Methods and Feminist Research', in HINDS, H., PHOENIX, A. and STACEY, J. (Eds) *Working Out: New Directions for Women's Studies*, London, Falmer Press.

KELLY, L., BURTON, S. and REGAN, L. (1992b) ' "And What Happened to Him?": Policy on Sex Offenders from the Survivor's Perspective', in PRISON REFORM TRUST *Beyond Containment: The Penal Response to Sex Offending*, London, Prison Reform Trust.

KENNEDY, H. (1992) *Eve Was Framed*, London, Chatto and Windus.

KENT, S.K. (1987) *Sex and Suffrage in Britain 1860–1914*, New Jersey, Princeton University Press.

KIRKWOOD, C. (1993) 'Investing Ourselves: Use of Researcher Personal Response in Feminist Methodology', in DE GROOT, J. and MAYNARD, M. (Eds) *Perspectives on Women's Studies for the 1990s: Doing Things Differently?*, London, Macmillan.

KLEIN, D. and KRESS, J. (1976) 'Any Woman's Blues: A Critical Overview of Women, Crime and the Criminal Justice System', *Crime and Social Justice*, 5.

LACEY, C. (1970) *Hightown Grammar*, Manchester, Manchester University Press.

LAWRENCE, E. (1982) 'In the Abundance of Water the Fool is Thirsty: Sociology and Black "Pathology" ', in CENTRE FOR CONTEMPORARY CULTURAL STUDIES *The Empire Strikes Back*, London, Hutchinson.

LAWS, S. (1990) *Issues of Blood: The Politics of Menstruation*, London, Macmillan.

LEIGH, M. (n.d.) (1909?) *Fed by Force: How the Government Treats Political Opponents in Prison, Statement of Mrs. Mary Leigh (who is still in Birmingham Gaol)*, The National Women's Social and Political Union.

LENEMAN, L. (1991) *A Guid Cause: The Women's Suffrage Movement in Scotland*, Aberdeen, Aberdeen University Press.

LEONARD, D. (1980) *Sex and Generation: A Study of Courtship and Weddings*, London, Tavistock.

LESBIAN HISTORY GROUP (1989) *Not a Passing Phase: Reclaiming Lesbians in History 1840–1985*, London, The Women's Press.

LEVETT, A. (1991) 'Childhood Sexual Abuse and Problems in Conceptualisation', *Agenda*, 10, pp. 38–47.

LIDDINGTON, J. and NORRIS, J. (1978) *One Hand Tied Behind Us: The Rise of the Women's Suffrage Movement*, London, Virago.

LORDE, A. (1984) *Sister Outsider*, Trumansberg, NY, The Crossing Press.

LYTTON, C. and WARTON, J., SPINSTER (1914) *Prisons and Prisoners: Some Personal Experiences*, London, William Heinemann.

McDERMOTT, J.M. (1992) 'The Personal is Empirical: Feminism, Research Methods and Criminal Justice Education', *Journal of Criminal Justice Education*, vol. 3, no. 2.

McGIBBON, A. and KELLY, L. (1989) *Abuse of Women in the Home: A Fact Pack*, Hammersmith and Fulham Community Safety Unit.

McGIBBON, A., COOPER, L. and KELLY, L. (1989) *'What Support?': An Exploratory Study of Council Policy and Practice and Local Support Services in the Area of Domestic Violence within Hammersmith and Fulham*, Hammersmith and Fulham Council Community Police Committee.

MACKINNON, C. (1982) 'Feminism, Marxism, Method and the State: An Agenda for Theory', in KEOHANE, N., ROSALDO, M. and GELPI, B. (Eds) *Feminist Theory*, Brighton, Harvester Press.

McLAUGHLIN, E. (1991) 'Oppositional Poverty: The Quantitative/Qualitative Divide and Other Dichotomies', *Sociological Review*, vol. 39, pp. 292–308.

McROBBIE, A. (1980) 'Settling Accounts with Subcultures: A Feminist Critique', *Screen Education*, 34, pp. 37–49.

MALSEED, J. (1987) 'Straw Men: A Note on Ann Oakley's Treatment of Textbook Prescriptions for Interviewing', *Sociology*, vol. 21, no. 4, pp. 629–31.

MAMA, A. (1987) *Race and Subjectivity: A Study of Black Women*, unpublished PhD thesis, University of London.

MAMA, A. (1989) *The Hidden Struggle: Statutary and Voluntary Sector Responses to Violence Against Women in the Home*, London Race and Housing Research Unit, c/o The Runnymede Trust.

MARCUS, G.E. (1986) 'Contemporary Problems of Ethnography in the Modern World System', in CLIFFORD, J. and MARCUS, G.E. (Eds) *Writing Culture:*

The Poetics and Politics of Ethnography, Berkeley, University of California Press, pp. 105–93.

MARCUS, G.E. (1992) 'Past, Present and Emergent Identities: Requirements for Ethnographies of Late Twentieth-Century Modernity World-Wide', in LASH, S. and FRIEDMAN, J. (Eds) *Modernity and Identity*, Oxford, Blackwell, pp. 309–31.

MARCUS, G. and CUSHMAN, D. (1982) 'Ethnographies as Texts', *Annual Review of Anthropology*, 11, pp. 25–69.

MARCUS, J. (1987) 'Introduction: Re-Reading the Pankhursts and Women's Suffrage', in MARCUS, J. (Ed.) *Suffrage and the Pankhursts*, London, Routledge and Kegan Paul.

MARSH, C. (1979) 'Problems with Surveys', *Sociology*, vol. 13, no. 2 (May).

MARTIN, J. and ROBERTS, C. (1984) *Women and Employment: A Lifetime Perspective*, London, HMSO.

MARWICK, A. (1989) *The Nature of History*, 3rd ed., Basingstoke, Macmillan.

MAY, T. (1993) *Social Research: Issues, Methods and Process*, Buckingham, Open University Press.

MAYNARD, M. (1989) *Sociological Theory*, London, Longman.

MEASOR, L. (1985) 'Interviewing: A Strategy in Qualitative Research', in BURGESS, R. (Ed.) *Strategies of Educational Research: Qualitative Methods*, Lewes, Falmer Press.

MESSERSCHMIDT, J. (in prep.) *Masculinities and Crime: Critique and Reconceptualization of Theory*, Maryland, Rowan and Littlefield.

METCALFE, A.E. (1917) *Woman's Effort: A Chronicle of British Women's Fifty Years' Struggle for Citizenship (1865–1914)*, Oxford, B.H. Blackwell.

MIES, M. (1983) 'Towards a Methodology for Feminist Research', in BOWLES, G. and DUELLI KLEIN, R. (Eds) *Theories of Women's Studies*, London, Routledge and Kegan Paul.

MITCHELL, D. (1967) *The Fighting Pankhursts: A Study in Tenacity*, London, Jonathan Cape.

MITCHELL, J. (1982) 'Reflections of a Black Social Scientist: Some Struggles, Some Doubts, Some Hopes', *Harvard Educational Review*, vol. 52, no. 1, pp. 27–44.

MONTEFIORE, D.B. (1927) *From a Victorian to a Modern*, London, E. Archer.

MORAGA, C. and ANZALDUA, G. (Eds) (1981) *This Bridge Called My Back: Writings by Radical Women of Color*, MA, Persephone Press.

MORLEY, D. (1979) *The Nationwide Audience*, London, British Film Institute.

MORRIS, A. (1987) *Women, Crime and Criminal Justice*, Oxford, Blackwell.

NEWBURN, T. and STANKO, E. (Eds) (in prep.) *Just Boys Doing Business: Men, Masculinity and Crime*, London, Routledge.

NEWMAN, S. (Ed.) (1991) *Autobiography and Questions of Gender*, London, Frank Cass.

NICHOLSON, L. (Ed.) (1990) *Feminism/Postmodernism*, London, Routledge.

OAKLEY, A. (1979) *Becoming a Mother*, Oxford, Martin Robertson.

OAKLEY, A. (1981) 'Interviewing Women: A Contradiction in Terms', in

ROBERTS, H. (Ed.) *Doing Feminist Research*, London, Routledge and Kegan Paul, pp. 30–62.

OAKLEY, A. (1993) *Social Support and Motherhood*, Oxford, Blackwell.

OPIE, A. (1992) 'Qualitative Research, Appropriation of the "Other" and Empowerment', *Feminist Review*, no. 40 (Spring), pp. 52–69.

PANKHURST, C. (1930) *The Great Scourge and How to End It*, London, E. Pankhurst.

PANKHURST, C. (1959) *Unshackled: The Story of How We Won the Vote*, London, Hutchinson.

PANKHURST, E. (1914) *My Own Story*, London, Eveleigh Nash.

PANKHURST, E.S. (1931) *The Suffragette Movement: An Intimate Account of Persons and Ideals*, London, Longmans, Green and Co.

PATRICK, J. (1976) *A Glasgow Gang Observed*, London, Eyre Methuen.

PETHICK-LAWRENCE, E. (1938) *My Part in a Changing World*, London, Victor Gollancz.

PHOENIX, A. (1986) 'Theories of Gender and Black Families', in WEINER, G. and ARNOT, M. (Eds) *Gender Under Scrutiny*, London, Hutchinson.

PHOENIX, A. (1990a) 'Social Research in the Context of Feminist Psychology', in BURMAN, E. (Ed.) *Feminists and Psychological Practice*, London, Sage.

PHOENIX, A. (1990b) 'Black Women and the Maternity Services', in GARCIA, J., FITZPATRICK, R. and RICHARDS, M. (Eds) *The Politics of Maternity Care*, Oxford, Clarendon Press.

PHOENIX, A. (1991) *Young Mothers?*, Cambridge, Polity Press.

PHOENIX, A. and TIZARD, B. (in prep.) *The Social Identities of Young Londoners*, London, Routledge.

PIERSON, R.R. (1991) 'Experience, Difference, Dominance and Voice in the Writing of Canadian Women's History', in OFFEN, K., PIERSON, R.R. and RENDALL, J. (Eds) *Writing Women's History: International Perspectives*, Basingstoke and London, Macmillan.

POPULAR MEMORY GROUP (1982) 'Popular Memory: Theory, Politics, Method', in CENTRE FOR CONTEMPORARY CULTURAL STUDIES *Making Histories*, London, Hutchinson.

POTTER, J. and WETHERELL, M. (1987) *Discourse and Social Psychology: Beyond Attitudes and Behaviour*, London, Sage.

PROCTER, Z. (1960) *Life and Yesterday*, London, Favil Press.

PUNCH, M. (1986) *The Politics and Ethics of Fieldwork*, London, Sage.

PURVIS, J. (1992) 'Using Primary Sources when Researching Women's History from a Feminist Perspective', *Women's History Review*, vol. 1, no. 2.

RABINOW, P. (1986) 'Representations Are Social Facts: Modernity and Post-Modernity in Anthropology', in CLIFFORD, J. and MARCUS, G.E. (Eds) *Writing Culture: The Poetics and Politics of Ethnography*, Berkeley, University of California Press.

RADFORD, J. (1989) 'Women Policing: Contradictions Old and New', in HANMER, J., RADFORD, J. and STANKO, E.A. (Eds) *Women, Policing and Male Violence*, London, Routledge.

RADFORD, J. and STANKO, E.A. (1991) 'Violence Against Women and Children: The Contradictions of Crime Control Under Patriarchy', in STENSON, K. and COWELL, D. (Eds) *The Politics of Crime Control*, London, Sage.

RAEBURN, A. (1973) *The Militant Suffragettes*, London, Michael Joseph.

RAMAZANOGLU, C. (1989a) *Feminism and the Contradictions of Oppression*, London, Routledge.

RAMAZANOGLU, C. (1989b) 'Improving on Sociology: The Problems of Taking a Feminist Standpoint', *Sociology*, vol. 23, no. 3, pp. 427–42.

RAMAZANOGLU, C. (1990) *Methods of Working as a Research Team*, WRAP Paper 3, London, Tufnell Press.

RAMAZANOGLU, C. and HOLLAND, J. (1993) 'Women's Sexuality and Men's Appropriation of Desire', in RAMAZANOGLU, C. (Ed.) *Up Against Foucault: Explorations of Some Tensions Between Foucault and Feminism*, London, Routledge.

RATTANSI, A. (1992) 'Changing the Subject? Racism, Culture and Education', in DONALD, J. and RATTANSI, A. (Eds) *'Race', Culture and Difference*, London, Sage, pp. 11–49.

REESE, S., DANIELSON, W., SHOEMAKER, P., CHANG, T. and HSU, H. (1986) 'Ethnicity-of-Interviewer Effects among Mexican-Americans and Anglos', *Public Opinion Quarterly*, 35, pp. 48–68.

REID, M. (1983) 'Review Article: A Feminist Sociological Imagination? Reading Ann Oakley', *Sociology of Health and Illness*, vol. 5, no. 1, pp. 83–94.

REINER, R. and ROCK, P. (in prep.) *The Criminology Profession*.

REINHARZ, S. (1983) 'Experiential Analysis: A Contribution to Feminist Research', in BOWLES, G. and DUELLI KLEIN, R. (Eds) *Theories of Women's Studies*, London, Routledge and Kegan Paul.

REINHARZ, S. (with DAVIDMAN, L.) (1992) *Feminist Methods in Social Research*, Oxford, Oxford University Press.

RENDALL, J. (1991) 'Uneven Developments: Women's History, Feminist History, and Gender History in Great Britain', in OFFEN, K., PIERSON, R.R. and RENDALL, J. (Eds) *Writing Women's History: International Perspectives*, Basingstoke and London, Macmillan.

REYES, M. DE LA LUZ and HALCON, J. (1988) 'Racism in Academia: The Old Wolf Revisited', *Harvard Educational Review*, vol. 58, no. 3, pp. 299–314.

RHODE, P. (in prep.) 'Race-of-Interviewer Effects in Qualitative Research'.

RICH, A. (1980) 'Compulsory Heterosexuality and Lesbian Existence', *Signs: Journal of Women in Culture and Society*, vol. 5, no. 4 (reprinted by Onlywomen Press, London, 1981, as a pamphlet).

RICHARDSON, M. (1953) *Laugh a Defiance*, London, Weidenfeld and Nicolson.

RILEY, D. (1988) *'Am I That Name?' Feminism and the Category of 'Women' in History*, Basingstoke, Macmillan.

ROBERTS, H. (Ed.) (1981) *Doing Feminist Research*, London, Routledge and Kegan Paul.

ROLLINS, J. (1985) *Between Women: Domestics and their Employers*, Philadelphia, Temple University Press.

ROMERO, P.W. (1987) *E. Sylvia Pankhurst: Portrait of a Radical*, New Haven, Yale University Press.

ROSE, H. (1983) 'Hand, Brain and Heart: A Feminist Epistemology for the Natural Sciences', *Signs*, vol. 9, no. 1, pp. 73–90.

ROSEN, A. (1974) *Rise Up Women! The Militant Campaign of the Women's Social and Political Union 1903–1914*, London, Routledge and Kegan Paul.

ROVER, C. (1967) *Women's Suffrage and Party Politics in Britain 1866–1914*, London, Routledge and Kegan Paul.

ROWBOTHAM, S. (1973a) *Hidden from History: 300 Years of Women's Oppression and the Fight Against It*, London, Pluto Press.

ROWBOTHAM, S. (1973b) *Woman's Consciousness, Man's World*, Harmondsworth, Penguin.

RUSSELL, D.E.H. (1975) *The Politics of Rape*, New York, Stein and Day.

RUSSELL, D.E.H. (1982) *Rape in Marriage*, New York, Macmillan.

RUSSELL, D.E.H. (1984) *Sexual Exploitation*, London, Sage.

RUSSELL, D.E.H. (1986) *The Secret Trauma*, London, Free Press.

RUTTER, M., YULE, W., BERGER, M., YULE, B., MORTON, J. and BAGLEY, C. (1974) 'Children of West Indian Immigrants–I. Rates of Behavioural Deviance and of Psychiatric Disorder', *Journal of Child Psychology and Psychiatry*, vol. 15, no. 14, pp. 241–54.

SAID, E.W. (1978) *Orientalism*, London, Routledge and Kegan Paul.

SAMUEL, R. and THOMPSON, P. (Eds) (1990) *The Myths We Live By*, London, Routledge.

SARACHILD, K. (1970) 'Notes for Consciousness-Raising', in REDSTOCKINGS COLLECTIVE (Eds) *Feminist Revolution: Notes from the Second Year*, New York, Redstockings Collective.

SAYER, A. (1992) *Method in Social Science: A Realist Approach*, London, Routledge.

SCHECHTER, S. (1982) *Women and Male Violence: The Visions and Struggles of the Battered Women's Movement*, London, Pluto Press.

SCOTT, J.W. (1988) *Gender and the Politics of History*, New York, Columbia University Press.

SCOTT, J.W. (1992) ' "Experience" ', in BUTLER, J. and SCOTT, J.W. (Eds) *Feminists Theorize the Political*, London, Routledge.

SCOTT, P.B. (1982) 'Debunking Sapphire: Toward a Non-Racist and Non-Sexist Social Science', in HULL, G.T., SCOTT, P.B. and SMITH, B. (Eds) *All the Women Are White, All the Blacks Are Men, But Some of Us Are Brave: Black Women's Studies*, New York, Feminist Press.

SCOTT, S. (1984) 'The Personable and the Powerful: Gender and Status in Sociological Research', in BELL, C. and ROBERTS, H. (Eds) *Social Researching: Politics, Problems, Practice*, London, Routledge and Kegan Paul.

SCOTT, S. and PORTER, M. (1983) 'On the Bottom Rung: A Discussion of Women's Work in Sociology', *Women's Studies International Forum*, 6, pp. 211–22.

SCULLY, D. and MAROLLA, J. (1985) 'Riding the Bull at Gilleys: Convicted Rapists Describe the Rewards of Rape', *Social Problems*, vol. 32, no. 3.

SILVERMAN, D. and PERAKYLA, A. (1990) 'AIDS Counselling: The Interactional Organisation of Talk about "Delicate" Issues', *Sociology of Health and Illness*, vol. 12, no. 3, pp. 293–318.

SKEGGS, B. (1986) *Young Women and Further Education: A Case Study of Young Women's Experience of Caring Courses in a Local College*, unpublished PhD thesis, University of Keele.

SKEGGS, B. (1990) 'Gender Reproduction and Further Education: Domestic Apprenticeships', in GLEESON, D. (Ed.) *Training and Its Alternatives*, Milton Keynes, Open University Press, pp. 183–217.

SKEGGS, B. (1992) 'Paul Willis, *Learning to Labour*', in BARKER, M. and BEEZER, A. (Eds) *Reading into Cultural Studies*, London, Routledge, pp. 181–96.

SMART, C. (1976) *Women, Crime and Criminology*, London, Routledge and Kegan Paul.

SMART, C. (1984) *The Ties that Bind*, London, Routledge and Kegan Paul.

SMART, C. (1990) 'Feminist Approaches to Criminology or Postmodern Woman Meets Atavistic Man', in GELSTHORPE, L. and MORRIS, A. (Eds) *Feminist Perspectives in Criminology*, Buckingham, Open University Press.

SMITH, D. (1986) 'Institutional Ethnography: A Feminist Method', *Resources for Feminist Research*, no. 15.

SMITH, D. (1988a) *The Everyday World as Problematic: A Feminist Sociology*, Milton Keynes, Open University Press.

SMITH, D. (1988b) 'A Peculiar Eclipsing', in SMITH, D. *The Everyday World as Problematic: A Feminist Sociology*, Milton Keynes, Open University Press.

SMITH, D. (1989) 'Sociological Theory: Methods of Writing Patriarchy', in WALLACE, R. (Ed.) *Feminism and Sociological Theory*, London, Sage.

SMYTH, E. (1934) *Female Pipings in Eden*, Edinburgh, Peter Davies.

SOLOMON, D.D. (n.d.) (1909?) *My Prison Experiences*, leaflet, reprinted from *Christian Commonwealth*, 25 August 1909.

SOOTHILL, K. and WALBY, S. (1990) *Sex Crimes in the News*, London, Routledge.

SPARKS, R. (1992) *Television and the Drama of Crime*, Milton Keynes, Open University Press.

SPIEGEL, G. (1990) 'History, Historicism, and the Social Logic of the Text', *Speculum*, vol. 65, no. 1 (January).

STACEY, J. (1988) 'Can there be a Feminist Ethnography?', *Women's Studies International Forum*, vol. 11, no. 1, pp. 21–7.

STANKO, E.A. (1985) *Intimate Intrusions*, London, Routledge and Kegan Paul.

STANKO, E.A. (1988) 'Hidden Violence to Women', in MAGUIRE, M. and POINTING, J. (Eds) *Victims of Crime: A New Deal?*, Milton Keynes, Open University Press.

STANKO, E.A. (1990a) *Everyday Violence*, London, Pandora.

STANKO, E.A. (1990b) 'When Precaution is Normal: A Feminist Critique of Crime Prevention', in GELSTHORPE, L. and MORRIS, A. (Eds) *Feminist Perspectives in Criminology*, Milton Keynes, Open University Press.

STANKO, E.A. (1992) 'The Case of Fearful Women', *Women and Criminal Justice*, vol. 4, no. 1.

STANKO, E.A. and HOBDELL, K. (1993) 'Assault on Men: Men, Masculinity and Victimisation', *British Journal of Criminology*, vol. 33, no. 2.

STANLEY, L. (Ed.) (1990a) *Feminist Praxis: Research, Theory and Epistemology in Feminist Sociology*, London, Routledge.

STANLEY, L. (1990b) 'Feminist Praxis and the Academic Mode of Production: An Editorial Introduction', in STANLEY, L. (Ed.) *Feminist Praxis: Research, Theory and Epistemology in Feminist Sociology*, London, Routledge.

STANLEY, L. (1990c) 'Moments of Writing: Is there a Feminist Auto/Biography?', *Gender and History*, vol. 2, no. 1.

STANLEY, L. (1990d) 'Recovering "Women" in History from Feminist Deconstructionism', *Women's Studies International Forum*, vol. 13, nos 1/2, Special Issue *British Feminist Histories*, ed. by L. Stanley.

STANLEY, L. (1992) *The Auto/Biographical I: The Theory and Practice of Feminist Auto/Biography*, Manchester and New York, Manchester University Press.

STANLEY, L., with MORLEY, A. (1988) *The Life and Death of Emily Wilding Davison*, London, The Women's Press.

STANLEY, L. and WISE, S. (1983) *Breaking Out*, London, Routledge and Kegan Paul.

STANLEY, L. and WISE, S. (1990) 'Method, Methodology and Epistemology in Feminist Research Processes', in STANLEY, L. (Ed.) *Feminist Praxis: Research, Theory and Epistemology in Feminist Sociology*, London, Routledge.

STANLEY, L. and WISE, S. (1991) 'Feminist Research, Feminist Consciousness and Experiences of Sexism', in FONOW, M. and COOK, J. (Eds) *Beyond Methodology: Feminist Scholarship as Lived Research*, Indiana, Indiana University Press.

STANLEY, L. and WISE, S. (1993) *Breaking Out Again*, London, Routledge.

STANTON, D.C. (Ed.) (1987) *The Female Autograph*, Chicago, University of Chicago Press.

STEIER, F. (Ed.) (1991) *Research and Reflexivity*, London, Sage.

STRACHEY, R. (1928) *'The Cause': A Short History of the Women's Movement in Great Britain*, London, G. Bell and Sons (reprinted by Virago, London, 1978).

STRATHERN, M. (1987a) 'The Limits of Auto-Anthropology', in JACKSON, A. (Ed.) *Anthropology at Home*, London, Tavistock, pp. 16–38.

STRATHERN, M. (1987b) 'Out of Context: The Persuasive Fictions of Anthropology', *Current Anthropology*, vol. 28, no. 3 (June), pp. 251–81.

STROHMAYER, U. and HANNAH, M. (1992) 'Domesticating Postmodernism', *Antipode*, vol. 24, no. 1, pp. 29–55.

THOMPSON, M.E. and THOMPSON, M.D. (1957) *They Couldn't Stop Us! Experiences of Two (Usually Law-Abiding) Women in the Years 1909–1913*, Ipswich, W.E. Harrison and Sons Ltd.

THOMSON, R. (1989) 'Interviewing as a Process: Dilemmas and Delights', unpublished paper.

TICKNER, L. (1987) *The Spectacle of Women: Imagery of the Suffrage Campaign 1907–14*, London, Chatto and Windus.

TIZARD, B. and PHOENIX, A. (1993) *Black, White or Mixed-Race? Race and Racism in the Lives of Young People of Mixed Parentage*, London, Routledge.

TONKIN, E. (1992) *Narrating Our Pasts: The Social Construction of Oral History*, Cambridge, Cambridge University Press.

TOSH, J. (1991) *The Pursuit of History: Aims, Methods and New Directions in the Study of Modern History*, 2nd ed., Harlow, Longman.

VALVERDE, M. (1992) ' "When the Mother of the Race is Free": Race, Reproduction, and Sexuality in First-Wave Feminism', in IACOVETTA, F. and VALVERDE, M. (Eds) *Gender Conflicts: New Essays in Women's History*, Toronto, University of Toronto Press.

VAN MAANEN, J. (1988) *Tales of the Field: On Writing Ethnography*, Chicago, University of Chicago Press.

VICINUS, M. (1985) *Independent Women: Work and Community for Single Women 1850–1920*, London, Virago.

WALKERDINE, V. (1984) 'Some Day My Prince Will Come', in McROBBIE, A. and NAVA, M. (Eds) *Gender and Generation*, London, Macmillan, pp. 162–85.

WALKERDINE, V. (1986) 'Video Replay: Families, Films and Fantasies', in BURGIN, V., DONALD, J. and KAPLAN, C. (Eds) *Formations of Fantasy*, London, Methuen, pp. 167–200.

WALKERDINE, V. (1990a) *Schoolgirl Fictions*, London, Verso.

WALKERDINE, V. (1990b) *The Mastery of Reason: Cognitive Development and the Production of Rationality*, London, Routledge.

WALKOWITZ, J. (1992) *City of Dreadful Delight: Narratives of Sexual Danger in Late-Victorian London*, London, Virago.

WARREN, C.A.B. (1988) *Gender Issues in Field Research*, London, Sage.

WETHERELL, M. and POTTER, J. (1992) *Mapping the Language of Racism*, Basingstoke, Harvester Wheatsheaf.

WHYTE, W.F. (1955) *Street Corner Society*, 2nd ed., Chicago, University of Chicago Press.

WIGHT, D. (in prep.) 'Boys' Thoughts and Talk about Sex in a Working Class Locality of Glasgow', *Sociological Review*.

WILLIS, P. (1981) *Learning to Labour: How Working Class Kids Get Working Class Jobs*, 2nd ed., Farnborough, Saxon House.

WINCH, P. (1958) *The Idea of Social Science*, London, Routledge and Kegan Paul.

WITTIG, M. (1992) *The Straight Mind and Other Essays*, Hemel Hempstead, Harvester.

WOOLGAR, S. (Ed.) (1988) *Knowledge and Reflexivity: New Frontiers in the Sociology of Knowledge*, London, Sage.

WOOLGAR, S. and ASHMORE, M. (1988) 'The Next Step: An Introduction to the Reflexive Project', in WOOLGAR, S. (Ed.) *Knowledge and Reflexivity: New Frontiers in the Sociology of Knowledge*, London, Sage.

WRIGHT, R.A. (1992) 'From Vamps and Tramps to Teases and Flirts: Stereotypes of Women in Criminology Textbooks, 1956 to 1965 and 1981 to 1990', *Journal of Criminal Justice Education*, vol. 3, no. 2.

YEATMAN, A. (1987) 'Women, Domestic Life and Sociology', in PATEMAN, C. and GROSS, E. (Eds) *Feminist Challenges: Social and Political Theory*, Boston, Northeastern University Press.

Notes on Contributors

Miriam Glucksmann is a Reader in Sociology at the University of Essex. Her main publications are *Structuralist Analysis in Contemporary Social Thought* (1974, Routledge and Kegan Paul), *Women on the Line* (under the pseudonym of Ruth Cavendish) (1982, Routledge and Kegan Paul) and *Women Assemble: Women Workers and the 'New Industries' in Inter-War Britain* (1990, Routledge). She has been actively involved in the Women's Movement and in teaching Women's Studies since the early 1970s. Her main interests are in gender and work. She is currently writing up research on links between women's paid employment and domestic labour in the north-west of England, and planning a project on women as employees and consumers, and the retail industry.

Janet Holland is Senior Research Officer in the Social Science Research Unit, Institute of Education, University of London and Lecturer at the Open University. Her research and publications are in the areas of youth, education, gender and class. She is working on young women's sexuality with the Women, Risk and AIDS team (WRAP).

Liz Kelly, Sheila Burton and Linda Regan have worked together at the Child Abuse Studies Unit, University of North London, for almost four years. Apart from conducting research CASU offers advice and consultancy, and organizes networking, training and conferences on the abuse of children and adult women from a feminist perspective. They intend to continue developing a collective approach to feminist research/practice.

Annecka Marshall is twenty-six, artistic and angry. Sometimes her rage has been self-inflicted. She regrets that many other talented African women have been denied true self-expression within academia. She prays that her writing contributes to a feminism that liberates all women.

Mary Maynard is a Senior Lecturer in Sociology and Co-ordinator of the Centre for Women's Studies at the University of York. She is co-author of *Sexism, Racism and Oppression* (with Arthur Brittan) (1984, Blackwell), co-editor of *Women, Violence and Social Control* (with Jalna Hanmer) (1987,

Macmillan) and author of *Sociological Theory* (1989, Longman). She has also written a number of articles on Women's Studies issues, particularly in relation to housework, violence, theory and methodology. Her current work focuses on the last two issues.

Ann Phoenix worked for ten years at the Thomas Coram Research Unit, Institute of Education, University of London. She is currently working in the Department of Human Sciences at Brunel University. Her publications include *Young Mothers?*, Polity Press, 1991; *Motherhood: Meanings, Practices and Ideologies*, Sage, 1991 (jointly edited with Anne Woollett and Eva Lloyd); *Working Out: New Directions in Women's Studies*, Falmer Press, 1992 (jointly edited with Hilary Hinds and Jackie Stacey) and *Black, White or Mixed Race? Race and Racism in the Lives of Young People of Mixed Parentage*, Routledge, London (co-authored with Barbara Tizard).

June Purvis is Professor of Sociology at the University of Portsmouth, and is currently researching the suffragette movement in Edwardian England and the life of Christabel Pankhurst. Her publications include *Hard Lessons: The Lives and Education of Working-Class Women in Nineteenth-Century England* (1989, Polity) and *A History of Women's Education in England* (1991, Open University Press), as well as articles on doing feminist research. She is the Founding Editor of two journals, *Gender and Education* and *Women's History Review*, as well as the Editor of *Studies on Women Abstracts*.

Caroline Ramazanoglu is a Senior Lecturer in Sociology at Goldsmiths' College, University of London, and has a general interest in explaining power relations. Her publications include work on labour migration, *Feminism and the Contradictions of Oppression* (1989, Routledge), an edited collection *Up Against Foucault: Explorations of some Tensions between Foucault and Feminism* (1993, Routledge), and articles on sexuality and feminist methodology. She is currently working with colleagues on young people and heterosexuality in the Women, Risk and AIDS team (WRAP).

Beverley Skeggs now teaches Women's Studies at Lancaster University, having recently left the Centre for Women's Studies at York. From her earliest ethnographic research, her work has concentrated on how power relations are lived. This focus comes from a desire to locate the sites and possibilities of social change. Her work analyses how young women, using the cultural resources to which they have access, construct their identities in relation to institutionalized constraints. The results of this work have been published in a variety of journals and will soon culminate in a book. She has also published *The Media* (with John Mundy) (1992, Nelson).

Elizabeth A. Stanko, Reader in the Department of Law, Brunel University, UK, has been a pioneer of feminist criminology on both sides of the Atlantic.

She received her PhD in sociology from the City University of New York, Graduate School in 1977. She is author of *Everyday Violence* (1990, Pandora), *Intimate Intrusions* (1985, Routledge and Kegan Paul), and has published widely on issues of prosecutorial discretion, violence against women and crime prevention. Her most recent book, *Just Boys Doing Business: Men, Masculinity and Crime*, (co-editor T. Newburn) will be published by Routledge in 1994.

Index

149-165